Department 56
Villages

The Heritage Village Collection®

The Original Snow Village® Collection

SIXTH EDITION

Secondary Market Price Guide
& Collector Handbook

EDITORIAL

Managing Editor:	Jeff Mahony
Associate Editors:	Melissa A. Bennett
	Gia C. Manalio
	Mike Micciulla
	Paula Stuckart
Assistant Editors:	Heather N. Carreiro
	Jennifer Renk
	Joan C. Wheal
Editorial Assistants:	Timothy R. Affleck
	Beth Hackett
	Christina M. Sette
	Steven Shinkaruk

PRODUCTION

Production Manager:	Scott Sierakowski

ART

Creative Director:	Joe T. Nguyen
Assistant Art Director:	Lance Doyle
Senior Graphic Designers:	Marla B. Gladstone
	Susannah C. Judd
	David S. Maloney
	Carole Mattia-Slater
	David Ten Eyck
Graphic Designers:	Jennifer J. Bennett
	Sean-Ryan Dudley
	Kimberly Eastman
	Melani Gonzalez
	Jim MacLeod
	Jeremy Maendel
	Chery-Ann Poudrier

R&D

Product Development Manager:	Paul Rasid

ISBN 1-58598-151-6

CheckerBee Publishing • 306 Industrial Park Road • Middletown, CT 06457 • CheckerBee.com

Table Of Contents

Table Of Contents

Introducing The Collector's Value Guide™

Welcome to the sixth edition of the Collector's Value Guide™ for Department 56® Villages. Inside these pages you will find detailed information about the wonderful world of The Heritage Village Collection®, The Original Snow Village Collection® and other Department 56 collectibles, including Hot Properties!, Seasons Bay® Series and Storybook Village® Collection. With this handy reference guide, you'll learn how a small Christmas village based on the town of Stillwater, Minnesota grew into a large, year-round collection of beautiful and elegant buildings and accessories.

The Collector's Value Guide™ is filled with pages and pages of color photographs of Department 56 buildings and accessories, along with essential information about each piece including stock numbers, issue and retirement dates, secondary market values and original prices. Our guide is designed to help you keep track of your collection, keep up with the secondary market and gain insight into the different aspects of collecting Department 56 Villages.

Look Inside To Find:

- An Interview With Heritage Village Artist Barbara Lund

- The Most Recent Village Introductions And Retirements

- The Ten Most Valuable Heritage Village Pieces

- The Ten Most Valuable Snow Village Pieces

- A Fun, Fact-Filled Look At Some Of The Real Buildings That Have Inspired Department 56 Recreations

- Exciting New Display Ideas From Collectors Like You

- More Display Shortcuts From "Dr. S"

- A Look At Other Department 56 Products & More!

Department 56® Overview

Can you believe it? It's been a quarter of a century since the first Department 56 villages were introduced! What started as a relatively modest hamlet of snowy villages has snowballed into a bustling landscape of mills, churches, log cabins, covered bridges and water towers. If you've ever seen an interesting structure while on a back roads drive, chances are it's been replicated as a Department 56 piece.

Originally part of the Bachman's retail store, "Department 56" came to life in 1976. Bachman's was a leader in giftware design and distribution, a far cry from its humble beginnings as a family-owned farm in the 1800s. In the 1900s, that farm had grown into a floral and garden business, which grew into the retail store Bachman's. Within Bachman's, a numbering system was created to identify the many different departments within the expanding company. Not to be confused with Area 51, the top-secret site where all sorts of otherworldly aircraft are said to be tested, Department 56 was the department number given to Bachman's division of Wholesale Gift Importers.

Spirit Of '76

The first six lighted miniature buildings were created in 1976 and were based on a quaint town along the St. Croix River. Decked out to the fullest for the holidays, the little town seemed to be a throwback to another era. The feel of this town was captured with the original six buildings and their popularity paved the way for even more creations, as well as some retirements to keep the line manageable. The name of the collection later changed from "Snow Village" to "The Original Snow Village®" in the midst of the copycat collections that were springing up.

An Expanding Village

Some may have worried that the year 1984 was going to offer a nightmarish future like the famous novel of the same name, but for Department 56 fans, the year 1984 was closer in spirit to *Great Expectations* or *A Christmas Carol*. It was in 1984 that The *Dicken's Village Series*® joined the collection as the second line of villages. This popular series of Victorian buildings would pave the way for

The Heritage Village Collection®. In 1986, *The New England Village® Series* and *The Alpine Village Series*® were created under the Heritage Village banner. All good things come to an end, however, and Dicken's Village saw its first retirements in 1988.

In addition to new pieces being added to established lines, entirely new lines have been created to inject new life into the world of Department 56 Villages. *Christmas in the City*, *Little Town of Bethlehem*™ and the *North Pole Series*™ are just some of the sets that have added zest to the collection. The first licensed property to join the Department 56 universe was the *Disney Parks Village*™ series in 1994. Today, if you have a craving for Starbucks® Coffee or a Harley-Davidson® motorcycle, you'll find Snow Village has no shortage of licensed properties to add a little bit of modern-day realism to your collection.

One of the biggest changes to affect Department 56 was its purchase by the New York investment firm Forstmann Little Co. in 1992. A year later, collectors had the chance to invest in Department 56 when its stock was initially offered to the public. Follow the excitement of the stock market by looking for the ticker symbol "DFS" on the New York Stock Exchange.

Silver Celebration

This year is probably the most important landmark in Department 56 history. The year 2001 marks the 25th anniversary of Department 56, and the company is pulling out all the stops to make sure this celebration will be talked about for at least 25 more years to come. From August 17-19, St. Paul, Minnesota is going to be home to a gala event that will give fans an exciting glimpse into the famous collectibles company.

And don't forget to visit the Department 56 showroom located at One Village Place in Eden Prairie, Minnesota, home to every village piece ever made.

What would a party be without presents? Unlike most birthday parties, Department 56 is letting the guests get all the presents. Attendees who register in advance for the celebration will receive a special silver luggage tag as a memento.

Department 56 has also created several must-have items to commemorate the special event. Many of the pieces are "event only" exclusives that aren't to be missed. From "Lowell Inn" to "Department 56 Studio, 1200 Second Avenue," these event pieces allow collectors to see some of the buildings that have played a major role in the company's long history.

With such an exciting silver anniversary planned, collectors should have plenty to keep them busy until Department 56's golden anniversary in 2026.

Interview With Barbara Lund

Recently, CheckerBee Publishing had the opportunity to speak with Department 56 artist Barbara Lund.

CheckerBee Publishing: What was the first building (or piece) that you designed for Department 56 and what memories do you carry from that experience?

Barbara Lund: It was about 1988 when I decided to join the family business and learn all the components and skills it takes to put a building together. Dad and I started out very slowly. I spent a long time just watching him work and listening to him talk about the process. After a number of months, he coaxed me slowly into the actual artwork by giving me just small parts of a building to complete. Once I had established some confidence, I would rough out some structures and he would help me adapt and alter them a bit to improve them. The first piece I created on my own was for the *New England Village Series*. Today, I also create pieces for product lines like *North Pole Series* and *Dickens' Village Series*.

CP: Do you often get to meet collectors? And, if so, can you tell us a little about what it is like to meet your fans?

BL: I very much enjoy meeting people who collect. It gives me an opportunity to understand what appeals to folks. Talking to people on the road brings my work full circle. At my drawing board I can imagine what someone may like, but actually seeing what they buy and hearing why they buy certain pieces helps me make intelligent decisions in the future.

CP: What do you think is the secret to Department 56 Villages' phenomenal success?

BL: Since the early 1980s when my family became involved with the company, it was clear that the folks running Department 56 were people of extraordinary taste, vision and drive. My parents

brought some great concepts in and everything just seemed to click. Now, roughly 20 years later, Department 56 is still the leader in lighted houses and the standard that everyone else tries to meet. Absolute dedication to keeping Department 56 number one in the marketplace is what explains their success.

CP: What is the favorite piece you have designed?

BL: There are many pieces we feel good about, but sometimes everything comes together when we are working on a piece and it stands out. It may be something we really lobbied to create and our excitement made the work pass more easily. It may be that, for whatever reason, it was a really happy time in our lives. It may be that the piece met with a lot of approval and people really seemed to like it. For me, that piece is "The Melancholy Tavern," although it seems funny that my favorite piece is called melancholy.

CP: How do you feel when you see one of your designs completed?

BL: This is such an easy answer: RELIEF. When the two-dimensional line work and color leaves my drawing board, I really do feel a very great sense of relief. Within a few months of completing a design, after all the other artisans have done their work, we get to see how close we came to the original concept and how it looks in finished form.

CP: The designers of Department 56 are understandably referred to as "architects." In designing the buildings for these villages, do you formulate an interior floor plan of the dwelling to help you determine the exterior?

BL: There are actually several pieces in the line that have interior views. This is a pretty new concept and one that has been well received, especially by children. Historically, we have not concentrated on interiors. Part of the beauty of a make-believe village is what you create in your mind – in the same way that reading a book is so much more imaginative than watching a movie where the visuals are all determined for you.

CP: Can you tell us a little about a typical day in the life of a Department 56 Village artist?

BL: There really is no such thing as a "typical" day. Every day brings new ideas and challenges.

CP: Could you give us some insight into the process of getting a piece into production, such as how long it takes from start to finish and how decisions for names, colors and accessories are made?

BL: When we begin a piece, we try to spend a few days just thinking about how we would like it to be. This has become easier after years of research and studying those particular places and periods. Next, we spend a day doodling out some shapes and trying to get the scale of the building correct. When we have a concept we like, we bring it to Department 56 for feedback, then devise a plan and complete the final drawings. Naming a building is pretty arbitrary but the color study is more of a science. We need to be wary of how recently we have repeated color combinations within a particular village. For instance, we wouldn't want all of the Dickens'

introductions in one year to have slate roofs and taupe walls. Yet, there are certain combinations that always look good and appeal to people, so we have to make a special effort to mix up the color a bit.

CP: During your career, have you ever gotten "artist's block" and, if so, how did you overcome it?

BL: Everyone "hits a block" at times, no matter what you do for a living. It is not exclusive to people who write or draw or sculpt or participate in one of the more traditional arts. Once in a while, everybody runs a little dry. When I began working with my father, he would say that sometimes you have to just walk away from the work to "get a fresh eye." Problem solving is a part of every line of work and often it helps to step back and gain some perspective. I probably step back a lot.

The Heritage Village Collection® Overview

Since 1984, when, The Heritage Village Collection® was created separately from the traditional The Original Snow Village® Collection, it has branched out into many more miniature communities, each with a flavor all its own. Now that the whole series encompasses seven unique collections, it's time for a little tour of the Heritage Village world. Fasten your seat belt!

Dickens' Village Series®

As we start our journey, we'll need to take a trip back in time. Get ready to see an England of yesteryear in the *Dickens' Village Series*, the one that started it all! Remember all the great novels of Charles Dickens? This is where those people and places live again, as "The Flat Of Ebeneezer Scrooge" shares the cobbled streets with historical landmarks like "The Old Globe Theater." We can always take a jaunt to the country from "Victoria Station" and maybe even get in a game of golf at the "Burwickglen Golf Clubhouse." After all that activity, there's nothing like a pint at "The Horse And Hounds Pub" and let's not forget to poke around the "Teaman & Crupp China Shop" for a few souvenirs on the way out.

New England Village® Series

Now that we've experienced old England, it's time to have a look at her transatlantic cousin. Get ready to skip on over to the *New England Village* of seafaring pride and bucolic beauty! We'll take a journey up to the "Mountain View Cabin" and get some of that wonderful

New England country air. If the sea air is more to your liking, there are fabulous rides on "The Emily Louise" to watch the rolling waters for whales. Before leaving be sure to visit "Platt's Candles & Wax" and the "Moggin Falls General Store" for some great bargains!

Alpine Village Series®

If you enjoy the snow-capped peaks of Switzerland, you'll love our next stop. In the *Alpine Village Series* there's no end to the wonderful shops and chalets that stretch before us like an endless ski village. Everything from traditional beer houses to majestic villas and castles are there to see, and the locals are friendly mountain folk ready to play a song for you on their accordions. Even the timeless classics Heidi and The Sound Of Music® have buildings of their own here.

Christmas In The City® Series

Had enough country living for now? It's time for us to switch gears and head to the big city for a bit of holiday shopping. All the

hustle and bustle and bright lights of *Christmas In The City* are enough to enchant anyone! It's got nearly every kind of architecture you could hope to see, from red brick storefronts to the traditional brownstone apartment blocks. And the citizens won't ever go hungry, with places like "Johnson's Grocery & Deli" and the "Cafe Caprice French Restaurant" around. While we're there, we should browse around in "Jenny's Corner Book Shop" before we take in a matinee at "The Majestic Theater." With so many things going on, you might want to stay a while, but there's still more to come!

North Pole Series™

Have you ever wondered how Santa and his work force of elves get all those toys made and relax in their down time? You'll find out on our next stop, as we head up to the snow-covered wonderland of the *North Pole Series*. You'll see their factories for peanut brittle, glass ornaments and even the place where the reindeer learn to fly! After seeing so many sights, we can get some exercise at "The Elf Spa" and have a bite to eat at the the "Mini-Donut Shop" before moving on. And don't forget to wave to the new residents of the *North Pole Woods*™ Collection!

Disney Parks Village™ Series

After all that cold weather, it's time to make for sunny California and Florida, as we stroll through *Disney Parks Village*, and relive those childhood memories of Mickey and Minnie. It's not a long stop, but it's worth the trip to see the "Olde World Antique Shops" (set/2) and "Tinker Bell's Treasures." You'll be humming "It's A Small World" to yourself before you know it!

Little Town Of Bethlehem™ Series

Our tour winds up with a final leap back in time, and this one is the longest. We'll be seeing ancient Bethlehem with all the splendor and glory of Biblical times. We'll walk the dusty streets and see "Herod's Temple" and the "Rug Merchant's Colonnade" before making for the "Desert Oasis" for a much-needed drink of water. Well, that's our last stop. We hope you enjoyed the tour!

What's New For The Heritage Village Collection®

In December of 2000, Department 56 announced the following new Heritage Village pieces.

Heritage Village Buildings

Dickens' Village®

Abington Lock Keeper's Residence . . . It's hard work managing the canals in *Dickens' Village*, and the lock keeper needs a place to relax after a long day.

Abington Lockside Inn . . . Where there are canals, there are sure to be travelers. And when those travelers get to *Dickens' Village*, there's a nice place for them to put up their feet before moving on.

Brightsmith & Sons, Queen's Jewellers (Event Piece) . . . Even if this piece doesn't have real jewelry inside, there are real Swarovski crystals imbedded on the outside!

Burwickglen Golf Clubhouse . . . You'll find nothing but welcoming smiles at this club. It's just a place where lovers of golf can hit the links on a beautiful spring day!

Crowntree Freckleton Windmill (LE-30,000)
... Before there was electric power, it was the wind that fueled places like Crowntree. Picturesque windmills like this used to dot the countryside all over Europe!

Glendun Cocoa Works ... Can you even imagine what must go on inside Glendun? It must be enough to make a chocolate-lover go mad with delight!

Hedgerow Garden Cottage ... It may be on the narrow side, but this garden home has enough country charm to enhance any collection!

Lilycott Garden Conservatory (set/5)
... No one can grow flowers in the winter, not even in *Dickens' Village*! So the towns-folk built a special greenhouse to keep their favorite flowers blooming all year round.

The Old Curiosity Shop . . . Don't let those crumbling walls fool you. Inside this store is a treasure trove of wonderful antiques, both beautiful and obscure.

Rockingham School ... The town's proudest families have been sending their sons and daughters to this fine institution for years. It has produced the village's best and brightest scholars!

Royal Staffordshire Porcelains . . .
When villagers need a fine set of tableware, or just something nice to put on the mantle, Staffordshire has just what they need.

Royal Stock Exchange . . . This stately, columned building is where the town's most respectable businesses have their stocks traded on the market.

Scrooge & Marley Counting House . . .
Miserly old Ebeneezer never got around to painting over his old partner's name on the sign. Maybe his old friend's ghost can change his mind about that . . . and a few other things.

New England Village® Series

The Cranberry House . . . There's no place like New England for the country's sweetest cranberries. Why not drop by for a snack while you're in town?

Laurel Hill Church . . . With its wonderfully crafted stone walls, Laurel Hill invites everyone to come inside and view the town's simplest – yet most joyous – house of worship.

Mountain View Cabin (LE-10,000) . . . A splendid cottage like this offers a unique view of the snow-covered mountains. But you'd better make your reservations soon, since it's a limited edition!

Verna Mae's Boutique (set/3) . . . Springtime always comes along too soon and, before you know it, you'll need some new accessories to go with that spring wardrobe. And no one can help you find some like good old Verna Mae!

Wm. Walton Fine Clocks & Pocket Pieces . . . Walton's spotless reputation will have his time pieces ticking away for years! If you have to live by the clock, why not make it a special one?

Alpine Village Series®

Altstädter Bierstube . . . Imagine yourself coming back from a long hike in the Alps, and finding a place like this waiting for you. Nothing like a refreshing lager beer to finish off such a day!

Nussknacker Werkstatt (LE-5,600) . . . If you can get past the diligent soldiers who guard the door of this nutcracker workshop, you'll see the amazing toys that this shop produces. It's a limited edition, so you'd better get there soon!

Christmas In The City® Series

42nd St. Fire Company . . . The brave fire brigade at 42nd Street is always ready for an emergency, whether it's a fire or just a cat stuck in a tree. Obviously, they prefer the latter!

Department 56 Studio, 1200 Second Avenue (Event Piece) . . . This 25th anniversary piece honors Department 56's own history by replicating the company's old corporate headquarters in Minneapolis!

Foster Pharmacy . . . There's no place like Foster's to enjoy an ice-cold fountain soda while you're doing your big city Christmas shopping.

Gardengate House . . . Folks come from all over the city to glimpse the town's most elegant town house. Just that one wreath is enough to give the place all of its Christmas spirit!

The Majestic Theater (LE-15,000) . . . The whole city turned out for the big premiere at this aptly named auditorium. The best show in the city won't be in town forever (it's a limited edition), so get your tickets soon!

Mrs. Stover's Bungalow Candies . . . The sweetest teeth in the city have always kept Mrs. Stover busy with her confections, but she doesn't mind. Who could mind making candy?

North Pole Series™

ACME Toy Factory (set/5) . . . Every holiday season, the staff at ACME work extra hard to bring joy to everyone, both young and old. Bet you can find all sorts of stuff here for your bag of tricks.

Design Works North Pole (Event Piece) . . .
Catch a glimpse of the elves' (and Department
56's) artistic process – from sculpting to painting
– in this detailed piece made in honor of
Department 56's 25th Anniversary Event.

Ginny's Cookie Treats (set/3) . . . The
management of *Elf Land*'s finest bakery
won't have to worry about their building.
With all the great goodies coming out of
there, the bakers will never have to eat the
gingerbread walls, although it's tempting!

Northern Lights Fire Station . . . With
sirens and bells at the ready, the North Pole
will never have to worry about a fire. The
dedicated fire fighters will defend their home
town to the last elf!

Reindeer Condo . . . One night of work in a
whole year might not seem like much, but it's no
picnic hauling a sleigh of toys all around the
world. So Santa's faithful teamsters have a place
of their own in the *North Pole Woods* to kick
back during the off season.

Rudolph's Condo . . . Rudolph once told Santa
that he needed a place to rest up after guiding the
magic sleigh through the darkness and fog of
Christmas Eve. Now he's got a place high in the
North Pole Woods to do just that!

Santa's Retreat (set/2) . . . Let's not forget Santa. He and the Mrs. need a vacation spot too! His retreat in the *North Pole Woods*™ is the perfect place for the Clauses to relax and wait for next December!

Toot's Model Train Mfg. (LE-25,000) . . . There's a lot of work that goes into making a model train, and the folks at this shop are never asleep on the job – because they're having too much fun!

Wedding Bells Chapel . . . Elves never know when they might feel an urge to tie the knot. So when that happens, the chapel is always there to serve their matrimonial needs!

Little Town Of Bethlehem™ *Series*

Carpenter's Shop (set/3) . . . Carpenters have always had an important job throughout history. It was at shops like this where they practiced their trade and trained their sons to follow in their footsteps.

Herod's Temple (set/5, LE-5,600) . . . This ancient, ornate temple will stand out among the other more rustic pieces in this series.

Rug Merchant's Colonnade (set/4) . . . When merchants from faraway lands came to places like Bethlehem, their colorful rugs captivated all the customers and browsers in town.

Heritage Village Collection® Accessories

General Heritage Village Collection®

Christmas Carolers (set/3)

Holiday Singers (animated)

Mill Falls (animated)

Perfect Putt (animated)

Santa's On His Way (animated)

Santa's Sleigh

Village Express Van (Event Piece)

Woodland Carousel (animated)

Dickens' Village Series®

Abington Bridge

Abington Canal (set/2)

Abington Canal Boat (set/2)

Abington Locks (set/2)

Following The Leader (set/2)

Gourmet Chocolates Delivery Wagon

Hedgerow Dovecote (set/2)

Horses At The Lampguard (set/3)

Keeping The Streets Clean (set/2)

Master Potter

Merry Go Roundabout

Par For The Course (set/3)

Polo Players (set/2)

Sherlock Holmes – The Hansom Cab

Sliding Down Cornhill With Bob Cratchit

These Are For You (set/2)

New England Village® Series

A Day At The Cabin (set/2)

Best Of The Harvest (set/2)

Gathering Cranberries

Here Comes Sinter Klaus

The Perfect Tree

Alpine Village Series®

At The Octoberfest (set/3)

Christmas In The City® Series

1937 Pirsch Pumper Fire Truck

Fire Drill Practice

Hot Chocolate For Sale

The Life Of The Party (set/2)

On To The Show

Russell Stover® Delivery Truck

North Pole Series™

All Aboard! (set/2)

Balancing Act (set/3)

Catch The Wind

Cutting The Trail

Gone Fishing

Icy Delights

Little Newlyweds

Polar Plowing Service

Rescue Ready

Ring Toss (set/2)

Star Of The Show

Little Town Of Bethlehem™ Series

Cypress Trees (set/3)

Little Town Of Bethlehem™ Series, cont.

Desert Camp (set/4)

Desert Oasis (set/5)

Desert Road (set/4)

Desert Rocks (set/5)

Limestone Outcropping

Merchant Cart (set/2)

Oil Lamps (set/2)

Olive Harvest (set/3)

Star Of Wonder

Stonemason At Work (set/3)

Town Wall Sections (set/2)

The Heritage Village Collection® Mid-Year Releases

Dickens' Village Series® – Buildings

Cratchit's Corner

Somerset Valley Church (set/9)

Dickens' Village Series® – Accessories

Bob Cratchit And Tiny Tim

Ghost Of Christmas Present Visits Scrooge

New England Village® Series – Buildings

Revere Silver Works (set/2)

New England Village® Series – Accessories

Silver For Sale (set/2)

Alpine Village Series® – Buildings

Crystal Ice Palace (25th Anniversary Special Edition, set/9)

Schwarzwalder Kuckucksuhren

Cuckoo Clock Vendor & Cart (set/2)

Christmas In The City® Series – Buildings

Baker Bros. Bagel Bakery

Paradise Travel Company

Yankee Stadium

Christmas In The City® Series – Accessories

Midtown News Stand (set/2)

Planning A Winter Vacation

Pretzel Cart

North Pole Series™ – Buildings

Caribou Coffee Shop (set/3)

The Egg Nog Pub

LEGO® Building Creation Station

Santa's Sleigh Launch (gift set/5)

North Pole Series™ – Accessories

Brick Lift

Just A Cup Of Joe

Little Builders

General Heritage Village Collection® – Accessories

Crystal Ice King & Queen (LE-25,000)

Gondola (animated)

Recent Retirements

Department 56 announced that the following The Heritage Village Collection® pieces retired on November 3, 2000. Each year the list of retirements can be found in *USA Today*, and on the official Department 56 website (*www.department56.com*). Collectors can also register to receive an E-mail on the morning of retirements. Each piece is listed below with its issue year in parenthesis.

Dickens' Village Series®
- ❏ Aldeburgh Music Box Shop (1999)
- ❏ Aldeburgh Music Box Shop (1999, set/3, LE-35,000)
- ❏ Barmby Moor Cottage (1997)
- ❏ The China Trader (1999)
- ❏ The Christmas Carol Cottage (1996, *The Christmas Carol Revisited*)
- ❏ Crooked Fence Cottage (1997)
- ❏ Dudley Docker (1999)
- ❏ Fezziwig's Ballroom (2000, set/6)
- ❏ Manchester Square (1997, set/25)
- ❏ The Old Royal Observatory (1999, set/2, LE-35,000)
- ❏ Thomas Mudge Timepieces (1998)

New England Village® Series
- ❏ Deacon's Way Chapel (1998)
- ❏ The Emily Louise (1998, set/2)
- ❏ Franklin Hook & Ladder Co. (1998)
- ❏ Harper's Farm (1998)
- ❏ Pierce Boat Works (1995)

Alpine Village Series®
- ❏ Bernhardiner Hundchen (1997)
- ❏ Danube Music Publisher (1996)
- ❏ Spielzeug Laden (1997)

Christmas In The City® Series
- ❏ Beekman House (1995)
- ❏ The City Globe (1997)
- ❏ Clark Street Automat (1999)
- ❏ The Consulate (LE-2000, set/2)

- ❏ Old Trinity Church (1998)
- ❏ Parkview Hospital (1999)
- ❏ The University Club (1998)

North Pole Series™
- ❏ Christmas Bread Bakers (1996)
- ❏ Cold Care Clinic (1999, *Elf Land*)
- ❏ Custom Stitchers (1998, *Elf Land*)
- ❏ Jack In The Box Plant No. 2 (LE-2000)
- ❏ North Pole Chapel (1993)
- ❏ Reindeer Barn (1990)
- ❏ Santa's Light Shop (1997)
- ❏ Santa's Lookout Tower (1993)
- ❏ Sweet Rock Candy Co. (2000, set/9)
- ❏ Tillie's Tiny Cup Café (1998, *Elf Land*)

General Heritage Village Collection® Accessories
- ❏ Biplane Up In The Sky (1998)
- ❏ Painting Our Own Village Sign (1998)

Dickens' Village Series® Accessories
- ❏ The 12 Days Of Dickens' Village Sign (1999)
- ❏ Chelsea Market Flower Monger & Cart (1993, set/2)
- ❏ Chelsea Market Hat Monger & Cart (1995, set/2)
- ❏ Eight Maids A-Milking (1996, set/2, *VIII, The 12 Days Of Dickens' Village*)

❏ Eleven Lords A-Leaping (1998, *XI, The 12 Days Of Dickens' Village*)
❏ English Post Box (1992)
❏ A Good Day's Catch (1999, set/2)
❏ King's Road Market Cross (1999)
❏ Members Of Parliament (1999, set/2)
❏ Nine Ladies Dancing (1997, set/3, *IX, The 12 Days Of Dickens' Village*)
❏ The Queen's Parliamentary Coach (LE-2000)
❏ Seven Swans A-Swimming (1996, set/4, *VII, The 12 Days Of Dickens' Village*)
❏ Ten Pipers Piping (1997, set/3, *X, The 12 Days Of Dickens' Village*)
❏ Twelve Drummers Drumming (1999, *XII, The 12 Days Of Dickens' Village*)

New England Village® Series Accessories
❏ Lobster Trappers (1995, set/4)
❏ Sea Captain & His Mates (1998, set/4)
❏ Volunteer Firefighters (1998, set/2)

Alpine Village Series® Accessories
❏ A New Batch Of Christmas Friends (1997, set/3)

Christmas In The City® Accessories
❏ 1919 Ford® Model-T (1998)
❏ Bringing Home The Baby (1999, set/2)
❏ The City Ambulance (1999)
❏ Ready For The Road (1998)
❏ "Yes, Virginia . . . " (1995, set/2)

North Pole Series™ Accessories
❏ Christmas Fun Run (1998, set/6)
❏ Downhill Elves (1998, set/2)
❏ Elves On Ice (1996, set/4)
❏ Happy New Year! (1999)
❏ Open Wide! (1999)

❏ Peppermint Skating Party (1998, set/6)
❏ Photo With Santa (1999, set/3)
❏ Untangle The Christmas Lights (1997)

Dickens' Village Series® Ornaments
❏ Christmas Carol Cottages (1998, set/3, *Classic Ornament Series*)
❏ Dickens' Village Church (1998, *Classic Ornament Series*)
❏ Dickens' Village Mill (1998, *Classic Ornament Series*)
❏ The Old Curiosity Shop (1998, *Classic Ornament Series*)
❏ Victoria Station (1999, *Classic Ornament Series*)

New England Village® Series Ornaments
❏ Captain's Cottage (1998, *Classic Ornament Series*)
❏ Craggy Cove Lighthouse (1998, *Classic Ornament Series*)
❏ Steeple Church (1998, *Classic Ornament Series*)

Christmas In The City® Series Ornaments
❏ Cathedral Church Of St. Mark (1998, *Classic Ornament Series*)
❏ City Hall (1998, *Classic Ornament Series*)
❏ Hollydale's Department Store (1999, *Classic Ornament Series*)
❏ Red Brick Fire Station (1998, *Classic Ornament Series*)

North Pole Series™ Ornaments
❏ Elf Bunkhouse (1998, *Classic Ornament Series*)
❏ Real Plastic Snow Factory (1999, *Classic Ornament Series*)
❏ Reindeer Barn (1998, *Classic Ornament Series*)
❏ Santa's Lookout Tower (1998, *Classic Ornament Series*)
❏ Santa's Workshop (1998, *Classic Ornament Series*)

The Heritage Village Collection® Top Ten

This list showcases the ten most valuable Heritage Village pieces as established by their secondary market value.

Dickens' Village Mill (LE-2,500)
Dickens' Village • #6519-6
Issued: 1985 • Retired: 1986
Issue Price: **$35** • Value: **$5,000**

Norman Church (LE-3,500)
Dickens' Village • #6502-1
Issued: 1986 • Retired: 1987
Issue Price: **$40** • Value: **$3,450**

Cathedral Church Of St. Mark (LE-3,024)
Christmas in the City • #5549-2
Issued: 1991 • Retired: 1993
Issue Price: **$120** • Value: **$2,100**

Chesterton Manor House (LE-7,500)
Dickens' Village • #6568-4
Issued: 1987 • Retired: 1988
Issue Price: **$45** • Value: **$1,475**

The Original Shops Of Dickens' Village (set/7)
Dickens' Village • #6515-3
Issued: 1984 • Retired: 1988
Issue Price: **$175** • Value: **$1,290**

New England Village (set/7)
New England Village • #6530-7
Issued: 1986 • Retired: 1989
Issue Price: **$170** • Value: **$1,175**

Smythe Woolen Mill (LE-7,500)
New England Village • #6543-9
Issued: 1987 • Retired: 1988
Issue Price: **$42** • Value: **$1,100**

Dickens' Cottages (set/3)
Dickens' Village • #6518-8
Issued: 1985 • Retired: 1988
Issue Price: **$75** • Value: **$970**

Josef Engel Farmhouse
Alpine Village • #5952-8
Issued: 1987 • Retired: 1989
Issue Price: **$33** • Value: **$950**

Palace Theatre
Christmas in the City • #5963-3
Issued: 1987 • Retired: 1989
Issue Price: **$45** • Value: **$895**

How To Use Your Collector's Value Guide™

1. *Locate* your piece within the Value Guide. The Heritage Village Collection is listed in the following order: *Dickens' Village Series®, New England Village® Series, Alpine Village Series®,* *Christmas In The City® Series, North Pole Series™, Disney Parks Village™ Series* and *Little Town Of Bethlehem™ Series.* In the section following the villages, each village's accessories are listed. Following all of the villages and accessories are hinged boxes and ornaments. Pieces are listed alphabetically within each section; however, buildings that are part of a set are shown individually after the set. To help you locate your pieces easily, we have provided numerical and alphabetical indexes beginning on page 267.

Ashbury Inn
Issued: 1991 • Retired: 1995
#5555-7 • Original Price: $55
Market Value: $78

Dickens Village Buildings	
Price Paid	Value
1. $55	$78
2.	
3.	
4.	
5.	
	$78
Totals	

2. *Find* the market value of your piece. If there is a variation with secondary market value, you will also find that value noted (store exclusives are listed in the same manner). Pieces for which no market value has been established are listed as "N/E" (not established). Pieces which are currently available at retail stores are listed at their current retail price.

3. *Record* the price you paid and the secondary market value in the corresponding boxes at the bottom of each page.

4. *Calculate* the value for each page by adding all of the prices in the "price paid" and "value" columns. Be sure to use a pencil so you can change the totals as your collection grows!

5. *Transfer* the totals from each page to the "Total Value of My Collection" worksheets for Heritage Village, beginning on page 139.

6. *Add* the totals together to determine the overall value of your collection.

Dickens' Village Series® – Buildings

The citizens of *Dickens' Village* know that you can't stop progress, so they've welcomed their 13 new neighbors this year with open arms. After all, who could object to a new golf clubhouse and a cocoa works! To make room for these new additions, there were 11 retirements in 2000. Since the introduction of its first seven shops in 1984, this village has grown in leaps and bounds and now numbers over 100 buildings.

1
New

Abington Lock Keeper's Residence
Issued: 2000 • Current
#58474 • Original Price: $58
Market Value: $58

2
New

Abington Lockside Inn
Issued: 2000 • Current
#58473• Original Price: $68
Market Value: $68

3

Aldeburgh Music Box Shop
Issued: 1999 • Retired: 2000
#58441 • Original Price: $60
Market Value: $62

4

Aldeburgh Music Box Shop (set/3, LE-35,000)
Issued: 1999 • Retired: 2000
#58442 • Original Price: $85
Market Value: $110

5

Ashbury Inn
Issued: 1991 • Retired: 1995
#5555-7 • Original Price: $55
Market Value: $78

Dickens' Village Series®

	Price Paid	Value
1.		
2.		
3.		
4.		
5.		
Totals		

Dickens' Village Series® – Buildings

6

Ashwick Lane Hose & Ladder
Issued: 1997 • Current
#58305 • Original Price: $54
Market Value: $54

7

New

Ashwick Lane Hose & Ladder Gift Set (set/10, GCC Piece)
Issued: 2000 • Current
#05700 • Original Price: $65
Market Value: $65

8

b

a

Barley Bree (set/2)
Issued: 1987 • Retired: 1989
#5900-5 • Original Price: $60
Market Value: $350

8a

Barn
Issued: 1987 • Retired: 1989
#5900-5 • Original Price: $30
Market Value: N/E

8b

Farmhouse
Issued: 1987 • Retired: 1989
#5900-5 • Original Price: $30
Market Value: N/E

Dickens' Village Series®

	Price Paid	Value
6.		
7.		
8.		
8a.		
8b.		
9.		
Totals		

9

Barmby Moor Cottage
Issued: 1997 • Retired: 2000
#58324 • Original Price: $48
Market Value: $51

10

Big Ben (set/2)
*The Historical
Landmark Series™*
Issued: 1998 • Current
#58341 • Original Price: $95
Market Value: $95

11

Bishops Oast House
Issued: 1990 • Retired: 1992
#5567-0 • Original Price: $45
Market Value: $83

12

Blenham Street Bank
Issued: 1995 • Retired: 1998
#58330 • Original Price: $60
Market Value: $80

13

Version 2

Version 1

Blythe Pond Mill House
Issued: 1986 • Retired: 1990
#6508-0 • Original Price: $37
Market Value:
1 – $270 ("Blythe Pond")
2 – $135 ("By The Pond")

14

**Boarding & Lodging
School ("18", LE-1993)**
*Charles Dickens'
Signature Series*
Issued: 1993 • Retired: 1993
#5809-2 • Original Price: $48
Market Value: $168

15

**Boarding & Lodging
School ("43")**
Issued: 1994 • Retired: 1998
#5810-6 • Original Price: $48
Market Value: $60

16

Brick Abbey
Issued: 1987 • Retired: 1989
#6549-8 • Original Price: $33
Market Value: $370

17

New

**Brightsmith & Sons,
Queen's Jewellers
(Event Piece)**
Issued: 2001 • To Be Retired: 2001
#58484 • Original Price: $75
Market Value: $75

Dickens' Village Series – **Buildings**

Dickens' Village Series®	Price Paid	Value
10.		
11.		
12.		
13.		
14.		
15.		
16.		
17.		
Totals		

Dickens' Village Series® – Buildings

18
New

Burwickglen Golf Clubhouse
Issued: 2000 • Current
#58477 • Original Price: $96
Market Value: $96

19

Butter Tub Barn
Issued: 1996 • Retired: 1999
#58338 • Original Price: $48
Market Value: $58

20

Butter Tub Farmhouse
Issued: 1996 • Retired: 1999
#58337 • Original Price: $40
Market Value: $47

21

C. Fletcher Public House (LE-12,500)
Issued: 1988 • Retired: 1989
#5904-8 • Original Price: $35
Market Value: $535

22

Chadbury Station And Train
Issued: 1986 • Retired: 1989
#6528-5 • Original Price: $65
Market Value: $385

23

Chancery Corner (set/8, Event Piece)
Issued: 1999 • Retired: 1999
#58352 • Original Price: $65
Market Value: N/E

Dickens' Village Series®

	Price Paid	Value
18.		
19.		
20.		
21.		
22.		
23.		
24.		
25.		
Totals		

24

Chesterton Manor House (LE-7,500)
Issued: 1987 • Retired: 1988
#6568-4 • Original Price: $45
Market Value: $1,475

25

The China Trader
Issued: 1999 • Retired: 2000
#58447 • Original Price: $72
Market Value: $74

26

The Christmas Carol Cottage (with magic smoking element)
The Christmas Carol Revisited
Issued: 1996 • Retired: 2000
#58339 • Original Price: $60
Market Value: $62

27

Christmas Carol Cottages (set/3)
Issued: 1986 • Retired: 1995
#6500-5 • Original Price: $75
Market Value: $136

27a

The Cottage Of Bob Cratchit & Tiny Tim
Issued: 1986 • Retired: 1995
#6500-5 • Original Price: $25
Market Value: $66

27b

Fezziwig's Warehouse
Issued: 1986 • Retired: 1995
#6500-5 • Original Price: $25
Market Value: $44

27c

Scrooge & Marley Counting House
Issued: 1986 • Retired: 1995
#6500-5 • Original Price: $25
Market Value: $56

28

Cobblestone Shops (set/3)
Issued: 1988 • Retired: 1990
#5924-2 • Original Price: $95
Market Value: $348

Dickens' Village Series®

	Price Paid	Value
26.		
27.		
27a.		
27b.		
27c.		
28.		
Totals		

Dickens' Village Series® – Buildings

28a

Booter And Cobbler
Issued: 1988 • Retired: 1990
#5924-2 • Original Price: $32
Market Value: $120

28b

T. Wells Fruit & Spice Shop
Issued: 1988 • Retired: 1990
#5924-2 • Original Price: $32
Market Value: $98

28c

The Wool Shop
Issued: 1988 • Retired: 1990
#5924-2 • Original Price: $32
Market Value: $172

29

Cobles Police Station
Issued: 1989 • Retired: 1991
#5583-2 • Original Price: $37.50
Market Value: $147

30

**Counting House & Silas
Thimbleton Barrister**
Issued: 1988 • Retired: 1990
#5902-1 • Original Price: $32
Market Value: $92

31

Version 1

Version 2

Crooked Fence Cottage
Issued: 1997 • Retired: 2000
#58304 • Original Price: $60
Market Value:
1 – N/E ("Seires" on bottomstamp)
2 – $62 ("Series" on bottomstamp)

Dickens' Village Series®

	Price Paid	Value
28a.		
28b.		
28c.		
29.		
30.		
31.		
32.		
33.		
Totals		

32

**Crown & Cricket
Inn (LE-1992)**
*Charles Dickens'
Signature Series*
Issued: 1992 • Retired: 1992
#5750-9 • Original Price: $100
Market Value: $170

33

New

**Crowntree Freckleton
Windmill (LE-30,000)**
Issued: 2000 • Current
#58472 • Original Price: $80
Market Value: $80

34

b   *c*

a

David Copperfield (set/3)
Issued: 1989 • Retired: 1992
#5550-6 • Original Price: $125
Market Value:
1 – $250 (with Peggotty's version 1)
2 – $190 (with Peggotty's version 2)

34a

Betsy Trotwood's Cottage
Issued: 1989 • Retired: 1992
#5550-6 • Original Price: $42.50
Market Value: $70

34b

Mr. Wickfield Solicitor
Issued: 1989 • Retired: 1992
#5550-6 • Original Price: $42.50
Market Value: $100

34c

Version 2

Version 1

Peggotty's Seaside Cottage
Issued: 1989 • Retired: 1992
#5550-6 • Original Price: $42.50
Market Value:
1 – $136 (tan)   **2** – $74 (green)

35

Dedlock Arms (LE-1994)
Charles Dickens' Signature Series
Issued: 1994 • Retired: 1994
#5752-5 • Original Price: $100
Market Value: $138

Dickens' Village Series®

	Price Paid	Value
34.		
34a.		
34b.		
34c.		
35.		
Totals		

Dickens' Village Series® – Buildings

Dickens' Village Series® – Buildings

36

Dickens' Cottages (set/3)
Issued: 1985 • Retired: 1988
#6518-8 • Original Price: $75
Market Value:
1 – $970 (with Stone Cottage version 1)
2 – $885 (with Stone Cottage version 2)

36a

Version 1

Version 2

Stone Cottage
Issued: 1985 • Retired: 1988
#6518-8 • Original Price: $25
Market Value: **1** – $450 (tan) **2** – $375 (green)

36b

Thatched Cottage
Issued: 1985 • Retired: 1988
#6518-8 • Original Price: $25
Market Value: $215

Dickens' Village Series®

	Price Paid	Value
36.		
36a.		
36b.		
36c.		
Totals		

36c

Tudor Cottage
Issued: 1985 • Retired: 1988
#6518-8 • Original Price: $25
Market Value: $375

37

a

c

b

Dickens' Lane Shops (set/3)
Issued: 1986 • Retired: 1989
#6507-2 • Original Price: $80
Market Value: $565

37a

Cottage Toy Shop
Issued: 1986 • Retired: 1989
#6507 • Original Price: $27
Market Value: $210

37b

Thomas Kersey Coffee House
Issued: 1986 • Retired: 1989
#6507-2 • Original Price: $27
Market Value: $173

37c

Tuttle's Pub
Issued: 1986 • Retired: 1989
#6507-2 • Original Price: $27
Market Value: $216

38

Version 1   *Version 2*   *Version 3*

Version 4   *Version 5*

Dickens' Village Church
Issued: 1985 • Retired: 1989
#6516-1 • Original Price: $35
Market Value: **1** - $450 (white) **2** - $260 (cream) **3** - $350 (green)
4 - $188 (tan) **5** - $155 (butterscotch)

Dickens' Village Series®

	Price Paid	Value
37.		
37a.		
37b.		
37c.		
38.		
Totals		

Dickens' Village Series® – Buildings

Dickens' Village Series® – Buildings

39

Dickens' Village Mill (LE-2,500)
Issued: 1985 • Retired: 1986
#6519-6 • Original Price: $35
Market Value: $5,000

40

Old East Rectory

Sudbury Church

The Spirit Of Giving

Dickens' Village Start A Tradition® Set (set/13, Event Piece)
Issued: 1997 • Retired: 1998
#58322 • Original Price: $75
Market Value: $115Z

41

Dudden Cross Church
Issued: 1995 • Retired: 1997
#5834-3 • Original Price: $45
Market Value: $54

42

Dudley Docker
Issued: 1999 • Retired: 2000
#58353 • Original Price: $70
Market Value: $73

43

Dursley Manor
Issued: 1995 • Retired: 1999
#58329 • Original Price: $50
Market Value: $60

Dickens' Village Series®

	Price Paid	Value
39.		
40.		
41.		
42.		
43.		
44.		
Totals		

44

East Indies Trading Co.
Issued: 1997 • Retired: 1999
#58302 • Original Price: $65
Market Value: $68

Dickens' Village Series® – Buildings

45

Fagin's Hide-A-Way
Issued: 1991 • Retired: 1995
#5552-2 • Original Price: $68
Market Value: $90

46

Scrooge At Fezziwig's Ball

Fezziwig's Ballroom (set/6, Event Piece)
Issued: 2000 • Retired: 2000
#58470 • Original Price: $75
Market Value: $88

47

Version 1   Version 2

The Flat Of Ebenezer Scrooge
Issued: 1989 • Current
#5587-5 • Original Price: $37.50
Market Value:
1 – $37.50 (with panes)
2 – $100 (without panes)

48

Gad's Hill Place (LE-1997)
Charles Dickens' Signature Series
Issued: 1997 • Retired: 1997
#57535 • Original Price: $98
Market Value: $125

49

Giggelswick Mutton & Ham
Issued: 1994 • Retired: 1997
#5822-0 • Original Price: $48
Market Value: $60

50

New

Glendun Cocoa Works
Issued: 2000 • Current
#58478 • Original Price: $80
Market Value: $80

51

The Grapes Inn (LE-1996)
Charles Dickens' Signature Series
Issued: 1996 • Retired: 1996
#57534 • Original Price: $120
Market Value: $145

Dickens' Village Series®

	Price Paid	Value
45.		
46.		
47.		
48.		
49.		
50.		
51.		
Totals		

Dickens' Village Series® – Buildings

52

Great Denton Mill
Issued: 1993 • Retired: 1997
#5812-2 • Original Price: $50
Market Value: $56

53

Great Expectations Satis Manor (set/4, with book)
Literary Classics®
Issued: 1998 • Current
#58310 • Original Price: $110
Market Value: $110

54

Green Gate Cottage (LE-22,500)
Issued: 1989 • Retired: 1990
#5586-7 • Original Price: $65
Market Value: $275

55

Hather Harness
Issued: 1994 • Retired: 1997
#5823-8 • Original Price: $48
Market Value: $54

56

Heathmoor Castle (LE-1999)
Issued: 1998 • Retired: 1999
#58313 • Original Price: $90
Market Value: $99

57

New

Hedgerow Garden Cottage
Issued: 2000 • Current
#58476 • Original Price: $57
Market Value: $57

Dickens' Village Series®

	Price Paid	Value
52.		
53.		
54.		
55.		
56.		
57.		
58.		
59.		
Totals		

58

Hembleton Pewterer
Issued: 1992 • Retired: 1995
#5800-9 • Original Price: $72
Market Value: $87

59

The Horse And Hounds Pub
Issued: 1998 • Current
#58340 • Original Price: $70
Market Value: $70

Dickens' Village Series® – Buildings

60

Ivy Glen Church
Issued: 1988 • Retired: 1991
#5927-7 • Original Price: $35
Market Value: $90

61

J. D. Nichols Toy Shop
Issued: 1995 • Retired: 1998
#58328 • Original Price: $48
Market Value: $59

62

Version 2

VILLAGE SEIRES

Version 1

J. Lytes Coal Merchant
Issued: 1997 • Retired: 1999
#58323 • Original Price: $50
Market Value:
1 – N/E ("Vallage" on bottomstamp)
2 – $58 ("Village" on bottomstamp)

63

Kenilworth Castle
Issued: 1987 • Retired: 1988
#5916-1 • Original Price: $70
Market Value: $650

64

Version 1

Princess of Whales.

box

Version 2

Kensington Palace (set/23, Event Piece)
Issued: 1998 • Retired: 1998
#58309 • Original Price: $195
Market Value: **1** – N/E ("Princess of Whales" on box)
2 – $265 ("Princess of Wales" on box)

65

b

a

King's Road (set/2)
Issued: 1990 • Retired: 1996
#5568-9 • Original Price: $72
Market Value: $100

Dickens' Village Series®

	Price Paid	Value
60.		
61.		
62.		
63.		
64.		
65.		
Totals		

Dickens' Village Series® – Buildings

65a

C. H. Watt Physician
Issued: 1990 • Retired: 1996
#55691 • Original Price: $36
Market Value: $55

65b

Tutbury Printer
Issued: 1990 • Retired: 1996
#55690 • Original Price: $36
Market Value: $52

66

King's Road Post Office
Issued: 1992 • Retired: 1998
#5801-7 • Original Price: $45
Market Value: $52

67

Kingsford's Brew House
Issued: 1993 • Retired: 1996
#5811-4 • Original Price: $45
Market Value: $60

68

Knottinghill Church
Issued: 1989 • Retired: 1995
#5582-4 • Original Price: $50
Market Value: $73

69

Leacock Poulterer
The Christmas Carol Revisited
Issued: 1997 • Retired: 1999
#58303 • Original Price: $48
Market Value: $52

70

Leed's Oyster House
Issued: 1999 • Current
#58446 • Original Price: $68
Market Value: $68

Dickens' Village Series®

	Price Paid	Value
65a.		
65b.		
66.		
67.		
68.		
69.		
70.		
Totals		

71

New

Sweet Roses

Topiary Trees

Lillycott Garden Conservatory (set/5)
Issued: 2000 • Current
#58475 • Original Price: $65
Market Value: $65

72

Lynton Point Tower
Issued: 1998 • Current
#58315 • Original Price: $80
Market Value: $80

73

The Maltings
Issued: 1995 • Retired: 1998
#5833-5 • Original Price: $50
Market Value: $58

74

Frogmore Chemist

G. Choir's Weights & Scales

Lydby Trunk & Satchel Shop

Custom House

Manchester Square Accessory

Manchester Square (set/25)
Issued: 1997 • Retired: 2000
#58301 • Original Price: $250
Market Value: $260

Dickens' Village Series®

	Price Paid	Value
71.		
72.		
73.		
74.		
Totals		

Value Guide — Department 56® Villages

Dickens' Village Series® – Buildings

Margrove Orangery
Issued: 1999 • Current
#58440 • Original Price: $98
Market Value: $98

McShane Cottage (set/2)
Issued: 1999 • Current
#58444 • Original Price: $55
Market Value: $55

The Melancholy Tavern
The Christmas Carol Revisited
Issued: 1996 • Retired: 1999
#58347 • Original Price: $45
Market Value: $50

Merchant Shops (set/5)
Issued: 1988 • Retired: 1993
#5926-9 • Original Price: $150
Market Value: $260

Dickens' Village Series®

	Price Paid	Value
75.		
76.		
77.		
78.		
78a.		
78b.		
Totals		

Geo. Weeton Watchmaker
Issued: 1988 • Retired: 1993
#5926-9 • Original Price: $32.50
Market Value: $53

The Mermaid Fish Shoppe
Issued: 1988 • Retired: 1993
#5926-9 • Original Price: $32.50
Market Value: $78

46

Dickens' Village Series® – Buildings

78c

Poulterer
Issued: 1988 • Retired: 1993
#5926-9 • Original Price: $32.50
Market Value: $62

78d

Walpole Tailors
Issued: 1988 • Retired: 1993
#5926-9 • Original Price: $32.50
Market Value: $59

78e

White Horse Bakery
Issued: 1988 • Retired: 1993
#5926-9 • Original Price: $32.50
Market Value: $64

79

Mulberrie Court
Issued: 1996 • Retired: 1999
#58345 • Original Price: $90
Market Value: $93

80

Nephew Fred's Flat
Issued: 1991 • Retired: 1994
#5557-3 • Original Price: $35
Market Value: $84

81

**Nettie Quinn Puppets
& Marionettes**
Issued: 1996 • Current
#58344 • Original Price: $50
Market Value: $50

82
b

a

**Nicholas Nickleby
(set/2)**
Issued: 1988 • Retired: 1991
#5925-0 • Original Price: $72
Market Value:
1 – $192 (with Nickleby Cottage
version 1)
2 – $165 (with Nickleby Cottage
version 2)

82a
Version 1

NICKOLAS NICKLEBY

Version 2

Nicholas Nickleby Cottage
Issued: 1988 • Retired: 1991
#5925-0 • Original Price: $36
Market Value:
1 – $125 ("Nickolas" on bottomstamp)
2 – $90 ("Nicholas" on bottomstamp)

Dickens' Village Series®

	Price Paid	Value
78c.		
78d.		
78e.		
79.		
80.		
81.		
82.		
82a.		
Totals		

Dickens' Village Series® – Buildings

82b

Wackford Squeers Boarding School
Issued: 1988 • Retired: 1991
#5925-0 • Original Price: $36
Market Value: $87

83

Norman Church (LE-3,500)
Issued: 1986 • Retired: 1987
#6502-1 • Original Price: $40
Market Value: $3,450

84

North Eastern Sea Fisheries Ltd.
Issued: 1998 • Retired: 1999
#58316 • Original Price: $70
Market Value: $84

85
New

The Old Curiosity Shop
Issued: 2000 • Current
#58482 • Original Price: $50
Market Value: $50

86

The Old Curiosity Shop
Issued: 1987 • Retired: 1999
#5905-6 • Original Price: $32
Market Value: $47

87

The Old Globe Theatre (set/4, LE-1998)
The Historical Landmark Series™
Issued: 1997 • Retired: 1998
#58501 • Original Price: $175
Market Value: $192

88

Old Michaelchurch
Issued: 1992 • Retired: 1996
#5562-0 • Original Price: $42
Market Value: $66

Dickens' Village Series®	Price Paid	Value
82b.		
83.		
84.		
85.		
86.		
87.		
88.		
Totals		

89

**Old Queensbridge
Station (set/2)**
Issued: 1999 • Current
#58443 • Original Price: $100
Market Value: $100

90

Version 1 *Version 2*

**The Old Royal Observatory
(set/2, LE-35,000)**
*The Historical
Landmark Series*™
Issued: 1999 • Retired: 2000
#58453 • Original Price: $95
Market Value:
1 – $120 (general release) **2** – $700 (retailer gift, gold dome,LE-5,600)

91

Version 1 *Version 2*

The Olde Camden Town Church
The Christmas Carol Revisited
Issued: 1996 • Retired: 1999
#58346 • Original Price: $55
Market Value: **1** – $64 (general release) **2** – N/E (Fortunoff)

92

Oliver Twist (set/2)
Issued: 1991 • Retired: 1993
#5553-0 • Original Price: $75
Market Value: $135

92a

Brownlow House
Issued: 1991 • Retired: 1993
#5553-0 • Original Price: $37.50
Market Value: $74

92b

Maylie Cottage
Issued: 1991 • Retired: 1993
#5553-0 • Original Price: $37.50
Market Value: $66

Dickens' Village Series®

	Price Paid	Value
89.		
90.		
91.		
92.		
92a.		
92b.		
Totals		

49

93

The Original Shops Of Dickens' Village (set/7)
Issued: 1984 • Retired: 1988
#6515-3 • Original Price: $175
Market Value: $1,290

93a

Abel Beesley Butcher
Issued: 1984 • Retired: 1988
#6515-3 • Original Price: $25
Market Value: $130

93b

Bean And Son Smithy Shop
Issued: 1984 • Retired: 1988
#6515-3 • Original Price: $25
Market Value: $192

93c

Candle Shop
Issued: 1984 • Retired: 1988
#6515-3 • Original Price: $25
Market Value: $190

Dickens' Village Series®

	Price Paid	Value
93.		
93a.		
93b.		
93c.		
93d.		
93e.		
Totals		

93d

Crowntree Inn
Issued: 1984 • Retired: 1988
#6515-3 • Original Price: $25
Market Value: $300

93e

Golden Swan Baker
Issued: 1984 • Retired: 1988
#6515-3 • Original Price: $25
Market Value: $185

Dickens' Village Series® – Buildings

93f

Green Grocer
Issued: 1984 • Retired: 1988
#6515-3 • Original Price: $25
Market Value: $200

93g

Jones & Co. Brush & Basket Shop
Issued: 1984 • Retired: 1988
#6515-3 • Original Price: $25
Market Value: $298

94

The Pied Bull Inn (LE-1993)
Charles Dickens' Signature Series
Issued: 1993 • Retired: 1993
#5751-7 • Original Price: $100
Market Value: $158

95

Portobello Road Thatched Cottages (set/3)
Issued: 1994 • Retired: 1997
#5824-6 • Original Price: $120
Market Value: $130

95a

Browning Cottage
Issued: 1994 • Retired: 1997
#58249 • Original Price: $40
Market Value: $45

95b

Cobb Cottage
Issued: 1994 • Retired: 1997
#58248 • Original Price: $40
Market Value: $45

95c

Mr. & Mrs. Pickle
Issued: 1994 • Retired: 1997
#58247 • Original Price: $40
Market Value: $45

96

Pump Lane Shoppes (set/3)
Issued: 1993 • Retired: 1996
#5808-4 • Original Price: $112
Market Value: $144

Dickens' Village Series®

	Price Paid	Value
93f.		
93g.		
94.		
95.		
95a.		
95b.		
95c.		
96.		
Totals		

Dickens' Village Series® – Buildings

Dickens' Village Series® – Buildings

96a

Bumpstead Nye
Cloaks & Canes
Issued: 1993 • Retired: 1996
#58085 • Original Price: $37.50
Market Value: $48

96b

Lomas Ltd. Molasses
Issued: 1993 • Retired: 1996
#58086 • Original Price: $37.50
Market Value: $48

96c

W.M. Wheat Cakes
& Puddings
Issued: 1993 • Retired: 1996
#58087 • Original Price: $37.50
Market Value: $52

97

Quilly's Antiques
Issued: 1996 • Retired: 1999
#58348 • Original Price: $46
Market Value: $56

98

Ramsford Palace

Wall Hedge

Corner Wall
Topiaries

Palace Fountain

Palace Gate

Palace Guards

Ramsford Palace (set/17, LE-27,500)
Issued: 1996 • Retired: 1996
#58336 • Original Price: $175
Market Value: $530

Dickens' Village Series®

	Price Paid	Value
96a.		
96b.		
96c.		
97.		
98.		
99.		
100.		
Totals		

99
New

100
New

Rockingham School
Issued: 2000 • Current
#58479 • Original Price: $85
Market Value: $85

Royal Staffordshire
Porcelains
Issued: 2000 • Current
#58481 • Original Price: $65
Market Value: $65

101

New

Royal Stock Exchange
Issued: 2000 • Current
#58480 • Original Price: $110
Market Value: $110

102

Ruth Marion Scotch Woolens (LE-17,500)
Issued: 1989 • Retired: 1990
#5585-9 • Original Price: $65
Market Value: $375

103

St. Martin-In-The-Fields Church
Issued: 2000 • Current
#58471 • Original Price: $96
Market Value: $96

104

New

Scrooge & Marley Counting House
Issued: 2000 • Current
#58483 • Original Price: $80
Market Value: $80

105

Seton Morris Spice Merchant

Christmas Apples

Seton Morris Spice Merchant (set/10, Event Piece)
Issued: 1998 • Retired: 1998
#58308 • Original Price: $65
Market Value: $75

106

Sir John Falstaff Inn (LE-1995)
The Charles Dickens' Signature Series
Issued: 1995 • Retired: 1995
#5753-3 • Original Price: $100
Market Value: $133

107

The Spider Box Locks
Issued: 1999 • Current
#58448 • Original Price: $60
Market Value: $60

108

Staghorn Lodge
Issued: 1999 • Current
#58445 • Original Price: $72
Market Value: $72

Dickens' Village Series®

	Price Paid	Value
101.		
102.		
103.		
104.		
105.		
106.		
107.		
108.		
Totals		

Dickens' Village Series® – Buildings

Dickens' Village Series® – Buildings

109

Faversham Lamps & Oil

Town Square Shops (set/2)

Town Square Carolers

Morston Steak & Kidney Pie

Start A Tradition Set (set/13)
Issued: 1995 • Retired: 1996
#5832-7 • Original Price: $85
Market Value: $110

110

Tattyeave Knoll
Issued: 1998 • Retired: 1999
#58311 • Original Price: $55
Market Value: $62

111

Teaman & Crupp China Shop
Issued: 1998 • Current
#58314 • Original Price: $64
Market Value: $64

112

Theatre Royal
Issued: 1989 • Retired: 1992
#5584-0 • Original Price: $45
Market Value: $87

113

Thomas Mudge Timepieces
Issued: 1998 • Retired: 2000
#58307 • Original Price: $60
Market Value: $62

Dickens' Village Series®		
	Price Paid	Value
109.		
110.		
111.		
112.		
113.		
114.		
Totals		

114

Tower Of London (set/5)
The Historical Landmark Series™
Issued: 1997 • Retired: 1997
#58500 • Original Price: $165
Market Value: $365

115

Victoria Station
Issued: 1989 • Retired: 1998
#5574-3 • Original Price: $100
Market Value: $115

116

Whittlesbourne Church
Issued: 1994 • Retired: 1998
#5821-1 • Original Price: $85
Market Value: $95

117

**Wingham Lane
Parrot Seller**
Issued: 1999 • Current
#58449 • Original Price: $68
Market Value: $68

118

b

c

a

Wrenbury Shops (set/3)
Issued: 1995 • Retired: 1997
#58331 • Original Price: $100
Market Value: $123

118a

The Chop Shop
Issued: 1995 • Retired: 1997
#58333 • Original Price: $35
Market Value: $45

118b

**T. Puddlewick
Spectacle Shop**
Issued: 1995 • Retired: 1998
#58334 • Original Price: $35
Market Value: $45

118c

Wrenbury Baker
Issued: 1995 • Retired: 1997
#58332 • Original Price: $35
Market Value: $48

Dickens' Village Series®

	Price Paid	Value
115.		
116.		
117.		
118.		
118a.		
118b.		
118c.		
Totals		

Dickens' Village Series® – Buildings

New England Village® Series–Buildings

It's been quite a year for the sailors and farmers of the *New England Village Series*. This past year, the quaint community welcomed six new neighbors into the fold. Now that the village has a cranberry barn and a clock shop, the townsfolk will never be hungry or late! Overall, there have been 67 buildings introduced into the *New England Village Series* since 1986, 52 of which have gone on to the greener pastures of retirement.

1

A. Bieler Farm (set/2)
Issued: 1993 • Retired: 1996
#5648-0 • Original Price: $92
Market Value: $126

1a

Pennsylvania Dutch Barn
Issued: 1993 • Retired: 1996
#56482 • Original Price: $50
Market Value: $67

1b

Pennsylvania Dutch Farmhouse
Issued: 1993 • Retired: 1996
#56481 • Original Price: $42
Market Value: $67

New England Village® Series

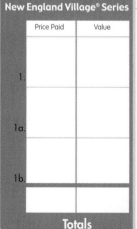

	Price Paid	Value
1.		
1a.		
1b.		
Totals		

2

Version 3

Version 1

Version 2

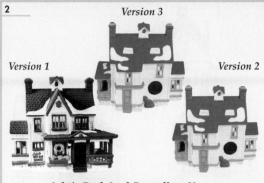

Ada's Bed And Boarding House
Issued: 1988 • Retired: 1991
#5940-4 • Original Price: $36
Market Value: **1** – $275 (yellow/rear steps part of mold)
2 – $152 (pale yellow/rear steps part of mold)
3 – $122 (pale yellow/rear steps attached separately)

3

Apple Valley School
Issued: 1996 • Current
#56172 • Original Price: $35
Market Value: $35

4

Arlington Falls Church
Issued: 1994 • Retired: 1997
#5651-0 • Original Price: $40
Market Value: $52

5

Version 2

Version 1

Berkshire House
Issued: 1989 • Retired: 1991
#5942-0 • Original Price: $40
Market Value: **1** – $148 (blue) **2** – $114 (teal)

6

Blue Star Ice Co.
Issued: 1993 • Retired: 1997
#5647-2 • Original Price: $45
Market Value: $58

7

Bluebird Seed And Bulb
Issued: 1992 • Retired: 1996
#5642-1 • Original Price: $48
Market Value: $57

New England Village® Series

	Price Paid	Value
2.		
3.		
4.		
5.		
6.		
7.		
Totals		

New England Village® Series – Buildings

New England Village® Series – Buildings

8

Bobwhite Cottage
Issued: 1996 • Current
#56576 • Original Price: $50
Market Value: $50

9

b

a

Brewster Bay Cottages (set/2)
Issued: 1995 • Retired: 1997
#5657-0 • Original Price: $90
Market Value: $103

9a

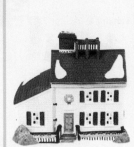

Jeremiah Brewster House
Issued: 1995 • Retired: 1997
#56568 • Original Price: $45
Market Value: $50

9b

Thomas T. Julian House
Issued: 1995 • Retired: 1997
#56569 • Original Price: $45
Market Value: $55

10

Cape Keag Fish Cannery
Issued: 1994 • Retired: 1998
#5652-9 • Original Price: $48
Market Value: $57

11

Captain's Cottage
Issued: 1990 • Retired: 1996
#5947-1 • Original Price: $40
Market Value: $55

12

c

a

b

Cherry Lane Shops (set/3)
Issued: 1988 • Retired: 1990
#5939-0 • Original Price: $80
Market Value: $324

12a

Anne Shaw Toys
Issued: 1988 • Retired: 1990
#5939-0 • Original Price: $27
Market Value: $162

New England Village® Series		
	Price Paid	Value
8.		
9.		
9a.		
9b.		
10.		
11.		
12.		
12a.		
Totals		

12b

Ben's Barbershop
Issued: 1988 • Retired: 1990
#5939-0 • Original Price: $27
Market Value: $112

12c

Otis Hayes Butcher Shop
Issued: 1988 • Retired: 1990
#5939-0 • Original Price: $27
Market Value: $88

13

Chowder House
Issued: 1995 • Retired: 1998
#56571 • Original Price: $40
Market Value: $52

14

Craggy Cove Lighthouse
Issued: 1987 • Retired: 1994
#5930-7 • Original Price: $35
Market Value: $70

15
New

The Cranberry House
Issued: 2000 • Current
#56627 • Original Price: $60
Market Value: $60

16

Deacon's Way Chapel
Issued: 1998 • Retired: 2000
#56604 • Original Price: $68
Market Value: $70

17

East Willet Pottery
Issued: 1997 • Retired: 1999
#56578 • Original Price: $45
Market Value: $47

New England Village® Series

	Price Paid	Value
12b.		
12c.		
13.		
14.		
15.		
16.		
17.		
Totals		

New England Village® Series – Buildings

New England Village® Series – Buildings

18

The Emily Louise (set/2)
Issued: 1998 • Retired: 2000
#56581 • Original Price: $70
Market Value: $72

19

Franklin Hook & Ladder Co.
Issued: 1998 • Retired: 2000
#56601 • Original Price: $55
Market Value: $60

20

Hale & Hardy House
Issued: 1999 • Current
#56610 • Original Price: $60
Market Value: $60

21

Harper's Farm
Issued: 1998 • Retired: 2000
#56605 • Original Price: $65
Market Value: $67

22

Harper's Farmhouse
Issued: 1999 • Current
#56612 • Original Price: $57
Market Value: $57

23

J. Hudson Stoveworks
Issued: 1996 • Retired: 1998
#56574 • Original Price: $60
Market Value: $72

New England Village® Series		
	Price Paid	Value
18.		
19.		
20.		
21.		
22.		
23.		
24.		
Totals		

24

Jacob Adams Farmhouse And Barn (set/5)
Issued: 1986 • Retired: 1989
#6538-2 • Original Price: $65
Market Value: $500

25

**Jannes Mullet
Amish Barn**
Issued: 1989 • Retired: 1992
#5944-7 • Original Price: $48
Market Value: $97

26

**Jannes Mullet Amish
Farm House**
Issued: 1989 • Retired: 1992
#5943-9 • Original Price: $32
Market Value: $120

27
New

Laurel Hill Church
Issued: 2000 • Current
#56629 • Original Price: $68
Market Value: $68

28

**McGrebe-Cutters
& Sleighs**
Issued: 1991 • Retired: 1995
#5640-5 • Original Price: $45
Market Value: $67

29

**Moggin Falls
General Store**
Issued: 1998 • Current
#56602 • Original Price: $60
Market Value: $60

30
New

**Mountain View Cabin
(LE-10,000)**
Issued: 2000 • Current
#56625 • Original Price: $55
Market Value: $55

31

**Navigational Charts
& Maps**
Issued: 1996 • Retired: 1999
#56575 • Original Price: $48
Market Value: $55

New England Village® Series

	Price Paid	Value
25.		
26.		
27.		
28.		
29.		
30.		
31.		
Totals		

New England Village® Series – Buildings

32

New England Village (set/7)
Issued: 1986 • Retired: 1989
#6530-7 • Original Price: $170
Market Value: **1** – $1,175 (with Steeple Church version 1)
2 – $1,092 (with Steeple Church version 2)

32a

Apothecary Shop
Issued: 1986 • Retired: 1989
#6530-7 • Original Price: $25
Market Value: $120

32b

Brick Town Hall
Issued: 1986 • Retired: 1989
#6530-7 • Original Price: $25
Market Value: $195

32c

General Store
Issued: 1986 • Retired: 1989
#6530-7 • Original Price: $25
Market Value: $320

New England Village® Series

	Price Paid	Value
32.		
32a.		
32b.		
32c.		
32d.		
32e.		
Totals		

32d

Livery Stable & Boot Shop
Issued: 1986 • Retired: 1989
#6530-7 • Original Price: $25
Market Value: $140

32e

Nathaniel Bingham Fabrics
Issued: 1986 • Retired: 1989
#6530-7 • Original Price: $25
Market Value: $160

32f

Red Schoolhouse
Issued: 1986 • Retired: 1989
#6530-7 • Original Price: $25
Market Value: $265

32g   Version 1

Version 2

Steeple Church
Issued: 1986 • Retired: 1989
#6530-7 • Original Price: $25
Market Value:
1 – $182 (tree attached with slip)
2 – $100 (tree attached with glue)

33

Old North Church
Issued: 1988 • Retired: 1998
#5932-3 • Original Price: $40
Market Value: $52

34

Pierce Boat Works
Issued: 1995 • Retired: 2000
#56573 • Original Price: $55
Market Value: $60

35

Pigeonhead Lighthouse
Issued: 1994 • Retired: 1998
#5653-7 • Original Price: $50
Market Value: $56

36

P. L. Wheeler's Bicycle Shop
Issued: 1999 • Current
#56613 • Original Price: $57
Market Value: $57

37

Platt's Candles & Wax
Issued: 1999 • Current
#56614 • Original Price: $60
Market Value: $60

38

Semple's Smokehouse
Issued: 1997 • Retired: 1999
#56580 • Original Price: $45
Market Value: $52

New England Village® Series

	Price Paid	Value
32f.		
32g.		
33.		
34.		
35.		
36.		
37.		
38.		
Totals		

New England Village® Series – Buildings

New England Village® Series – Buildings

39

Shingle Creek House
Issued: 1990 • Retired: 1994
#5946-3 • Original Price: $37.50
Market Value: $60

40

Sleepy Hollow (set/3)
Issued: 1990 • Retired: 1993
#5954-4 • Original Price: $96
Market Value: $194

40a

Ichabod Crane's Cottage
Issued: 1990 • Retired: 1993
#5954-4 • Original Price: $32
Market Value: $57

40b

Sleepy Hollow School
Issued: 1990 • Retired: 1993
#5954-4 • Original Price: $32
Market Value: $95

40c

Van Tassel Manor
Issued: 1990 • Retired: 1993
#5954-4 • Original Price: $32
Market Value: $64

41

Sleepy Hollow Church
Issued: 1990 • Retired: 1993
#5955-2 • Original Price: $36
Market Value: $65

New England Village® Series

	Price Paid	Value
39.		
40.		
40a.		
40b.		
40c.		
41.		
42.		
43.		
Totals		

42

**Smythe Woolen Mill
(LE-7,500)**
Issued: 1987 • Retired: 1988
#6543-9 • Original Price: $42
Market Value: $1,100

43

**Steen's Maple House
(with magic
smoking element)**
Issued: 1997 • Current
#56579 • Original Price: $60
Market Value: $60

44

Steeple Church
Issued: 1986 • Retired: 1990
#6539-0 • Original Price: $30
Market Value: $93

45

Stoney Brook Town Hall
Issued: 1992 • Retired: 1995
#5644-8 • Original Price: $42
Market Value: $58

46

Susquehanna Station (set/2)
Issued: 2000 • Current
#56624 • Original Price: $60
Market Value: $60

47

Timber Knoll Log Cabin
Issued: 1987 • Retired: 1990
#6544-7 • Original Price: $28
Market Value: $170

48

Trinity Ledge
Issued: 1999 • Current
#56611 • Original Price: $85
Market Value: $85

49

Van Guilder's Ornamental Ironworks
Issued: 1997 • Retired: 1999
#56577 • Original Price: $50
Market Value: $55

50

New

New Spring Finery

Verna Mae's Boutique (set/3)
Issued: 2000 • Current
#56626 • Original Price: $65
Market Value: $65

New England Village® Series

	Price Paid	Value
44.		
45.		
46.		
47.		
48.		
49.		
50.		
Totals		

New England Village® Series– Buildings

51

Weston Train Station
Issued: 1987 • Retired: 1989
#5931-5 • Original Price: $42
Market Value: $285

52
New

Wm. Walton Fine Clocks & Pocket Pieces
Issued: 2000 • Current
#56628 • Original Price: $60
Market Value: $60

53

Woodbridge Post Office
Issued: 1995 • Retired: 1998
#56572 • Original Price: $40
Market Value: $47

54

Yankee Jud Bell Casting
Issued: 1992 • Retired: 1995
#5643-0 • Original Price: $44
Market Value: $60

New England Village® Series		
	Price Paid	Value
51.		
52.		
53.		
54.		
Totals		

Alpine Village Series® – Buildings

Charming little villages tucked away in the Alps may be a bit isolated, but this community is open enough to see two new structures for 2001. With a brand-new toy works and a new beer house (what European mountain town would be without one?), the growth of the *Alpine Village Series* is faster than a Swiss skier! Those two pieces bring the grand total up to 26, a respectable number of which 18 have bid auf Wiedersehen so far.

1

Version 1   Version 2

Alpine Church
Issued: 1987 • Retired: 1991
#6541-2 • Original Price: $32
Market Value: **1** – $475 (white trim) **2** – $185 (brown trim)

2

b

a

Alpine Shops (set/2)
Issued: 1992 • Retired: 1997
#5618-9 • Original Price: $75
Market Value: $86

2a

Kukuck Uhren
Issued: 1992 • Retired: 1998
#56191 • Original Price: $37.50
Market Value: $42

2b

1629

Metterniche Wurst

Metterniche Wurst
Issued: 1992 • Retired: 1997
#56190 • Original Price: $37.50
Market Value: $45

Alpine Village Series®

	Price Paid	Value
1.		
2.		
2a.		
2b.		
Totals		

Alpine Village Series® – Buildings

Alpine Village Series® – Buildings

3

Alpine Village (set/5)
Issued: 1986 • Retired: 1996
#6540-4 • Original Price: $150
Market Value: $178

3a

Apotheke
Issued: 1986 • Retired: 1997
#65407 • Original Price: $25
Market Value: $42

3b

Besson Bierkeller
Issued: 1986 • Retired: 1996
#65405 • Original Price: $25
Market Value: $45

3c

E. Staubr Backer
Issued: 1986 • Retired: 1997
#65408 • Original Price: $25
Market Value: $44

Alpine Village Series®

	Price Paid	Value
3.		
3a.		
3b.		
3c.		
3d.		
3e.		
Totals		

3d

Gasthof Eisl
Issued: 1986 • Retired: 1996
#65406 • Original Price: $25
Market Value: $44

3e

Milch-Kase
Issued: 1986 • Retired: 1996
#65409 • Original Price: $25
Market Value: $46

4

New

Altstädter Bierstube
Issued: 2000 • Current
#56218 • Original Price: $65
Market Value: $65

5

Bahnhof
Issued: 1990 • Retired: 1993
#5615-4 • Original Price: $42
Market Value: $85

6

Bakery & Chocolate Shop (Konditorei Schokolade)
Issued: 1994 • Retired: 1998
#5614-6 • Original Price: $37.50
Market Value: $47

7

Bernhardiner Hundchen (St. Bernard Puppies)
Issued: 1997 • Retired: 2000
#56174 • Original Price: $50
Market Value: $52

8

Danube Music Publisher
Issued: 1996 • Retired: 2000
#56173 • Original Price: $55
Market Value: $57

9

Federbetten Und Steppdecken
Issued: 1998 • Current
#56176 • Original Price: $48
Market Value: $48

10

Glockenspiel (animated, musical)
Issued: 1999 • Current
#56210 • Original Price: $80
Market Value: $80

Alpine Village Series®

	Price Paid	Value
4.		
5.		
6.		
7.		
8.		
9.		
10.		
Totals		

Alpine Village Series® – Buildings

11

Grist Mill
Issued: 1988 • Retired: 1997
#5953-6 • Original Price: $42
Market Value: $56

12

Heidi's Grandfather's House
Issued: 1998 • Current
#56177 • Original Price: $64
Market Value: $64

13

Hofburg Castle
Issued: 2000 • Current
#56216 • Original Price: $68
Market Value: $68

14

Josef Engel Farmhouse
Issued: 1987 • Retired: 1989
#5952-8 • Original Price: $33
Market Value: $950

15

Kamm Haus
Issued: 1995 • Retired: 1999
#56171 • Original Price: $42
Market Value: $50

16

New

Nussknacker Werkstatt (LE-5,600)
Issued: 2000 • Current
#56217 • Original Price: $60
Market Value: $60

Alpine Village Series®		
	Price Paid	Value
11.		
12.		
13.		
14.		
15.		
16.		
17.		
Totals		

17

St. Nikolaus Kirche
Issued: 1991 • Retired: 1999
#5617-0 • Original Price: $37.50
Market Value: $46

18

The Sound Of Music®
von Trapp Villa (set/5)
Issued: 1998 • Current
#56178 • Original Price: $130
Market Value: $130

19

The Sound Of Music®
Wedding Church
Issued: 1999 • Current
#56211 • Original Price: $60
Market Value: $60

20

Spielzeug Laden
Issued: 1997 • Retired: 2000
#56192 • Original Price: $65
Market Value: $67

21

Sport Laden
Issued: 1993 • Retired: 1998
#5612-0 • Original Price: $50
Market Value: $57

Alpine Village Series®

	Price Paid	Value
18.		
19.		
20.		
21.		
Totals		

Alpine Village Series® – Buildings

Christmas In The City® Series – Buildings

Since 1987, when *Christmas In The City Series* made its first appearance with five lonely buildings, Department 56 has built that original tiny town into a metropolis of 61 miniatures! The charming city saw six new places of business and leisure spring up in 2001, including a special 25th anniversary event piece. No big-city wrecking crew will ever knock down the series' 48 retired pieces, and the growth of this most unique city is sure to continue!

1

5th Avenue Salon
Issued: 1999 • Current
#58950 • Original Price: $68
Market Value: $68

2
New

42nd St. Fire Company
Issued: 2000 • Current
#58914 • Original Price: $80
Market Value: $80

3

5607 Park Avenue Townhouse
Issued: 1989 • Retired: 1992
#5977-3 • Original Price: $48
Market Value: $94

Christmas In The City® Series

	Price Paid	Value
1.		
2.		
3.		
4.		
5.		
Totals		

4

5609 Park Avenue Townhouse
Issued: 1989 • Retired: 1992
#5978-1 • Original Price: $48
Market Value: $94

5

All Saints Corner Church
Issued: 1991 • Retired: 1998
#5542-5 • Original Price: $96
Market Value: $116

Christmas In The City® Series – Buildings

6

Arts Academy
Issued: 1991 • Retired: 1993
#5543-3 • Original Price: $45
Market Value: $80

7

Brighton School
Issued: 1995 • Retired: 1998
#58876 • Original Price: $52
Market Value: $65

8

Brokerage House
Issued: 1994 • Retired: 1997
#5881-5 • Original Price: $48
Market Value: $63

9

Brownstones On The Square (set/2)
Issued: 1995 • Retired: 1998
#58877 • Original Price: $90
Market Value: $100

9a

Beekman House
Issued: 1995 • Retired: 2000
#58878 • Original Price: $45
Market Value: $47

9b

Pickford Place
Issued: 1995 • Retired: 1998
#58879 • Original Price: $45
Market Value: $57

10

Cafe Caprice French Restaurant
Issued: 1996 • Current
#58882 • Original Price: $45
Market Value: $45

11

The Capitol
Issued: 1997 • Retired: 1998
#58887 • Original Price: $110
Market Value: $140

Christmas In The City® Series		
	Price Paid	Value
6.		
7.		
8.		
9.		
9a.		
9b.		
10.		
11.		
Totals		

Christmas In The City® Series – Buildings

12

The Cathedral
Issued: 1987 • Retired: 1990
#5962-5 • Original Price: $60
Market Value: $360

13

**Cathedral Church Of
St. Mark (LE-3,024)**
Issued: 1991 • Retired: 1993
#5549-2 • Original Price: $120
Market Value: $2,100

14

Chocolate Shoppe
Issued: 1988 • Retired: 1991
#5968-4 • Original Price: $40
Market Value: $150

15

**Christmas In The City
(set/3)**
Issued: 1987 • Retired: 1990
#6512-9 • Original Price: $112
Market Value: $626

15a

Bakery
Issued: 1987 • Retired: 1990
#6512-9 • Original Price: $37.50
Market Value: $145

15b

Tower Restaurant
Issued: 1987 • Retired: 1990
#6512-9 • Original Price: $37.50
Market Value: $272

15c

Toy Shop And Pet Store
Issued: 1987 • Retired: 1990
#6512-9 • Original Price: $37.50
Market Value: $272

16

The City Globe
Issued: 1997 • Retired: 2000
#58883 • Original Price: $65
Market Value: $68

Christmas In The City® Series

	Price Paid	Value
12.		
13.		
14.		
15.		
15a.		
15b.		
15c.		
16.		
Totals		

Christmas In The City® Series – Buildings

Value Guide — Department 56® Villages

17

City Hall
Issued: 1988 • Retired: 1991
#5969-2 • Original Price: $65
Market Value: $186

18

Clark Street Automat
Issued: 1999 • Retired: 2000
#58954 • Original Price: $68
Market Value: $73

19

The Consulate
(set/2, LE-2000)
Issued: 1999 • Retired: 2000
#58951 • Original Price: $95
Market Value: $99

20
New

Department 56 Studio,
1200 Second Avenue
(Event Piece)
Issued: 2001 • To Be Retired: 2001
#58918 • Original Price: $100
Market Value: $100

21

The Doctor's Office
Issued: 1991 • Retired: 1994
#5544-1 • Original Price: $60
Market Value: $87

22

Dorothy's Dress Shop
(LE-12,500)
Issued: 1989 • Retired: 1991
#5974-9 • Original Price: $70
Market Value: $380

23

First Metropolitan Bank
Issued: 1994 • Retired: 1997
#5882-3 • Original Price: $60
Market Value: $72

24
New

Foster Pharmacy
Issued: 2000 • Current
#58916 • Original Price: $85
Market Value: $85

Christmas In The City® Series

	Price Paid	Value
17.		
18.		
19.		
20.		
21.		
22.		
23.		
24.		
Totals		

Christmas In The City® Series – Buildings

75

Christmas In The City® Series – Buildings

25

New

Gardengate House
Issued: 2000 • Current
#58915 • Original Price: $68
Market Value: $68

26

**Grand Central
Railway Station**
Issued: 1996 • Retired: 1999
#58881 • Original Price: $90
Market Value: $96

27

**The Grand Movie
Theater**
Issued: 1998 • Retired: 1999
#58870 • Original Price: $50
Market Value: $63

28

Hank's Market
Issued: 1988 • Retired: 1992
#5970-6 • Original Price: $40
Market Value: $88

29

**Heritage Museum
Of Art**
Issued: 1994 • Retired: 1998
#5883-1 • Original Price: $96
Market Value: $108

30

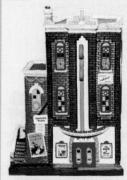

Hi-De-Ho Nightclub
Issued: 1997 • Retired: 1999
#58884 • Original Price: $52
Market Value: $60

31

**Hollydale's
Department Store**
Issued: 1991 • Retired: 1997
#5534-4 • Original Price: $75
Market Value: $98

Christmas In The City® Series		
	Price Paid	Value
25.		
26.		
27.		
28.		
29.		
30.		
31.		
Totals		

32

Holy Name Church
Issued: 1995 • Current
#58875 • Original Price: $96
Market Value: $96

33

Ivy Terrace Apartments
Issued: 1995 • Retired: 1997
#5887-4 • Original Price: $60
Market Value: $72

34

Jenny's Corner Book Shop
Issued: 2000 • Current
#58912 • Original Price: $65
Market Value: $65

35

Johnson's Grocery & Deli
Issued: 1997 • Current
#58886 • Original Price: $60
Market Value: $60

36

Lafayette's Bakery
Issued: 1999 • Current
#58953 • Original Price: $62
Market Value: $62

37

"Little Italy" Ristorante
Issued: 1991 • Retired: 1995
#5538-7 • Original Price: $50
Market Value: $85

38
New

The Majestic Theater (LE-15,000)
Issued: 2000 • Current
#58913 • Original Price: $100
Market Value: $100

39

Molly O'Brien's Irish Pub
Issued: 1999 • Current
#58952 • Original Price: $62
Market Value: $62

Christmas In The City® Series

	Price Paid	Value
32.		
33.		
34.		
35.		
36.		
37.		
38.		
39.		
Totals		

Christmas In The City® Series – Buildings

40
New

Mrs. Stover's Bungalow Candies
Issued: 2000 • Current
#58917 • Original Price: $75
Market Value: $75

41

Old Trinity Church
Issued: 1998 • Retired: 2000
#58940 • Original Price: $96
Market Value: $100

42

Palace Theatre
Issued: 1987 • Retired: 1989
#5963-3 • Original Price: $45
Market Value: $895

43

Paramount Hotel
Issued: 2000 • Current
#58911 • Original Price: $85
Market Value: $85

44

Parkview Hospital
Issued: 1999 • Retired: 2000
#58947 • Original Price: $65
Market Value: $70

45

Precinct 25 Police Station
Issued: 1998 • Current
#58941 • Original Price: $56
Market Value: $56

Christmas In The City® Series

	Price Paid	Value
40.		
41.		
42.		
43.		
44.		
45.		
46.		
47.		
Totals		

46

Red Brick Fire Station
Issued: 1990 • Retired: 1995
#5536-0 • Original Price: $55
Market Value: $88

47

Ritz Hotel
Issued: 1989 • Retired: 1994
#5973-0 • Original Price: $55
Market Value: $83

48

Riverside Row Shops
Issued: 1997 • Retired: 1999
#58888 • Original Price: $52
Market Value: $57

49

Scottie's Toy Shop

5¢ Pony Rides

Scottie's Toy Shop
(set/10, Event Piece)
Issued: 1998 • Retired: 1998
#58871 • Original Price: $65
Market Value: $95

50

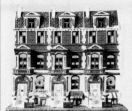

Sutton Place Brownstones
Issued: 1987 • Retired: 1989
#5961-7 • Original Price: $80
Market Value: $875

51

The University Club
Issued: 1998 • Retired: 2000
#58945 • Original Price: $60
Market Value: $62

52

b

a   *c*

Uptown Shoppes
(set/3)
Issued: 1992 • Retired: 1996
#5531-0 • Original Price: $150
Market Value: $187

52a

City Clockworks
Issued: 1992 • Retired: 1996
#55313 • Original Price: $56
Market Value: $68

52b

Haberdashery
Issued: 1992 • Retired: 1996
#55311 • Original Price: $40
Market Value: $58

52c

Music Emporium
Issued: 1992 • Retired: 1996
#55312 • Original Price: $54
Market Value: $70

Christmas In The City® Series

	Price Paid	Value
48.		
49.		
50.		
51.		
52.		
52a.		
52b.		
52c.		
Totals		

Christmas In The City® Series – Buildings

53

Variety Store
Issued: 1988 • Retired: 1990
#5972-2 • Original Price: $45
Market Value: $190

54

**Washington Street
Post Office**
Issued: 1996 • Retired: 1998
#58880 • Original Price: $52
Market Value: $67

55

The Wedding Gallery
Issued: 1998 • Current
#58943 • Original Price: $60
Market Value: $60

56

b

a

**West Village Shops
(set/2)**
Issued: 1993 • Retired: 1996
#5880-7 • Original Price: $90
Market Value: $119

56a

Potter's Tea Seller
Issued: 1993 • Retired: 1996
#58808 • Original Price: $45
Market Value: $60

56b

Spring St. Coffee House
Issued: 1993 • Retired: 1996
#58809 • Original Price: $45
Market Value: $65

Christmas In The City® Series

	Price Paid	Value
53.		
54.		
55.		
56.		
56a.		
56b.		
57.		
58.		
Totals		

57

Wintergarten Cafe
Issued: 1999 • Retired: 1999
#58948 • Original Price: $60
Market Value: $78

58

Wong's In Chinatown
Issued: 1990 • Retired: 1994
#5537-9 • Original Price: $55
Market Value: $84

North Pole Series™ – Buildings

Just to add to the magic of the winter holidays, Department 56 began crafting a whole village of whimsical *North Pole Series* buildings in 1990. Santa Claus and his elves sure must be grateful for all those extra facilities! Since then, 61 pieces have been added to this frosty collection, including nine new ones for 2001. A total of 37 pieces have been voted out of the North Pole, but every year sees more pieces in Santa's hometown.

1
New

ACME Toy Factory
(set/5)
Issued: 2000 • Current
#56729 • Original Price: $80
Market Value: $80

2

Beard Barber Shop
Issued: 1994 • Retired: 1997
#5634-0 • Original Price: $27.50
Market Value: $42

3

Christmas Bread Bakers
Issued: 1996 • Retired: 2000
#56393 • Original Price: $55
Market Value: $58

4

Cold Care Clinic
Elf Land™
Issued: 1999 • Retired: 2000
#56703 • Original Price: $42
Market Value: $45

North Pole Series™

	Price Paid	Value
1.		
2.		
3.		
4.		
Totals		

North Pole Series™ – Buildings

5

Custom Stitchers
Elf Land™
Issued: 1998 • Retired: 2000
#56400 • Original Price: $37.50
Market Value: $39

6

New

Design Works North Pole (Event Piece)
Issued: 2001 • To Be Retired: 2001
#56733 • Original Price: $75
Market Value: $75

7

Elf Mountain Ski Resort
Issued: 1999 • Current
#56700 • Original Price: $70
Market Value: $70

8

The Elf Spa
Elf Land™
Issued: 1998 • Current
#56402 • Original Price: $40
Market Value: $40

9

Elfie's Sleds & Skates
Issued: 1992 • Retired: 1996
#5625-1 • Original Price: $48
Market Value: $63

10

Elfin Forge & Assembly Shop
Issued: 1995 • Retired: 1998
#56384 • Original Price: $65
Market Value: $75

11

Elfin Snow Cone Works
Issued: 1994 • Retired: 1997
#5633-2 • Original Price: $40
Market Value: $54

North Pole Series™

	Price Paid	Value
5.		
6.		
7.		
8.		
9.		
10.		
11.		
Totals		

12

**Elsie's Gingerbread
(with magic smoking
element, LE-1998)**
Issued: 1997 • Retired: 1998
#56398 • Original Price: $65
Market Value: $105

13

Elves' Trade School
Issued: 1995 • Retired: 1998
#56387 • Original Price: $50
Market Value: $62

14
New

**Ginny's Cookie
Treats (set/3)**
Elf Land™
Issued: 2000 • Current
#56732 • Original Price: $50
Market Value: $50

15

The Glacier Gazette
Issued: 1997 • Retired: 1999
#56394 • Original Price: $48
Market Value: $54

16

Glass Ornament Works
Issued: 1997 • Current
#56396 • Original Price: $60
Market Value: $60

17

Hall Of Records
Issued: 1996 • Retired: 1999
#56392 • Original Price: $50
Market Value: $56

18

**Jack In The Box Plant
No. 2 (LE-2000)**
Issued: 1999 • Retired: 2000
#56705 • Original Price: $65
Market Value: $70

North Pole Series™

	Price Paid	Value
12.		
13.		
14.		
15.		
16.		
17.		
18.		
Totals		

83

Value Guide — Department 56® Villages

North Pole Series™ – Buildings

19

Marie's Doll Museum
Issued: 1999 • Retired: 1999
#56408 • Original Price: $55
Market Value: $93

20

Mini-Donut Shop
Elf Land™
Issued: 1999 • Current
#56702 • Original Price: $42
Market Value: $42

21

Mrs. Claus' Greenhouse
Issued: 1997 • Current
#56395 • Original Price: $68
Market Value: $68

22

Neenee's Dolls & Toys
Issued: 1991 • Retired: 1995
#5620-0 • Original Price: $37.50
Market Value: $67

23

a
b

North Pole (set/2)
Issued: 1990 • Retired: 1996
#5601-4 • Original Price: $70
Market Value: $96

23a

Elf Bunkhouse
Issued: 1990 • Retired: 1996
#56016 • Original Price: $35
Market Value: $57

North Pole Series™		
	Price Paid	Value
19.		
20.		
21.		
22.		
23.		
23a.		
23b.		
24.		
Totals		

23b

Reindeer Barn
Issued: 1990 • Retired: 2000
#56015 • Original Price: $35
Market Value: $43

24

North Pole Chapel
Issued: 1993 • Retired: 2000
#5626-0 • Original Price: $45
Market Value: $50

25

North Pole Dolls   Santa's Bear Works

Entrance

North Pole Dolls & Santa's Bear Works (set/3)
Issued: 1994 • Retired: 1997
#5635-9 • Original Price: $96
Market Value: $120

26

North Pole Express Depot
Issued: 1993 • Retired: 1998
#5627-8 • Original Price: $48
Market Value: $57

27

b

a

North Pole Shops (set/2)
Issued: 1991 • Retired: 1995
#5621-9 • Original Price: $75
Market Value: $135

27a

Orly's Bell & Harness Supply
Issued: 1991 • Retired: 1995
#5621-9 • Original Price: $37.50
Market Value: $68

27b

Rimpy's Bakery
Issued: 1991 • Retired: 1995
#5621-9 • Original Price: $37.50
Market Value: $76

28

New

Northern Lights Fire Station
Issued: 2000 • Current
#56730 • Original Price: $64
Market Value: $64

29

Northern Lights Tinsel Mill
Issued: 1999 • Current
#56704 • Original Price: $55
Market Value: $55

North Pole Series™

	Price Paid	Value
25.		
26.		
27.		
27a.		
27b.		
28.		
29.		
Totals		

North Pole Series™ – Buildings

North Pole Series™ – Buildings

30

Oakwood Post Office Branch (set/2)
North Pole Woods™
Issued: 2000 • Current
#56881 • Original Price: $65
Market Value: $70

31

Obbie's Books & Letrinka's Candy
Issued: 1992 • Retired: 1996
#5624-3 • Original Price: $70
Market Value: $90

32

The Peanut Brittle Factory
Issued: 1999 • Current
#56701 • Original Price: $80
Market Value: $80

33

Crayola® Polar Palette Art Center
Issued: 2000 • Current
#56726 • Original Price: $65
Market Value: $65

34

Popcorn & Cranberry House
Issued: 1996 • Retired: 1997
#56388 • Original Price: $45
Market Value: $96

35

Post Office
Issued: 1992 • Retired: 1999
#5623-5 • Original Price: $45
Market Value: $60

North Pole Series™		
	Price Paid	Value
30.		
31.		
32.		
33.		
34.		
35.		
36.		
37.		
Totals		

36

Real Plastic Snow Factory
Issued: 1998 • Current
#56403 • Original Price: $80
Market Value: $80

37

Reindeer Care & Repair
North Pole Woods™
Issued: 2000 • Current
#56882 • Original Price: $60
Market Value: $65

38
New

Reindeer Condo
North Pole Woods™
Issued: 2000 • Current
#56886 • Original Price: $70
Market Value: $70

39

Reindeer Flight School
Issued: 1998 • Current
#56404 • Original Price: $55
Market Value: $55

40

Route 1, North Pole, Home Of Mr. & Mrs. Claus
Issued: 1996 • Current
#56391 • Original Price: $110
Market Value: $110

41
New

Rudolph's Condo
North Pole Woods™
Issued: 2000 • Current
#56885 • Original Price: $50
Market Value: $50

42

Santa's Bell Repair
Issued: 1996 • Retired: 1998
#56389 • Original Price: $45
Market Value: $57

43

Santa's Light Shop
Issued: 1997 • Retired: 2000
#56397 • Original Price: $52
Market Value: $54

44

Santa's Lookout Tower
Issued: 1993 • Retired: 2000
#5629-4 • Original Price: $45
Market Value: $50

45
New

Santa's Retreat (set/2)
North Pole Woods™
Issued: 2000 • Current
#56883 • Original Price: $70
Market Value: $70

North Pole Series™

	Price Paid	Value
38.		
39.		
40.		
41.		
42.		
43.		
44.		
45.		
Totals		

North Pole Series™ – Buildings

North Pole Series™ – Buildings

46

Santa's Rooming House
Issued: 1995 • Retired: 1999
#56386 • Original Price: $50
Market Value: $55

47

Santa's Visiting Center (set/6, Event Piece)
Issued: 1999 • Retired: 1999
#56407 • Original Price: $65
Market Value: $98

48

Santa's Woodworks
Issued: 1993 • Retired: 1996
#5628-6 • Original Price: $42
Market Value: $63

49

Santa's Workshop
Issued: 1990 • Retired: 1993
#5600-6 • Original Price: $72
Market Value: $425

50

Gift Wrap & Ribbons *Candy Cane & Peppermint Shop*

Candy Cane Elves (set/2)

Candy Cane Lane (set/2)

Start A Tradition (set/12)
Issued: 1996 • Retired: 1996
#56390 • Original Price: $85
Market Value: $110

North Pole Series™

	Price Paid	Value
46.		
47.		
48.		
49.		
50.		
51.		
52.		
Totals		

51

Candy Mining

Sweet Rock Candy Co. (set/9, Event Piece)
Issued: 2000 • Retired: 2000
#56725 • Original Price: $75
Market Value: $80

52

Tassy's Mittens & Hassel's Woolies
Issued: 1991 • Retired: 1995
#5622-7 • Original Price: $50
Market Value: $87

53

Tillie's Tiny Cup Café
Elf Land™
Issued: 1998 • Retired: 2000
#56401 • Original Price: $37.50
Market Value: $39

54

Tin Soldier Shop
Issued: 1995 • Retired: 1997
#5638-3 • Original Price: $42
Market Value: $55

55

New

Toot's Model Train Mfg. (LE-25,000)
Issued: 2000 • Current
#5672-8 • Original Price: $110
Market Value: $110

56

Town Meeting Hall
North Pole Woods™
Issued: 2000 • Current
#56880 • Original Price: $68
Market Value: $73

57

Trim-A-Tree Factory (set/2)
North Pole Woods™
Issued: 2000 • Current
#56884 • Original Price: $50
Market Value: $55

58

Weather & Time Observatory
Issued: 1995 • Retired: 1999
#56385 • Original Price: $50
Market Value: $54

59

New

Wedding Bells Chapel
Elf Land™
Issued: 2000 • Current
#5673-1 • Original Price: $45
Market Value: $45

North Pole Series™

	Price Paid	Value
53.		
54.		
55.		
56.		
57.		
58.		
59.		
Totals		

North Pole Series™ – Buildings

Disney Parks Village™ Series – Buildings *(left margin)*

Disney Parks Village™ Series– Buildings

In 1994, Department 56 released the first four buildings that honored everyone's favorite theme park – Disneyland! The "Disneyland Fire Department #105," "Mickey's Christmas Carol" and "Olde World Antiques Shops" began the series. It continued in 1995 with "Tinker Bell's Treasures" and "Silversmith" in 1995. Their run didn't last for long, since they were all retired in 1996. But lovers of Disney and Department 56 have kept up their search for these elusive pieces!

1

Disneyland Fire Department #105
Issued: 1994 • Retired: 1996
#5352-0 • Original Price: $45
Market Value: $52

2

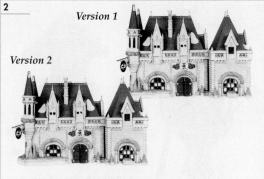

Version 1

Version 2

Mickey's Christmas Carol (set/2)
Issued: 1994 • Retired: 1996
#5350-3 • Original Price: $144
Market Value:
1 – $160 (with spires on dormers)
2 – $160 (without spires on dormers)

Disney Parks Village™ Series

	Price Paid	Value
1.		
2.		
3.		
Totals		

3

a

b

Olde World Antiques Shops (set/2)
Issued: 1994 • Retired: 1996
#5351-1 • Original Price: $90
Market Value: $100

Value Guide — Department 56® Villages

3a

Olde World Antiques I
Issued: 1994 • Retired: 1996
#5351-1 • Original Price: $45
Market Value: $55

3b

Olde World Antiques II
Issued: 1994 • Retired: 1996
#5351-1 • Original Price: $45
Market Value: $55

4

Silversmith
Issued: 1995 • Retired: 1996
#53521 • Original Price: $50
Market Value: $285

5

Tinker Bell's Treasures
Issued: 1995 • Retired: 1996
#53522 • Original Price: $60
Market Value: $275

Disney Parks Village™ Series – Buildings

Disney Parks Village™ Series

	Price Paid	Value
3a.		
3b.		
4.		
5.		
Totals		

91

Little Town Of Bethlehem™ Series – Buildings

When the original 12-piece set "Little Town Of Bethlehem" made its first appearance in 1987, no one could have known that the Biblical theme would catch on so well. But it did and Department 56 has continued to produce more of these buildings to illustrate everyday life in ancient times. Counting the original set, 7 scenes have graced collectibles shelves to date. Two more pieces came on the scene for 2001, making this series the only one to grow out of a single set.

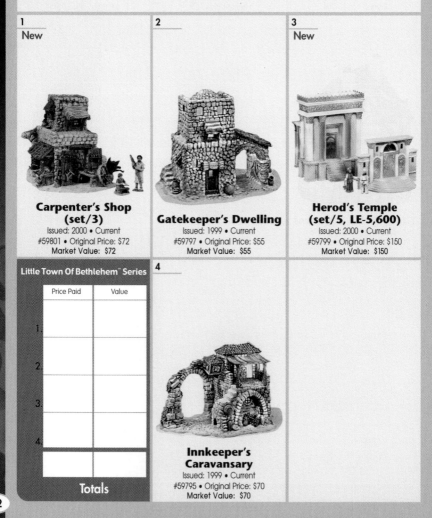

1
New

Carpenter's Shop (set/3)
Issued: 2000 • Current
#59801 • Original Price: $72
Market Value: $72

2

Gatekeeper's Dwelling
Issued: 1999 • Current
#59797 • Original Price: $55
Market Value: $55

3
New

Herod's Temple (set/5, LE-5,600)
Issued: 2000 • Current
#59799 • Original Price: $150
Market Value: $150

4

Innkeeper's Caravansary
Issued: 1999 • Current
#59795 • Original Price: $70
Market Value: $70

Little Town Of Bethlehem™ Series

	Price Paid	Value
1.		
2.		
3.		
4.		
Totals		

5

Little Town Of Bethlehem (set/12)
Issued: 1987 • Retired: 1999
#5975-7 • Original Price: $150
Market Value: $165

6

Nativity (set/2)
Issued: 1999 • Current
#59796 • Original Price: $55
Market Value: $55

7

New

Rug Merchant's Colonnade (set/4)
Issued: 2000 • Current
#59802 • Original Price: $110
Market Value: $110

Little Town Of Bethlehem™ Series – Buildings

Little Town Of Bethlehem™ Series		
	Price Paid	Value
5.		
6.		
7.		
Totals		

93

Accessories

What good is a town or city without people? Numerous accessories are available to make your little communities come to life, ranging from human characters (some of whom are taken from literature) to simple yet necessary ornaments likes trees and streetlights.

The Heritage Village Collection® Accessories

1

Biplane Up In The Sky
Issued: 1998 • Retired: 2000
#52731 • Original Price: $50
Market Value: $60

2

Bumper Fun Ride (set/4, animated)
Issued: 2000 • Current
#52500 • Original Price: $98
Market Value: $98

3

Christmas At The Park (set/3)
Issued: 1993 • Current
#5866-1 • Original Price: $27.50
Market Value: $27.50

4

Christmas Bells (Event Piece)
Issued: 1996 • Retired: 1996
#98711 • Original Price: $35
Market Value: $53

5

New

Christmas Carolers
Issued: 2000 • Current
#58631 • Original Price: $27.50
Market Value: $27.50

6

Churchyard Fence Extensions (set/4)
Issued: 1992 • Retired: 1997
#5807-6 • Original Price: $16
Market Value: $22

7

Churchyard Fence Gate (set/3)
Issued: 1992 • Retired: 1992
#5563-8 • Original Price: $15
Market Value: $62

The Heritage Village Collection®

	Price Paid	Value
1.		
2.		
3.		
4.		
5.		
6.		
7.		
Totals		

8

Churchyard Gate And Fence (set/3)
Issued: 1992 • Retired: 1997
#5806-8 • Original Price: $15
Market Value: $22

9

Dashing Through The Snow
Issued: 1993 • Current
#5820-3 • Original Price: $32.50
Market Value: $32.50

10

Dorothy's Skate Rental
Issued: 1999 • Current
#55515 • Original Price: $35
Market Value: $35

11

Family Winter Outing (set/3, track compatible)
Issued: 1999 • Current
#55033 • Original Price: $10
Market Value: $10

12

Gate House (Event Piece)
Issued: 1992 • Retired: 1992
#5530-1 • Original Price: $22.50
Market Value: $52

13

Hear Ye, Hear Ye
Issued: 1999 • Current
#55523 • Original Price: $13.50
Market Value: $13.50

14

Heritage Village Promotional Sign
Issued: 1989 • Retired: 1990
#9953-8 • Original Price: $5
Market Value: $29

15
New

Holiday Singers (musical, animated)
Issued: 2000 • Current
#52505 • Original Price: $75
Market Value: $75

16

The Holly & The Ivy (set/2, Event Piece)
Issued: 1997 • Retired: 1997
#56100 • Original Price: $17.50
Market Value: $34

17

Lighted Tree w/Children And Ladder (set/3)
Issued: 1986 • Retired: 1989
#6510-2 • Original Price: $35
Market Value: $295

The Heritage Village Collection®

	Price Paid	Value
8.		
9.		
10.		
11.		
12.		
13.		
14.		
15.		
16.		
17.		
Totals		

The Heritage Village Collection® – Accessories

The Heritage Village Collection® – Accessories

18

Look, It's The Goodyear Blimp (animated)
Issued: 2000 • Current
#55001 • Original Price: $45
Market Value: $45

19

New

Mill Falls (animated)
Issued: 2000 • Current
#52503 • Original Price: $75
Market Value: $75

20

One Horse Open Sleigh
Issued: 1988 • Retired: 1993
#5982-0 • Original Price: $20
Market Value: $44

21

Painting Our Own Village Sign
Issued: 1998 • Retired: 2000
#55501 • Original Price: $12.50
Market Value: $14

22

New

Perfect Putt (animated)
Issued: 2000 • Current
#52508 • Original Price: $65
Market Value: $65

23

Playing In The Snow (set/3)
Issued: 1993 • Retired: 1996
#5556-5 • Original Price: $25
Market Value: $39

The Heritage Village Collection®		
	Price Paid	Value
18.		
19.		
20.		
21.		
22.		
23.		
24.		
25.		
26.		
27.		
Totals		

24

Poinsettia Delivery Truck
Issued: 1997 • Retired: 1999
#59000 • Original Price: $32.50
Market Value:
1 – $37 (general release) **2** – $45 (William Glen)

25

Porcelain Trees (set/2)
Issued: 1986 • Retired: 1992
#6537-4 • Original Price: $14
Market Value: $39

26

Rockefeller® Plaza Skating Rink (set/3, musical, animated)
Issued: 2000 • Current
#52504 • Original Price: $125
Market Value: $125

27

New

Santa's On His Way (musical, animated)
Issued: 2000 • Current
#52502 • Original Price: $65
Market Value: $65

28

New

Santa's Sleigh
Issued: 2000 • Current
#58630 • Original Price: $68
Market Value: $68

29

Skating Party (set/3)
Issued: 1991 • Current
#5523-9 • Original Price: $27.50
Market Value: $27.50

30

Skating Pond
Issued: 1987 • Retired: 1990
#6545-5 • Original Price: $24
Market Value: $83

31

Ski Slope (animated)
Issued: 1998 • Current
#52733 • Original Price: $75
Market Value: $75

32

Snow Children (set/3)
Issued: 1988 • Retired: 1994
#5938-2 • Original Price: $15
Market Value: $37

33

Stars And Stripes Forever (Event Piece, music box)
Issued: 1998 • Retired: 1999
#55502 • Original Price: $50
Market Value: $56

34

Through The Woods (set/4, animated)
Issued: 1999 • Current
#52791 • Original Price: $75
Market Value: $75

35

Town Square Gazebo
Issued: 1989 • Retired: 1997
#5513-1 • Original Price: $19
Market Value: $27

36

Town Tree (set/5)
Issued: 1993 • Current
#5565-4 • Original Price: $45
Market Value: $45

37

Town Tree Carolers (set/6, Parkwest/NALED Piece)
Issued: 2000 • Current
#05702 • Original Price: $65
Market Value: $65

The Heritage Village Collection®	
Price Paid	Value
28.	
29.	
30.	
31.	
32.	
33.	
34.	
35.	
36.	
37.	
Totals	

The Heritage Village Collection® – Accessories

38

Town Tree Trimmers (set/4)
Issued: 1993 • Current
#5566-2 • Original Price: $32.50
Market Value: $32.50

39

Two Rivers Bridge
Issued: 1994 • Retired: 1997
#5656-1 • Original Price: $35
Market Value: $45

40

Up, Up & Away Witch (animated)
Issued: 1998 • Current
#52711 • Original Price: $50
Market Value: $50

41

Village Animated Accessory Track
Issued: 1996 • Retired: 1999
#52642 • Original Price: $65
Market Value: N/E

42

Village Animated All Around The Park (set/18)
Issued: 1994 • Retired: 1996
#5247-7 • Original Price: $95
Market Value: $115

43

Village Animated Skating Pond (set/15)
Issued: 1993 • Current
#5229-9 • Original Price: $60
Market Value: $60

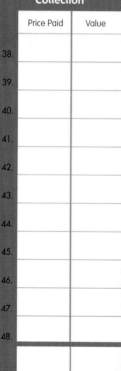

The Heritage Village Collection®		
	Price Paid	Value
38.		
39.		
40.		
41.		
42.		
43.		
44.		
45.		
46.		
47.		
48.		
Totals		

44

Village Animated Ski Mountain
Issued: 1996 • Retired: 1998
#52641 • Original Price: $75
Market Value: $80

45

Village Animated Sledding Hill
Issued: 1997 • Current
#52645 • Original Price: $65
Market Value: $65

46

Village Express Electric Train Set (set/24)
Issued: 1998 • Current
#52710 • Original Price: $270
Market Value: $270

47

Village Express Train (set/22, manufactured by Bachman Trains)
Issued: 1988 • Retired: 1996
#5980-3 • Original Price: $95
Market Value: $140

48

Village Express Train (set/22, manufactured by Tyco)
Issued: 1987 • Retired: 1988
#5997-8 • Original Price: $90
Market Value: $300

The Heritage Village Collection® – Accessories

49

Village Express Van
Issued: 1992 • Retired: 1996
#5865-3 • Original Price: $25
Market Value: $40
(green, general release)

"Village Express Van" Versions

Black – $125
Gold – $800
Bachman's – $85
Bronner's – $55
The Christmas Dove – $60
European Imports – $53
Fortunoff – $110
Incredible Xmas Place – $67
Lemon Tree – $50

The Limited Edition – $100
Lock, Stock & Barrel – $110
North Pole City – $58
Parkwest – $500
Robert's – $56
St. Nick's – $63
Stats – $58
William Glen – $58
The Windsor Shoppe – $56

50

New

**Village Express Van
(Event Piece)**
Issued: 2001 • To Be Retired: 2001
#52911 • Original Price: $25
Market Value: $25

51

**Village Monuments
(set/3)**
Issued: 1999 • Current
#55524 • Original Price: $25
Market Value: $25

52

**Village Porcelain
Pine, Large**
Issued: 1992 • Retired: 1997
#5218-3 • Original Price: $12.50
Market Value: $18

53

**Village Porcelain
Pine, Small**
Issued: 1992 • Retired: 1997
#5219-1 • Original Price: $10
Market Value: $15

54

**Village Porcelain Pine
Trees (set/2)**
Issued: 1994 • Retired: 1997
#5251-5 • Original Price: $15
Market Value: $20

55

**Village Sign
With Snowman**
Issued: 1989 • Retired: 1994
#5572-7 • Original Price: $10
Market Value: $22

56

**Village Streetcar
(set/10)**
Issued: 1994 • Retired: 1998
#5240-0 • Original Price: $65
Market Value: $70

The Heritage Village Collection®

	Price Paid	Value
49.		
50.		
51.		
52.		
53.		
54.		
55.		
56.		
Totals		

The Heritage Village Collection® – Accessories

57

Village Train Trestle
Issued: 1988 • Retired: 1990
#5981-1 • Original Price: $17
Market Value: $70

58

Village Up, Up & Away, Animated Sleigh
Issued: 1995 • Current
#52593 • Original Price: $40
Market Value: $40

59

Village Waterfall
Issued: 1996 • Retired: 1999
#52644 • Original Price: $65
Market Value: N/E

60
New

**Woodland Carousel
(musical, animated)**
Issued: 2000 • Current
#52509 • Original Price: $75
Market Value: $75

Dickens' Village Series® – Accessories

1

The 12 Days Of Dickens' Village Sign
Issued: 1999 • Retired: 2000
#58467 • Original Price: $20
Market Value: $30

The Heritage Village Collection®

	Price Paid	Value
57.		
58.		
59.		
60.		

Dickens' Village Series®

1.		
2.		
3.		
4.		
5.		
6.		

Totals

2
New

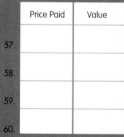

Abington Bridge
Issued: 2000 • Current
#58536 • Original Price: $37.50
Market Value: $37.50

3
New

Abington Canal (set/2)
Issued: 2000 • Current
#58535• Original Price: $30
Market Value: $30

4
New

**Abington Canal Boat
(set/2)**
Issued: 2000 • Current
#58522 • Original Price: $35
Market Value: $35

5
New

Abington Locks (set/2)
Issued: 2000 • Current
#58521 • Original Price: $48
Market Value: $48

6

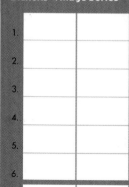

Ale Mates (set/2)
Issued: 1998 • Current
#58417 • Original Price: $25
Market Value: $25

The Heritage Village Collection® – Accessories

7

Ashley Pond Skating Party (set/6)
Issued: 1997 • Retired: 1999
#58405 • Original Price: $70
Market Value: $73

8

The Bird Seller (set/3)
Issued: 1992 • Retired: 1995
#5803-3 • Original Price: $25
Market Value: $37

9

Blacksmith (set/3)
Issued: 1987 • Retired: 1990
#5934-0 • Original Price: $20
Market Value: $83

10

Bringing Fleeces To The Mill (set/2)
Issued: 1993 • Retired: 1998
#5819-0 • Original Price: $35
Market Value: $42

11

Bringing Home The Yule Log (set/3)
Issued: 1991 • Retired: 1998
#5558-1 • Original Price: $27.50
Market Value: $33

12

Brixton Road Watchman (set/2)
Issued: 1995 • Retired: 1999
#58390 • Original Price: $25
Market Value: $29

13

Busy Railway Station (set/3)
Issued: 1999 • Current
#58464 • Original Price: $27.50
Market Value: $27.50

14

C. Bradford, Wheelwright & Son (set/2)
Issued: 1993 • Retired: 1996
#5818-1 • Original Price: $24
Market Value: $36

15   *Version 1*   *Version 2*   *Version 3*

Carolers (set/3)
Issued: 1984 • Retired: 1990
#6526-9 • Original Price: $10
Market Value: **1** – $120 (white lamppost)
2 – $43 (black lamppost, tan viola)
3 – N/E (black lamppost, brown/tan viola)

16

Carolers On The Doorstep (set/4)
Issued: 1990 • Retired: 1993
#5570-0 • Original Price: $25
Market Value: $44

17

Caroling With The Cratchit Family (set/3)
Christmas Carol Revisited
Issued: 1996 • Current
#58396 • Original Price: $37.50
Market Value: $37.50

Dickens' Village Series®

	Price Paid	Value
7.		
8.		
9.		
10.		
11.		
12.		
13.		
14.		
15.		
16.		
17.		
Totals		

Dickens' Village Series® – Accessories

18

Chelsea Lane Shoppers (set/4)
Issued: 1993 • Retired: 1999
#5816-5 • Original Price: $30
Market Value: $33

19

Chelsea Market Curiosities Monger & Cart (set/2)
Issued: 1994 • Retired: 1998
#5827-0 • Original Price: $27.50
Market Value: $34

20

Chelsea Market Fish Monger & Cart (set/2)
Issued: 1993 • Retired: 1997
#5814-9 • Original Price: $25
Market Value: $35

21

Version 1   *Version 2*

Chelsea Market Flower Monger & Cart (set/2)
Issued: 1993 • Retired: 2000
#5815-7 • Original Price: $27.50
Market Value:
1 – $34 (general release) **2** – $65 (Lord & Taylor)

22

Chelsea Market Fruit Monger & Cart (set/2)
Issued: 1993 • Retired: 1997
#5813-0 • Original Price: $25
Market Value: $35

Dickens' Village Series®

	Price Paid	Value
18.		
19.		
20.		
21.		
22.		
23.		
24.		
25.		
26.		
27.		
28.		
Totals		

23

Chelsea Market Hat Monger & Cart (set/2)
Issued: 1995 • Retired: 2000
#58392 • Original Price: $27.50
Market Value: $30

24

Chelsea Market Mistletoe Monger & Cart (set/2)
Issued: 1994 • Retired: 1998
#5826-2 • Original Price: $25
Market Value: $35

25

Child's Play (set/2)
Issued: 1998 • Current
#58415 • Original Price: $25
Market Value: $25

26

Childe Pond & Skaters (set/4)
Issued: 1988 • Retired: 1991
#5903-0 • Original Price: $30
Market Value: $88

27

Christmas Carol Christmas Morning Figures (set/3)
Issued: 1989 • Current
#5588-3 • Original Price: $18
Market Value: $18

28

Christmas Carol Christmas Spirits Figures (set/4)
Issued: 1989 • Current
#5589-1 • Original Price: $27.50
Market Value: $27.50

29

Christmas Carol Figures (set/3)
Issued: 1986 • Retired: 1990
#6501-3 • Original Price: $12.50
Market Value: $87

30

Christmas Carol Holiday Trimming Set (set/21)
Issued: 1994 • Retired: 1997
#5831-9 • Original Price: $65
Market Value: $78

31

"A Christmas Carol" Reading By Charles Dickens (set/4)
Issued: 1996 • Current
#58403 • Original Price: $45
Market Value: $45

32

"A Christmas Carol" Reading By Charles Dickens (set/7, LE-42,500)
Charles Dickens' Signature Series
Issued: 1996 • Retired: 1997
#58404 • Original Price: $75
Market Value: $150

33

Christmas Pudding Costermonger (set/3)
Issued: 1997 • Current
#58408 • Original Price: $32.50
Market Value: $32.50

34

Cobbler & Clock Peddler (set/2)
Issued: 1995 • Retired: 1997
#58394 • Original Price: $25
Market Value: $32

35

Come Into The Inn (set/3)
Issued: 1991 • Retired: 1994
#5560-3 • Original Price: $22
Market Value: $39

36

Constables (set/3)
Issued: 1989 • Retired: 1991
#5579-4 • Original Price: $17.50
Market Value: $70

37

David Copperfield Characters (set/5)
Issued: 1989 • Retired: 1992
#5551-4 • Original Price: $32.50
Market Value: $49

38

Delivering Coal For The Hearth (set/2)
Issued: 1997 • Retired: 1999
#58326 • Original Price: $32.50
Market Value: $38

39

Dickens' Village Sign
Issued: 1987 • Retired: 1993
#6569-2 • Original Price: $6
Market Value: $20

Dickens' Village Series®

	Price Paid	Value
29.		
30.		
31.		
32.		
33.		
34.		
35.		
36.		
37.		
38.		
39.		
Totals		

Dickens' Village Series® – Accessories

Value Guide — Department 56® Villages

40

Version 1   Version 2   Version 3

Dover Coach
Issued: 1987 • Retired: 1990
#6590-0 • Original Price: $18
Market Value: **1** – $100 (without mustache)
2 – $67 (with mustache, tight reins)
3 – $65 (with mustache, loose reins)

41

Eight Maids A-Milking (set/2)
#VIII, The 12 Days Of Dickens' Village
Issued: 1996 • Retired: 2000
#58384 • Original Price: $25
Market Value: $30

42

Eleven Lords A-Leaping
#XI, The 12 Days Of Dickens' Village
Issued: 1998 • Retired: 2000
#58413 • Original Price: $27.50
Market Value: $33

43

English Post Box
Issued: 1992 • Retired: 2000
#58050 • Original Price: $4.50
Market Value: $11

44

Farm People & Animals (set/5)
Issued: 1987 • Retired: 1989
#5901-3 • Original Price: $24
Market Value: $98

45

Version 1   Version 2

Father Christmas's Journey (track compatible)
Issued: 1997 • Current
#58407 • Original Price: $30
Market Value: **1** – $30 (general release) **2** – N/E (North Pole City)

46

Fezziwig And Friends (set/3)
Issued: 1988 • Retired: 1990
#5928-5 • Original Price: $12.50
Market Value: $59

47

Version 1   Version 2

The Fezziwig Delivery Wagon
Christmas Carol Revisited
Issued: 1996 • Current
#58400 • Original Price: $32.50
Market Value:
1 – $32.50 (general release) **2** – N/E (Lord & Taylor)

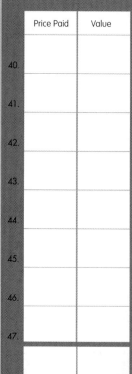

Dickens' Village Series®

	Price Paid	Value
40.		
41.		
42.		
43.		
44.		
45.		
46.		
47.		
Totals		

48

Fine Asian Antiques (set/2)
Issued: 1999 • Current
#58462 • Original Price: $27.50
Market Value: $27.50

49

The Fire Brigade Of London Town (set/5)
Issued: 1997 • Current
#58406 • Original Price: $70
Market Value: $70

50

Five Golden Rings (set/2)
#V, The 12 Days Of Dickens' Village
Issued: 1995 • Retired: 1999
#58381 • Original Price: $27.50
Market Value: $31

51

The Flying Scot Train (set/4)
Issued: 1990 • Retired: 1998
#5573-5 • Original Price: $48
Market Value: $57

52
New

Following The Leader (set/2)
Issued: 2000 • Current
#58526 • Original Price: $32.50
Market Value: $32.50

53

Four Calling Birds
#IV, The 12 Days Of Dickens' Village
Issued: 1995 • Retired: 1999
#58379 • Original Price: $32.50
Market Value: $36

54

Gingerbread Vendor (set/2)
Issued: 1996 • Current
#58402 • Original Price: $22.50
Market Value: $22.50

55

A Good Day's Catch (set/2)
Issued: 1999 • Retired: 2000
#58420 • Original Price: $27.50
Market Value: $31

56
New

Gourmet Chocolates Delivery Wagon
Issued: 2000 • Current
#58523 • Original Price: $45
Market Value: $45

57
New

Hedgerow Dovecote (set/2)
Issued: 2000 • Current
#58524 • Original Price: $32.50
Market Value: $32.50

Dickens' Village Series®

	Price Paid	Value
48.		
49.		
50.		
51.		
52.		
53.		
54.		
55.		
56.		
57.		
Totals		

Dickens' Village Series® – Accessories

Dickens' Village Series® – Accessories

58

Here We Come A-Wassailing (set/5)
Issued: 1998 • Current
#58410 • Original Price: $45
Market Value: $45

59

Holiday Coach
Issued: 1991 • Retired: 1998
#5561-1 • Original Price: $68
Market Value: $80

60

Holiday Quintet (set/6)
Issued: 2000 • Current
#58520 • Original Price: $37.50
Market Value: $37.50

61

Holiday Travelers (set/3)
Issued: 1990 • Retired: 1999
#5571-9 • Original Price: $22.50
Market Value: $28

Dickens' Village Series®

	Price Paid	Value
58.		
59.		
60.		
61.		
62.		
63.		
64.		
65.		
66.		
67.		
Totals		

62 New

Horses At The Lampguard (set/3)
Issued: 2000 • Current
#58531 • Original Price: $45
Market Value: $45

63 New

Keeping The Streets Clean (set/2)
Issued: 2000 • Current
#58532 • Original Price: $18
Market Value: $18

64

King's Road Cab
Issued: 1989 • Retired: 1998
#5581-6 • Original Price: $30
Market Value: $37

65

King's Road Market Cross
Issued: 1999 • Retired: 2000
#58456 • Original Price: $25
Market Value: $30

66

Lamplighter w/Lamp (set/2)
Issued: 1989 • Current
#5577-8 • Original Price: $9
Market Value: $10

67

Lionhead Bridge
Issued: 1992 • Retired: 1997
#5864-5 • Original Price: $22
Market Value: $34

68

The Locomotive Shed & Water Tower
Issued: 1999 • Current
#58465 • Original Price: $32.50
Market Value: $32.50

69

Master Gardeners (set/2)
Issued: 1999 • Current
#58458 • Original Price: $30
Market Value: $30

70

New

Master Potter
Issued: 2000 • Current
#58527 • Original Price: $18
Market Value: $18

71

Meeting Family At The Railroad Station (set/4)
Issued: 1999 • Current
#58457 • Original Price: $32.50
Market Value: $32.50

72

Members Of Parliament (set/2)
Issued: 1999 • Retired: 2000
#58455 • Original Price: $19
Market Value: $22

73

New

Merry Go Roundabout
Issued: 2000 • Current
#58533 • Original Price: $32.50
Market Value: $32.50

74

Nicholas Nickleby Characters (set/4)
Issued: 1988 • Retired: 1991
#5929-3 • Original Price: $20
Market Value: $40

75

Nine Ladies Dancing (set/3)
#IX, The 12 Days Of Dickens' Village
Issued: 1997 • Retired: 2000
#58385 • Original. Price: $30
Market Value: $34

76

The Old Puppeteer (set/3)
Issued: 1992 • Retired: 1995
#5802-5 • Original Price: $32
Market Value: $44

77

Oliver Twist Characters (set/3)
Issued: 1991 • Retired: 1993
#5554-9 • Original Price: $35
Market Value: $48

78

Version 1   *Version 2*

Ox Sled
Issued: 1987 • Retired: 1989
#5951-0 • Original Price: $20
Market Value: **1** – $235 (tan pants/green seat)
2 – $138 (blue pants/black seat)

Dickens' Village Series®		
	Price Paid	Value
68.		
69.		
70.		
71.		
72.		
73.		
74.		
75.		
76.		
77.		
78.		
Totals		

Dickens' Village Series® – Accessories

79
New

Par For The Course (set/3)
Issued: 2000 • Current
#58525 • Original Price: $27.50
Market Value: $27.50

80

A Partridge In A Pear Tree
#I, The 12 Days Of Dickens' Village
Issued: 1995 • Retired: 1999
#5835-1 • Original Price: $35
Market Value: $40

81

A Peaceful Glow On Christmas Eve (set/3)
Issued: 1994 • Current
#5830-0 • Original Price: $30
Market Value: $30

82
New

Polo Players (set/2)
Issued: 2000 • Current
#58529 • Original Price: $40
Market Value: $40

83

Portobello Road Peddlers (set/3)
Issued: 1994 • Retired: 1998
#5828-9 • Original Price: $27.50
Market Value: $34

84

Postern
(*Dickens' Village*® Ten Year Anniversary Piece)
Issued: 1994 • Retired: 1994
#9871-0 • Original Price: $17.50
Market Value: $36

85

Poultry Market (set/3)
Issued: 1991 • Retired: 1995
#5559-0 • Original Price: $30
Market Value: $46

86

The Queen's Parliamentary Coach (LE-2000)
Issued: 1999 • Retired: 2000
#58454 • Original Price: $60
Market Value: $100

87

Red Christmas Sulky
Issued: 1996 • Current
#58401 • Original Price: $30
Market Value: $30

88

Royal Coach
Issued: 1989 • Retired: 1992
#5578-6 • Original Price: $55
Market Value: $85

89

Seven Swans A-Swimming (set/4)
#VII, The 12 Days Of Dickens' Village
Issued: 1996 • Retired: 2000
#58383 • Original Price: $27.50
Market Value: $33

90
New

Sherlock Holmes – The Hansom Cab
Issued: 2000 • Current
#58534 • Original Price: $35
Market Value: $35

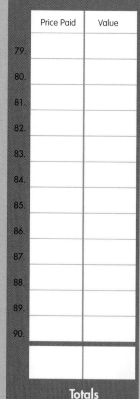

Dickens' Village Series®

	Price Paid	Value
79.		
80.		
81.		
82.		
83.		
84.		
85.		
86.		
87.		
88.		
89.		
90.		
Totals		

91

Shopkeepers (set/4)
Issued: 1987 • Retired: 1988
#5966-8 • Original Price: $15
Market Value: $40

92

Silo & Hay Shed (set/2)
Issued: 1987 • Retired: 1989
#5950-1 • Original Price: $18
Market Value: $170

93

Sitting In Camden Park (set/4)
Issued: 1998 • Current
#58411 • Original Price: $35
Market Value: $35

94

Six Geese A-Laying (set/2)
#VI, The 12 Days Of Dickens' Village
Issued: 1995 • Retired: 1999
#58382 • Original Price: $30
Market Value: $36

95

New

Sliding Down Cornhill With Bob Cratchit
Issued: 2000 • Current
#58528 • Original Price: $25
Market Value: $25

96

Stone Bridge
Issued: 1987 • Retired: 1990
#6546-3 • Original Price: $12
Market Value: $80

97

"Tallyho!" (set/5)
Issued: 1995 • Retired: 1998
#58391 • Original Price: $50
Market Value: $60

98

Ten Pipers Piping (set/3)
#X, The 12 Days Of Dickens' Village
Issued: 1997 • Retired: 2000
#58386 • Original Price: $30
Market Value: $35

99

Tending The Cold Frame (set/3)
Issued: 1998 • Retired: 1999
#58416 • Original Price: $32.50
Market Value: $37

100

Tending The New Calves (set/3)
Issued: 1996 • Retired: 1999
#58395 • Original Price: $30
Market Value: $34

101

Thatchers (set/3)
Issued: 1994 • Retired: 1997
#5829-7 • Original Price: $35
Market Value: $39

102

New

These Are For You (set/2)
Issued: 2000 • Current
#58530 • Original Price: $25
Market Value: $25

Dickens' Village Series®

	Price Paid	Value
91.		
92.		
93.		
94.		
95.		
96.		
97.		
98.		
99.		
100.		
101.		
102.		
Totals		

Dickens' Village Series® – Accessories

Dickens' Village Series® – Accessories

103

Three French Hens (set/3)
#III, The 12 Days Of Dickens' Village
Issued: 1995 • Retired: 1999
#58378 • Original Price: $32.50
Market Value: $34

104

Town Crier & Chimney Sweep (set/2)
Issued: 1990 • Current
#5569-7 • Original Price: $15
Market Value: $16

105

A Treasure From The Sea (set/2)
Issued: 1999 • Current
#58461 • Original Price: $22.50
Market Value: $22.50

106

Twelve Drummers Drumming
#XII, The 12 Days Of Dickens' Village
Issued: 1999 • Retired: 2000
#58387 • Original Price: $65
Market Value: $80

107

Two Turtle Doves (set/4)
#II, The 12 Days Of Dickens' Village
Issued: 1995 • Retired: 1999
#5836-0 • Original Price: $32.50
Market Value: $37

108

Under The Bumbershoot
Issued: 1999 • Current
#58460 • Original Price: $20
Market Value: $20

109

Photo Unavailable

Versions:
#02100 – gold
#02101 – green
#02102 – red
N/A – blue
TBA (8/01)

Under The NCC Umbrella (NCC Piece)
Issued: 2000 • Current
See Above • Original Price: $20
Market Value: $20 (all versions)

110

Until We Meet Again (set/2)
Issued: 1998 • Current
#58414 • Original Price: $27.50
Market Value: $27.50

111

Victoria Station Train Platform
Issued: 1990 • Retired: 1999
#5575-1 • Original Price: $20
Market Value: $26

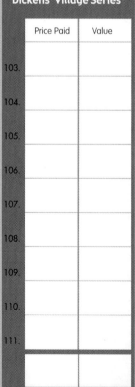

Dickens' Village Series®	Price Paid	Value
103.		
104.		
105.		
106.		
107.		
108.		
109.		
110.		
111.		
Totals		

112

Village Street Peddlers (set/2)
Issued: 1992 • Retired: 1994
#5804-1 • Original Price: $16
Market Value: $29

113

Village Train (set/3)
Issued: 1985 • Retired: 1986
#6527-7 • Original Price: $12
Market Value: $450

114

Village Well & Holy Cross (set/2)
Issued: 1987 • Retired: 1989
#6547-1 • Original Price: $13
Market Value: $150

115

Violet Vendor/Carolers/Chestnut Vendor (set/3)
Issued: 1989 • Retired: 1992
#5580-8 • Original Price: $23
Market Value: $43

116

Vision Of A Christmas Past (set/3)
Issued: 1993 • Retired: 1996
#5817-3 • Original Price: $27.50
Market Value: $40

117

Winter Sleighride
Issued: 1994 • Current
#5825-4 • Original Price: $18
Market Value: $18

118

"Ye Olde Lamplighter" Dickens' Village Sign
Issued: 1995 • Current
#58393 • Original Price: $20
Market Value: $20

119

Yeomen Of The Guard (set/5)
Issued: 1996 • Retired: 1997
#58397 • Original Price: $30
Market Value: $64

New England Village® Series– Accessories

1

New

A Day At The Cabin (set/2)
Issued: 2000 • Current
#56642 • Original Price: $25
Market Value: $25

2

Amish Buggy
Issued: 1990 • Retired: 1992
#5949-8 • Original Price: $22
Market Value: $65

Dickens' Village Series®	Price Paid	Value
112.		
113.		
114.		
115.		
116.		
117.		
118.		
119.		

New England Village® Series		
1.		
2.		
Totals		

New England Village® Series – Accessories

3

Version 1   Version 2

Amish Family (set/3)
Issued: 1990 • Retired: 1992
#5948-0 • Original Price: $20
Market Value: **1** – $52 (with mustache) **2** – $40 (without mustache)

4

An Artist's Touch
Issued: 1998 • Current
#56638 • Original Price: $17
Market Value: $17

5

New

**Best Of The Harvest
(set/2)**
Issued: 2000 • Current
#56647 • Original Price: $25
Market Value: $25

6

**Blue Star Ice
Harvesters (set/2)**
Issued: 1993 • Retired: 1997
#5650-2 • Original Price: $27.50
Market Value: $30

7

**Christmas Bazaar . . .
Flapjacks & Hot Cider
(set/2)**
Issued: 1997 • Retired: 1999
#56596 • Original Price: $27.50
Market Value: $29

New England Village® Series

	Price Paid	Value
3.		
4.		
5.		
6.		
7.		
8.		
9.		
10.		
11.		
12.		
13.		
Totals		

8

**Christmas Bazaar . . .
Handmade Quilts
(set/2)**
Issued: 1996 • Retired: 1999
#56594 • Original Price: $25
Market Value: $27

9

**Christmas Bazaar . . .
Sign (set/2)**
Issued: 1997 • Retired: 1999
#56598 • Original Price: $16
Market Value: $18

10

**Christmas Bazaar . . .
Toy Vendor & Cart
(set/2)**
Issued: 1997 • Retired: 1999
#56597 • Original Price: $27.50
Market Value: $29

11

**Christmas Bazaar . . .
Woolens & Preserves
(set/2)**
Issued: 1996 • Retired: 1999
#56595 • Original Price: $25
Market Value: $27

12

**Covered Wooden
Bridge**
Issued: 1986 • Retired: 1990
#6531-5 • Original Price: $10
Market Value: $44

13

Dairy Delivery Sleigh
Issued: 1999 • Current
#56622 • Original Price: $37.50
Market Value: $37.50

14

Doctor's House Call (set/2)
Issued: 1999 • Current
#56616 • Original Price: $27.50
Market Value: $27.50

15

Farm Animals (set/4)
Issued: 1989 • Retired: 1991
#5945-5 • Original Price: $15
Market Value: $47

16

Farm Animals (set/8)
Issued: 1995 • Current
#56588 • Original Price: $32.50
Market Value: $32.50

17

Farmer's Market (set/2)
Issued: 1998 • Current
#56637 • Original Price: $55
Market Value: $55

18

Fly-casting In The Brook
Issued: 1998 • Current
#56633 • Original Price: $15
Market Value: $15

19

"Fresh Paint" New England Village Sign
Issued: 1995 • Current
#56592 • Original Price: $20
Market Value: $20

20

New

Gathering Cranberries
Issued: 2000 • Current
#56644 • Original Price: $30
Market Value: $30

21

Harvest Pumpkin Wagon
Issued: 1995 • Retired: 1999
#56591 • Original Price: $45
Market Value: $53

22

Harvest Seed Cart (set/3)
Issued: 1992 • Retired: 1995
#5645-6 • Original Price: $27.50
Market Value: $41

23

New

Here Comes Sinter Klaus
Issued: 2000 • Current
#56646 • Original Price: $17
Market Value: $17

24

It's Almost Thanksgiving (set/4)
Issued: 1999 • Current
#56639 • Original Price: $60
Market Value: $60

New England Village® Series		
	Price Paid	Value
14.		
15.		
16.		
17.		
18.		
19.		
20.		
21.		
22.		
23.		
24.		
Totals		

New England Village® Series – Accessories

New England Village® Series – Accessories

25

Knife Grinder (set/2)
Issued: 1993 • Retired: 1996
#5649-9 • Original Price: $22.50
Market Value: $29

26

Let's Go One More Time (set/3)
Issued: 1999 • Current
#56621 • Original Price: $30
Market Value: $30

27

Load Up The Wagon (set/2)
Issued: 1998 • Current
#56630 • Original Price: $40
Market Value: $40

28

Lobster Trappers (set/4)
Issued: 1995 • Retired: 2000
#56589 • Original Price: $35
Market Value: $37

29

Lumberjacks (set/2)
Issued: 1995 • Retired: 1998
#56590 • Original Price: $30
Market Value: $38

30

Making The Christmas Candles (set/2)
Issued: 1999 • Current
#56620 • Original Price: $25
Market Value: $25

31

Maple Sugaring Shed (set/3)
Issued: 1987 • Retired: 1989
#6589-7 • Original Price: $19
Market Value: $250

32

Market Day (set/3)
Issued: 1991 • Retired: 1993
#5641-3 • Original Price: $35
Market Value: $47

33

Mill Creek Crossing
Issued: 1999 • Current
#56623 • Original Price: $32.50
Market Value: $32.50

34

New England Village Sign
Issued: 1987 • Retired: 1993
#6570-6 • Original Price: $6
Market Value: $22

35

New England Winter Set (set/5)
Issued: 1986 • Retired: 1990
#6532-3 • Original Price: $18
Market Value: $50

New England Village® Series		
	Price Paid	Value
25.		
26.		
27.		
28.		
29.		
30.		
31.		
32.		
33.		
34.		
35.		
Totals		

36

A New Potbellied Stove For Christmas (set/2)
Issued: 1996 • Retired: 1998
#56593 • Original Price: $35
Market Value: $43

37

The Old Man And The Sea (set/3)
Issued: 1994 • Retired: 1998
#5655-3 • Original Price: $25
Market Value: $33

38

Over The River And Through The Woods
Issued: 1994 • Retired: 1998
#5654-5 • Original Price: $35
Market Value: $44

39

Pennyfarthing Pedaling
Issued: 1999 • Current
#56615 • Original Price: $13.50
Market Value: $13.50

40

New

The Perfect Tree
Issued: 2000 • Current
#56645 • Original Price: $20
Market Value: $20

41

Postal Pick-up
Issued: 2000 • Current
#56641 • Original Price: $14
Market Value: $14

42

Red Covered Bridge
Issued: 1988 • Retired: 1994
#5987-0 • Original Price: $15
Market Value: $35

43

The Sailors' Knot
Issued: 1999 • Current
#56617 • Original Price: 27.50
Market Value: $27.50

44

Sea Captain & His Mates (set/4)
Issued: 1998 • Retired: 2000
#56587 • Original Price: $32.50
Market Value: $35

45

Sleepy Hollow Characters (set/3)
Issued: 1990 • Retired: 1992
#5956-0 • Original Price: $27.50
Market Value: $48

46

Version 1

Version 2

Sleighride (also known as "Dickens' Sleighride")
Issued: 1986 • Retired: 1990
#6511-0 • Original Price: $19.50
Market Value: **1** – $55 (thin scarf) **2** – $52 (thick scarf)

	New England Village® Series	
	Price Paid	Value
36.		
37.		
38.		
39.		
40.		
41.		
42.		
43.		
44.		
45.		
46.		
Totals		

New England Village® Series – Accessories

New England Village® Series – Accessories

47

Tapping The Maples (set/7)
Issued: 1997 • Current
#56599 • Original Price: $75
Market Value: $75

48

Town Tinker (set/2)
Issued: 1992 • Retired: 1995
#5646-4 • Original Price: $24
Market Value: $36

49
Under The Mistletoe
Issued: 1998 • Current
#56631 • Original Price: $16.50
Market Value: $16.50

50

Village Harvest People (set/4)
Issued: 1988 • Retired: 1991
#5941-2 • Original Price: $27.50
Market Value: $53

51

Volunteer Firefighters (set/2)
Issued: 1998 • Retired: 2000
#56635 • Original Price: $37.50
Market Value: $40

52

Woodcutter And Son (set/2)
Issued: 1988 • Retired: 1990
#5986-2 • Original Price: $10
Market Value: $50

53

The Woodworker
Issued: 1999 • Current
#56619 • Original Price: $35
Market Value: $35

Alpine Village Series® – Accessories

1

"Alpen Horn Player" Alpine Village Sign
Issued: 1995 • Current
#56182 • Original Price: $20
Market Value: $20

2

Alpine Village Sign
Issued: 1987 • Retired: 1993
#6571-4 • Original Price: $6
Market Value: $22

3

Alpine Villagers (set/3)
Issued: 1986 • Retired: 1992
#6542-0 • Original Price: $13
Market Value: $39

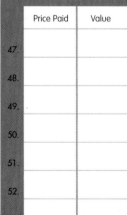

New England Village® Series	Price Paid	Value
47.		
48.		
49.		
50.		
51.		
52.		
53.		

Alpine Village Series®		
1.		
2.		
3.		
Totals		

4

Alpine Villagers (set/5)
Issued: 1999 • Current
#56215 • Original Price: $32.50
Market Value: $32.50

5

New

At The Octoberfest (set/3)
Issued: 2000 • Current
#56302 • Original Price: $27.50
Market Value: $27.50

6

Buying Bakers Bread (set/2)
Issued: 1992 • Retired: 1995
#5619-7 • Original Price: $20
Market Value: $38

7

Climb Every Mountain (set/4)
Issued: 1993 • Current
#5613-8 • Original Price: $27.50
Market Value: $27.50

8

Heidi & Her Goats (set/4)
Issued: 1997 • Current
#56201 • Original Price: $30
Market Value: $30

9

Here Comes The Bride – The Sound Of Music®
Issued: 2000 • Current
#56300 • Original Price: $18
Market Value: $18

10

Leading The Bavarian Cow
Issued: 1999 • Current
#56214 • Original Price: $20
Market Value: $20

11

A New Batch Of Christmas Friends (set/3)
Issued: 1997 • Retired: 2000
#56175 • Original Price: $27.50
Market Value: $29

12

Nutcracker Vendor & Cart
Issued: 1996 • Current
#56183 • Original Price: $25
Market Value: $25

13

Polka Fest (set/3)
Issued: 1994 • Retired: 1999
#5607-3 • Original Price: $30
Market Value: $34

14

St. Nicholas
Issued: 1998 • Current
#56203 • Original Price: $12
Market Value: $12

Alpine Village Series®

Alpine Village Series®

	Price Paid	Value
4.		
5.		
6.		
7.		
8.		
9.		
10.		
11.		
12.		
13.		
14.		
Totals		

Alpine Village Series® – Accessories

Alpine Village Series® – Accessories

15

Silent Night (music box)
Issued: 1995 • Retired: 1999
#56180 • Original Price: $32.50
Market Value: $36

16

Sisters Of The Abbey (set/2)
Issued: 1999 • Current
#56213 • Original Price: $20
Market Value: $20

17

The Sound Of Music® Gazebo (music box)
Issued: 1999 • Current
#56212 • Original Price: $40
Market Value: $40

18

The Toy Peddler (set/3)
Issued: 1990 • Retired: 1998
#5616-2 • Original Price: $22
Market Value: $32

19

Trekking In The Snow (set/3)
Issued: 1998 • Current
#56202 • Original Price: $27.50
Market Value: $27.50

Christmas In The City® Series – Accessories

Alpine Village Series®	Price Paid	Value
15.		
16.		
17.		
18.		
19.		
Christmas In The City® Series		
1.		
2.		
3.		
4.		
5.		
6.		
Totals		

1

1919 Ford® Model-T
Issued: 1998 • Retired: 2000
#58906 • Original Price: $20
Market Value: $24

2

1935 Duesenberg®
Issued: 2000 • Current
#58964 • Original Price: $20
Market Value: $20

3
New

1937 Pirsch Pumper Fire Truck
Issued: 2000 • Current
#58969 • Original Price: $25
Market Value: $25

4

All Around The Town (set/2)
Issued: 1991 • Retired: 1993
#5545-0 • Original Price: $18
Market Value: $33

5

All In Together Girls
Issued: 1999 • Current
#58960 • Original Price: $23.50
Market Value: $23.50

6

Automobiles (set/3)
Issued: 1987 • Retired: 1996
#5964-1 • Original Price: $15
Market Value: $30

7

Big Smile For The Camera (set/2)
Issued: 1997 • Retired: 1999
#58900 • Original Price: $27.50
Market Value: $30

8

Boulevard (set/14)
Issued: 1989 • Retired: 1992
#5516-6 • Original Price: $25
Market Value: $55

9

Bringing Home The Baby (set/2)
Issued: 1999 • Retired: 2000
#58909 • Original Price: $27.50
Market Value: $29

10

Busy City Sidewalks (set/4)
Issued: 1999 • Current
#58955 • Original Price: $32.50
Market Value: $32.50

11

Busy Sidewalks (set/4)
Issued: 1990 • Retired: 1992
#5535-2 • Original Price: $28
Market Value: $54

12

Caroling Thru The City (set/3)
Issued: 1991 • Retired: 1998
#5548-4 • Original Price: $27.50
Market Value: $32

13

A Carriage Ride For The Bride (track compatible)
Issued: 1998 • Current
#58901 • Original Price: $40
Market Value: $40

14

Central Park Carriage
Issued: 1989 • Current
#5979-0 • Original Price: $30
Market Value: $30

15

Chamber Orchestra (set/4)
Issued: 1994 • Retired: 1998
#5884-0 • Original Price: $37.50
Market Value: $43

16

Choirboys All-In-A-Row
Issued: 1995 • Retired: 1998
#58892 • Original Price: $20
Market Value: $30

17

Christmas In The City Sign
Issued: 1987 • Retired: 1993
#5960-9 • Original Price: $6
Market Value: $23

18

The City Ambulance
Issued: 1999 • Retired: 2000
#58910 • Original Price: $15
Market Value: $17

Christmas In The City® Series		
	Price Paid	Value
7.		
8.		
9.		
10.		
11.		
12.		
13.		
14.		
15.		
16.		
17.		
18.		
Totals		

119

Christmas In The City® Series – Accessories

19

City Bus & Milk Truck (set/2)
Issued: 1988 • Retired: 1991
#5983-8 • Original Price: $15
Market Value: $41

20

"City Fire Dept.," Fire Truck (set/3)
Issued: 1991 • Retired: 1995
#5547-6 • Original Price: $18
Market Value: $39

21

City Newsstand (set/4)
Issued: 1988 • Retired: 1991
#5971-4 • Original Price: $25
Market Value: $78

22

City People (set/5)
Issued: 1987 • Retired: 1990
#5965-0 • Original Price: $27.50
Market Value: $59

23

City Police Car
Issued: 1998 • Current
#58903 • Original Price: $16.50
Market Value: $16.50

24

City Professions – Doctor & Nurse (set/2)
Issued: 2000 • Current
#58962 • Original Price: $17.50
Market Value: $17.50

25

City Professions – House Painter & Newspaper Boy (set/2)
Issued: 2000 • Current
#58966 • Original Price: $17.50
Market Value: $17.50

26

City Professions – Postman & Dairy Delivery Man (set/2)
Issued: 2000 • Current
#58965 • Original Price: $17.50
Market Value: $17.50

27

City Taxi
Issued: 1996 • Current
#58894 • Original Price: $12.50
Market Value: $12.50

28

City Workers (set/4)
Issued: 1987 • Retired: 1988
#5967-6 • Original Price: $15
Market Value: $46

29

Don't Drop The Presents! (set/2)
Issued: 1992 • Retired: 1995
#5532-8 • Original Price: $25
Market Value: $38

30

Excellent Taste (set/2)
Issued: 1999 • Current
#58958 • Original Price: $22
Market Value: $22

Christmas In The City® Series		
	Price Paid	Value
19.		
20.		
21.		
22.		
23.		
24.		
25.		
26.		
27.		
28.		
29.		
30.		
Totals		

31

The Family Tree
Issued: 1996 • Current
#58895 • Original Price: $18
Market Value: $18

32

Feeney's Delivery Of Dreams (Feeney's Piece)
Issued: 2000 • Retired: 2000
#02272 • Original Price: $14.99
Market Value: N/E

33

The Fire Brigade (set/2)
Issued: 1991 • Retired: 1995
#5546-8 • Original Price: $20
Market Value: $38

34
New

Fire Drill Practice
Issued: 2000 • Current
#58968 • Original Price: $25
Market Value: $25

35

Fresh Flowers For Sale (set/2)
Issued: 1999 • Current
#58957 • Original Price: $30
Market Value: $30

36

Going Home For The Holidays (set/3)
Issued: 1996 • Retired: 1999
#58896 • Original Price: $27.50
Market Value: $30

37

Hailing A Cab (set/3)
Issued: 2000 • Current
#58961 • Original Price: $27.50
Market Value: $27.50

38

Holiday Field Trip (set/3)
Issued: 1994 • Retired: 1998
#5885-8 • Original Price: $27.50
Market Value: $34

39
New

Hot Chocolate For Sale
Issued: 2000 • Current
#58971 • Original Price: $27.50
Market Value: $27.50

40

Hot Dog Vendor (set/3)
Issued: 1994 • Retired: 1997
#5886-6 • Original Price: $27.50
Market Value: $32

41

Version 1   Version 2

Johnson's Grocery . . . Holiday Deliveries (track compatible)
Issued: 1997 • Current
#58897 • Original Price: $18
Market Value: **1**– $18 (general release) **2** – N/E (William Glen)

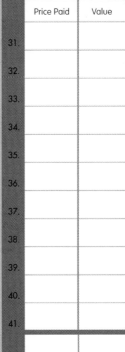

Christmas In The City® Series	
Price Paid	Value
31.		
32.		
33.		
34.		
35.		
36.		
37.		
38.		
39.		
40.		
41.		
Totals	

Christmas In The City® Series – Accessories

42

"A Key To The City" Christmas In The City Sign
Issued: 1995 • Current
#58893 • Original Price: $20
Market Value: $20

43

Let's Go Shopping In The City (set/3)
Issued: 1997 • Retired: 1999
#58899 • Original Price: $35
Market Value: $38

44
New

The Life Of The Party (set/2)
Issued: 2000 • Current
#58970 • Original Price: $30
Market Value: $30

45

Mailbox & Fire Hydrant (set/2)
Issued: 1989 • Retired: 1990
#5517-4 • Original Price: $6
Market Value: $25

46
Mailbox & Fire Hydrant (set/2)
Issued: 1990 • Retired: 1998
#5214-0 • Original Price: $5
Market Value: $25

47
New

On To The Show
Issued: 2000 • Current
#58967 • Original Price: $20
Market Value: $20

Christmas In The City® Series		
	Price Paid	Value
42.		
43.		
44.		
45.		
46.		
47.		
48.		
49.		
50.		
51.		
52.		
53.		
Totals		

48

One-Man Band And The Dancing Dog (set/2)
Issued: 1995 • Retired: 1998
#58891 • Original Price: $17.50
Market Value: $29

49

Organ Grinder (set/3)
Issued: 1989 • Retired: 1991
#5957-9 • Original Price: $21
Market Value: $39

50

Picking Out The Christmas Tree (set/3)
Issued: 1999 • Current
#58959 • Original Price: $37.50
Market Value: $37.50

51

Popcorn Vendor (set/3)
Issued: 1989 • Retired: 1992
#5958-7 • Original Price: $22
Market Value: $40

52

Ready For The Road
Issued: 1998 • Retired: 2000
#58907 • Original Price: $20
Market Value: $23

53

Rest Ye Merry Gentlemen
Issued: 1990 • Current
#5540-9 • Original Price: $12.50
Market Value: $13

54

River Street Ice House Cart
Issued: 1989 • Retired: 1991
#5959-5 • Original Price: $20
Market Value: $57

55

New

Russell Stover® Delivery Truck
Issued: 2000 • Current
#58972 • Original Price: $20
Market Value: $20

56

Salvation Army Band (set/6)
Issued: 1988 • Retired: 1991
#5985-4 • Original Price: $24
Market Value: $94

57

Spirit Of The Season
Issued: 1997 • Retired: 1999
#58898 • Original Price: $20
Market Value: $22

58

Steppin' Out On The Town (set/5)
Issued: 1997 • Retired: 1999
#58885 • Original Price: $35
Market Value: $37

59

Street Musicians (set/3)
Issued: 1993 • Retired: 1997
#5564-6 • Original Price: $25
Market Value: $35

60

'Tis The Season
Issued: 1990 • Retired: 1994
#5539-5 • Original Price: $12.50
Market Value: $25

61

To Protect And To Serve (set/3)
Issued: 1998 • Current
#58902 • Original Price: $32.50
Market Value: $32.50

62

A Treasured Book (set/3)
Issued: 2000 • Current
#5896-3 • Original Price: $35
Market Value: $35

63

Village Gathering Taxi (William Glen Piece)
Issued: 2000 • Retired: 2000
#02270 • Original Price: $12.50
Market Value: N/E

64

Visiting The Nativity (set/3)
Issued: 1999 • Current
#58956 • Original Price: $37.50
Market Value: $37.50

65

Welcome Home (set/3)
Issued: 1992 • Retired: 1995
#5533-6 • Original Price: $27.50
Market Value: $35

Christmas In The City® Series

	Price Paid	Value
54.		
55.		
56.		
57.		
58.		
59.		
60.		
61.		
62.		
63.		
64.		
65.		
Totals		

66

"Yes, Virginia . . . "
(set/2)
Issued: 1995 • Retired: 2000
#58890 • Original Price: $12.50
Market Value: $16

North Pole™ – Accessories

1

New

All Aboard! (set/2)
Issued: 2000 • Current
#56803 • Original Price: $16.50
Market Value: $16.50

2

Baker Elves (set/3)
Issued: 1991 • Retired: 1995
#5603-0 • Original Price: $27.50
Market Value: $45

3

New

Balancing Act (set/3)
North Pole Woods™
Issued: 2000 • Current
#56932 • Original Price: $25
Market Value: $25

4

"A Busy Elf"
North Pole Sign
Issued: 1995 • Retired: 1999
#56366 • Original Price: $20
Market Value: $26

Christmas In The City® Series		
	Price Paid	Value
66.		
North Pole Series™		
1.		
2.		
3.		
4.		
5.		
6.		
7.		
8.		
9.		
Totals		

5

Candy Cane
Lampposts (set/4)
Issued: 1996 • Current
#52621 • Original Price: $13
Market Value: $13

6

Canine Courier
Issued: 1999 • Current
#56709 • Original Price: $32.50
Market Value: $32.50

7

New

Catch The Wind
Issued: 2000 • Current
#56807 • Original Price: $17.50
Market Value: $17.50

8

Charting Santa's
Course (set/2)
Issued: 1995 • Retired: 1997
#56364 • Original Price: $25
Market Value: $32

9

Check This Out
Issued: 1999 • Current
#56711 • Original Price: $13.50
Market Value: $13.50

10

Christmas Fun Run (set/6)
Issued: 1998 • Retired: 2000
#56434 • Original Price: $35
Market Value: $37

11

Cruisin' Crayola® Elves (set/2)
Issued: 2000 • Current
#56800 • Original Price: $16.50
Market Value: $16.50

12
New

Cutting The Trail
Issued: 2000 • Current
#56806 • Original Price: $14
Market Value: $14

13

Dash Away Delivery
Issued: 1998 • Current
#56438 • Original Price: $40
Market Value: $40

14

Delivering Real Plastic Snow
Issued: 1998 • Current
#56435 • Original Price: $17
Market Value: $17

15

Delivering The Christmas Greens (set/2)
Issued: 1997 • Current
#56373 • Original Price: $27.50
Market Value: $27.50

16

Don't Break The Ornaments (set/2)
Issued: 1997 • Current
#56372 • Original Price: $27.50
Market Value: $27.50

17

Downhill Daredevils (set/2)
Issued: 1999 • Current
#56707 • Original Price: $16.50
Market Value: $16.50

18

Downhill Elves (set/2)
Issued: 1998 • Retired: 2000
#56439 • Original Price: $9
Market Value: $12

19

Early Rising Elves (set/5)
Issued: 1996 • Retired: 1999
#56369 • Original Price: $32.50
Market Value: $36

20

Elves (set/4)
North Pole Woods™
Issued: 2000 • Current
#56922 • Original Price: $30
Market Value: $30

21

Elves On Ice (set/4)
Issued: 1996 • Retired: 2000
#52298 • Original Price: $7.50
Market Value: $10

North Pole Series™		
	Price Paid	Value
10.		
11.		
12.		
13.		
14.		
15.		
16.		
17.		
18.		
19.		
20.		
21.		
Totals		

North Pole Series™ – Accessories

22

Elves On Track (set/3, track compatible)
Issued: 1999 • Current
#56714 • Original Price: $10
Market Value: $10

23

End Of The Line (set/2)
Issued: 1996 • Retired: 1999
#56370 • Original Price: $28
Market Value: $40

24

New

Gone Fishing
North Pole Woods™
Issued: 2000 • Current
#56930 • Original Price: $35
Market Value: $35

25

A Happy Harley® Day
Issued: 1999 • Current
#56706 • Original Price: $17
Market Value: $17

26

Happy New Year!
Issued: 1999 • Retired: 2000
#56443 • Original Price: $17.50
Market Value: $20

27

Have A Seat (set/6)
Issued: 1998 • Current
#56437 • Original Price: $30
Market Value: $30

North Pole Series™

	Price Paid	Value
22.		
23.		
24.		
25.		
26.		
27.		
28.		
29.		
30.		
31.		
32.		
Totals		

28

Holiday Deliveries
Issued: 1996 • Current
#56371 • Original Price: $16.50
Market Value: $16.50

29

New

Icy Delights
Issued: 2000 • Current
#56808 • Original Price: $17.50
Market Value: $17.50

30

I'll Need More Toys (set/2)
Issued: 1995 • Retired: 1998
#56365 • Original Price: $25
Market Value: $30

31

Last Minute Delivery
Issued: 1994 • Retired: 1998
#5636-7 • Original Price: $35
Market Value: $39

32

Leonardo & Vincent
Issued: 2000 • Current
#56801 • Original Price: $16.50
Market Value: $16.50

33

Letters For Santa (set/3)
Issued: 1992 • Retired: 1994
#5604-9 • Original Price: $30
Market Value: $68

34

New

Little Newlyweds
Issued: 2000 • Current
#56805 • Original Price: $13
Market Value: $13

35

Loading The Sleigh (set/6, animated)
Issued: 1998 • Current
#52732 • Original Price: $125
Market Value: $125

36

Photo Unavailable

Lord & Taylor Hot Air Balloon 2000 (LE-2000, Lord & Taylor Piece)
Issued: 2000 • Retired: 2000
#2440 • Original Price: $40
Market Value: $45

37

Marshmallows Around The Campfire (set/3)
Issued: 1999 • Current
#56712 • Original Price: $30
Market Value: $30

38

North Pole Express (set/3)
Issued: 1996 • Retired: 1999
#56368 • Original Price: $37.50
Market Value: $45

39

North Pole Gate
Issued: 1993 • Retired: 1998
#5632-4 • Original Price: $32.50
Market Value: $40

40

Nuts About Broomball
North Pole Woods™
Issued: 2000 • Current
#56926 • Original Price: $20
Market Value: $20

41

Open Wide!
Issued: 1999 • Retired: 2000
#56713 • Original Price: $13
Market Value: $15

42

Party In The Hot Tub! (set/2)
ELf Land™
Issued: 2000 • Current
#56802 • Original Price: $30
Market Value: $30

43

Peppermint Skating Party (set/6)
Issued: 1998 • Retired: 2000
#56363 • Original Price: $64
Market Value: $69

44

Photo With Santa (set/3, track compatible)
Issued: 1999 • Retired: 2000
#56444 • Original Price: $7.50
Market Value: $10

North Pole Series™

	Price Paid	Value
33.		
34.		
35.		
36.		
37.		
38.		
39.		
40.		
41.		
42.		
43.		
44.		
Totals		

North Pole Series™ – Accessories

North Pole Series™ – Accessories

45
New

Polar Plowing Service
North Pole Woods™
Issued: 2000 • Current
#56929 • Original Price: $30
Market Value: $30

46

Reindeer Training Camp (set/2)
Issued: 1998 • Current
#56436 • Original Price: $27.50
Market Value: $27.50

47
New

Rescue Ready
Issued: 2000 • Current
#56804 • Original Price: $16.50
Market Value: $16.50

48
New

Ring Toss (set/2)
North Pole Woods™
Issued: 2000 • Current
#56931 • Original Price: $17.50
Market Value: $17.50

49

Santa & Mrs. Claus (set/2)
Issued: 1990 • Current
#5609-0 • Original Price: $15
Market Value: $15

50

Santa's Little Helpers (set/3)
Issued: 1990 • Retired: 1993
#5610-3 • Original Price: $28
Market Value: $65

51
New

Photo
Unavailable

Santa's On His Way (musical waterglobe, May Co. Department Stores Piece)
Issued: 2000 • N/A
N/A • Original Price: N/A
Market Value: N/E

52

Scissors Wizard (set/2)
North Pole Woods™
Issued: 2000 • Current
#56923 • Original Price: $25
Market Value: $25

53

Sing A Song For Santa (set/3)
Issued: 1993 • Retired: 1998
#5631-6 • Original Price: $28
Market Value: $33

54

Ski Bums
Issued: 1999 • Current
#56710 • Original Price: $22.50
Market Value: $22.50

55

Sleigh & Eight Tiny Reindeer (set/5)
Issued: 1990 • Current
#5611-1 • Original Price: $40
Market Value: $42

56

Snow Cone Elves (set/4)
Issued: 1994 • Retired: 1997
#5637-5 • Original Price: $30
Market Value: $36

North Pole Series™

	Price Paid	Value
45.		
46.		
47.		
48.		
49.		
50.		
51.		
52.		
53.		
54.		
55.		
56.		
Totals		

North Pole Series™ – Accessories

57
New

Star Of The Show
North Pole Woods™
Issued: 2000 • Current
#56928 • Original Price: $25
Market Value: $25

58

Tailored For You (set/2)
North Pole Woods™
Issued: 2000 • Current
#56921 • Original Price: $22.50
Market Value: $22.50

59

Tangled In Tinsel
Issued: 1999 • Current
#56708 • Original Price: $25
Market Value: $25

60

Tee Time Elves (set/2)
Issued: 1999 • Current
#56442 • Original Price: $27.50
Market Value: $27.50

61

**Testing The Toys
(set/2)**
Issued: 1992 • Retired: 1999
#5605-7 • Original Price: $16.50
Market Value: $20

62

Toymaker Elves (set/3)
Issued: 1991 • Retired: 1995
#5602-2 • Original Price: $27.50
Market Value: $44

63

**Trimming The
North Pole**
Issued: 1990 • Retired: 1993
#5608-1 • Original Price: $10
Market Value: $42

64

**Untangle The
Christmas Lights**
Issued: 1997 • Retired: 2000
#56374 • Original Price: $35
Market Value: $38

65

Welcome To Elf Land
Elf Land™
Issued: 1998 • Current
#56431 • Original Price: $35
Market Value: $35

66

**Welcome To North
Pole Woods**
North Pole Woods™
Issued: 2000 • Current
#56920 • Original Price: $25
Market Value: $25

67

**Woodsmen Elves
(set/3)**
Issued: 1993 • Retired: 1995
#5630-8 • Original Price: $30
Market Value: $62

North Pole Series™		
	Price Paid	Value
57.		
58.		
59.		
60.		
61.		
62.		
63.		
64.		
65.		
66.		
67.		
Totals		

Disney Parks Village™ Series – Accessories

1

Balloon Seller (set/2)
Issued: 1995 • Retired: 1996
#53539 • Original Price: $25
Market Value: $55

2

Disney Parks Family (set/3)
Issued: 1994 • Retired: 1996
#5354-6 • Original Price: $32.50
Market Value: $38

3

Mickey & Minnie (set/2)
Issued: 1994 • Retired: 1996
#5353-8 • Original Price: $22.50
Market Value: $35

4

Olde World Antiques Gate
Issued: 1994 • Retired: 1996
#5355-4 • Original Price: $15
Market Value: $33

Little Town Of Bethlehem™ Series – Accessories

1
New

Cyprus Trees (set/3)
Issued: 2000 • Current
#59907 • Original Price: $20
Market Value: $20

2
New

Desert Camp (set/4)
Issued: 2000 • Current
#59904 • Original Price: $52
Market Value: $52

3
New

Desert Oasis (set/5)
Issued: 2000 • Current
#59901 • Original Price: $60
Market Value: $60

4
New

Desert Road (set/4)
Issued: 2000 • Current
#59909 • Original Price: $22.50
Market Value: $22.50

5
New
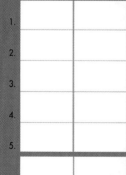
Desert Rocks (set/5)
Issued: 2000 • Current
#59910 • Original Price: $25
Market Value: $25

Disney Parks Village™ Series

	Price Paid	Value
1.		
2.		
3.		
4.		

Little Town Of Bethlehem™ Series

1.		
2.		
3.		
4.		
5.		
Totals		

6

The Good Shepherd & His Animals (set/6)
Issued: 1999 • Current
#59791 • Original Price: $25
Market Value: $25

7

Heralding Angels (set/3)
Issued: 1999 • Current
#59759 • Original Price: $20
Market Value: $20

8

New

Limestone Outcropping
Issued: 2000 • Current
#59911 • Original Price: $40
Market Value: $40

9

New

Merchant Cart (set/2)
Issued: 2000 • Current
#59902 • Original Price: $30
Market Value: $30

10

New

Oil Lamps (set/2)
Issued: 2000 • Current
#59905 • Original Price: $25
Market Value: $25

11

New

Olive Harvest (set/3)
Issued: 2000 • Current
#59912 • Original Price: $40
Market Value: $40

12

New

Star Of Wonder
Issued: 2000 • Current
#59906 • Original Price: $20
Market Value: $20

13

New

Stonemason At Work (set/3)
Issued: 2000 • Current
#59903 • Original Price: $45
Market Value: $45

14

Town Gate (set/2)
Issued: 1999 • Current
#59794 • Original Price: $25
Market Value: $25

15

New

Town Wall Sections (set/2)
Issued: 2000 • Current
#59908 • Original Price: $16.50
Market Value: $16.50

16

Town Well & Palm Trees (set/3)
Issued: 1999 • Current
#59793 • Original Price: $45
Market Value: $45

17

Wise Men From The East (set/2)
Issued: 1999 • Current
#59792 • Original Price: $25
Market Value: $25

Little Town Of Bethlehem™ Series		
	Price Paid	Value
6.		
7.		
8.		
9.		
10.		
11.		
12.		
13.		
14.		
15.		
16.		
17.		
Totals		

Heritage Village Collection® – Hinged Boxes

1

Bah, Humbug
Issued: 1997 • Retired: 2000
#58430 • Original Price: $15
Market Value: $17

2

Chimney Sweep
Issued: 1998 • Retired: 2000
#58434 • Original Price: $15
Market Value: $17

3

God Bless Us Every One
Issued: 1997 • Retired: 2000
#58432 • Original Price: $13
Market Value: $17

4

Royal Coach
Issued: 1998 • Retired: 2000
#57501 • Original Price: $25
Market Value: $28

5

Sleighride
Issued: 1998 • Retired: 2000
#57502 • Original Price: $20
Market Value: $22

6

The Spirit Of Christmas
Issued: 1997 • Retired: 2000
#58431 • Original Price: $15
Market Value: $17

7

Town Crier
Issued: 1998 • Retired: 2000
#58433 • Original Price: $15
Market Value: $17

8

Caroling Elf
Issued: 1998 • Retired: 2000
#57506 • Original Price: $15
Market Value: $17

9

Elf On A Sled
Issued: 1998 • Retired: 2000
#57505 • Original Price: $15
Market Value: $17

Dickens' Village Series®

	Price Paid	Value
1.		
2.		
3.		
4.		
5.		
6.		
7.		

North Pole Series™

8.		
9.		

Totals

Heritage Village Collection® – Hinged Boxes

Heritage Village Collection® – Ornaments

Several villages have ornaments available, and with so many to choose from, you won't want to wait for Christmas to decorate your home – or anyplace else!

1

New

Photo Unavailable

Village Express Van (Event Piece)
Issued: 2001 • To Be Retired: 2001
#97701 • Original Price: $25
Market Value: $25

2

Fezziwig's Warehouse *The Cottage Of Bob Cratchit & Tiny Tim* *Scrooge & Marley Counting House*

Christmas Carol Cottages (set/3)
Classic Ornament Series
Issued: 1998 • Retired: 2000
#98745 • Original Price: $50
Market Value: $53

3

Crown & Cricket Inn Ornament (LE-1996)
Issued: 1996 • Retired: 1996
#98730 • Original Price: $15
Market Value: $27

4

Dedlock Arms Ornament (LE-1994)
Issued: 1994 • Retired: 1994
#9872-8 • Original Price: $12.50
Market Value: $27

5

Dickens' Village Church
Classic Ornament Series
Issued: 1997 • Retired: 1998
#98737 • Original Price: $15
Market Value: $17

6

Dickens' Village Church
Classic Ornament Series
Issued: 1998 • Retired: 2000
#98767 • Original Price: $20
Market Value: $21

7

Dickens' Village Mill
Classic Ornament Series
Issued: 1997 • Retired: 1998
#98733 • Original Price: $15
Market Value: $17

8

Dickens' Village Mill
Classic Ornament Series
Issued: 1998 • Retired: 2000
#98766 • Original Price: $22.50
Market Value: $24

Heritage Village Collection®

	Price Paid	Value
1.		

Dickens' Village Series®

2.		
3.		
4.		
5.		
6.		
7.		
8.		

Totals

Heritage Village Collection® – Ornaments

9

Gad's Hill Place Ornament (LE-1997)
Issued: 1997 • Retired: 1997
#98732 • Original Price: $15
Market Value: $27

10

The Grapes Inn Ornament (LE-1996)
Issued: 1996 • Retired: 1996
#98729 • Original Price: $15
Market Value: $27

11

Old Curiosity Shop
Classic Ornament Series
Issued: 1997 • Retired: 1998
#98738 • Original Price: $15
Market Value: $17

12

The Old Curiosity Shop
Classic Ornament Series
Issued: 1998 • Retired: 2000
#98768 • Original Price: $20
Market Value: $21

13

The Pied Bull Inn Ornament (LE-1996)
Issued: 1996 • Retired: 1996
#98731 • Original Price: $15
Market Value: $32

14

Sir John Falstaff Inn Ornament (LE-1995)
Issued: 1995 • Retired: 1995
#9870-1 • Original Price: $15
Market Value: $30

15

Victoria Station
Classic Ornament Series
Issued: 1999 • Retired: 2000
#98780 • Original Price: $22.50
Market Value: $24

16

Captain's Cottage
Classic Ornament Series
Issued: 1998 • Retired: 2000
#98756 • Original Price: $20
Market Value: $21

17

Craggy Cove Lighthouse
Classic Ornament Series
Issued: 1997 • Retired: 1998
#98739 • Original Price: $15
Market Value: $20

18
Craggy Cove Lighthouse
Classic Ornament Series
Issued: 1998 • Retired: 2000
#98769 • Original Price: $20
Market Value: $21

19

Steeple Church
Classic Ornament Series
Issued: 1998 • Retired: 2000
#98757 • Original Price: $20
Market Value: $21

Dickens' Village Series®

	Price Paid	Value
9.		
10.		
11.		
12.		
13.		
14.		
15.		

New England Village® Series

16.		
17.		
18.		
19.		

Totals

20

Cathedral Church Of St. Mark
Classic Ornament Series
Issued: 1998 • Retired: 2000
#98759 • Original Price: $22.50
Market Value: $24

21

City Hall
Classic Ornament Series
Issued: 1997 • Retired: 1998
#98741 • Original Price: $15
Market Value: $19

22

City Hall
Classic Ornament Series
Issued: 1998 • Retired: 2000
#98771 • Original Price: $20
Market Value: $21

23

Dorothy's Dress Shop
Classic Ornament Series
Issued: 1997 • Retired: 1998
#98740 • Original Price: $15
Market Value: $18

24

Dorothy's Dress Shop
Classic Ornament Series
Issued: 1998 • Retired: 1999
#98770 • Original Price: $20
Market Value: $22

25

Hollydale's Department Store
Classic Ornament Series
Issued: 1999 • Retired: 2000
#98782 • Original Price: $20
Market Value: $21

26

Red Brick Fire Station
Classic Ornament Series
Issued: 1998 • Retired: 2000
#98758 • Original Price: $20
Market Value: $21

27

Elf Bunkhouse
Classic Ornament Series
Issued: 1998 • Retired: 2000
#98763 • Original Price: $20
Market Value: $21

28

North Pole Santa's Workshop
Classic Ornament Series
Issued: 1997 • Retired: 1998
#98734 • Original Price: $18
Market Value: $20

29

Real Plastic Snow Factory
Classic Ornament Series
Issued: 1999 • Retired: 2000
#98781 • Original Price: $22.50
Market Value: $24

30

Reindeer Barn
Classic Ornament Series
Issued: 1998 • Retired: 2000
#98762 • Original Price: $20
Market Value: $21

Christmas In The City® Series		
	Price Paid	Value
20.		
21.		
22.		
23.		
24.		
25.		
26.		
North Pole Series™		
27.		
28.		
29.		
30.		
Totals		

135

31

Santa's Lookout Tower
Classic Ornament Series
Issued: 1997 • Retired: 1998
#98742 • Original Price: $15
Market Value: $17

32

Santa's Lookout Tower
Classic Ornament Series
Issued: 1998 • Retired: 2000
#98773 • Original Price: $20
Market Value: $21

33

Santa's Workshop
Classic Ornament Series
Issued: 1998 • Retired: 2000
#98772 • Original Price: $22
Market Value: $23

Heritage Village Collection® Mid-Year Releases

The following *Heritage Village Collection®* buildings and accessories were released into the various *Heritage Village* collections on May 11, 2001.

1

New

Cratchit's Corner
Dickens' Village Series®
Issued: 2001 • Current
#58486 • Original Price: $80
Market Value: $80

North Pole Series™

	Price Paid	Value
31.		
32.		
33.		

Heritage Village Collection® Mid-Year Releases

1.		
2.		
3.		
4.		
5.		
6.		

Totals

2

New

Somerset Valley Church (set/9)
Dickens' Village Series®
Issued: 2001
To Be Retired: December 26, 2001
#58485 • Original Price: $75
Market Value: $75

3

New

Revere Silver Works (set/2)
New England Village® Series
Issued: 2001 • Current
#56632 • Original Price: $60
Market Value: $60

4

New

Schwarzwalder Kuckucksuhren
Alpine Village Series®
Issued: 2001 • Current
#56220 • Original Price: $65
Market Value: $65

5

New

Baker Bros. Bagel Bakery
Christmas In The City® Series
Issued: 2001 • Current
#58920 • Original Price: $75
Market Value: $75

6

New

Crystal Ice Palace (25th Anniversary Special Edition, set/9)
Christmas In The City® Series
Issued: 2001 • To Be Retired: December 26, 2001
#58922 • Original Price: $165
Market Value: $165

Heritage Village Collection® – Ornaments

7

New

Paradise Travel Company
Christmas In The City®
Series
Issued: 2001 • Current
#58921 • Original Price: $75
Market Value: $75

8

New

Yankee Stadium
Christmas In The City®
Series
Issued: 2001 • Current
#58923 • Original Price: $85
Market Value: $85

9

New

Caribou Coffee Shop (set/3)
North Pole Series™
Issued: 2001 • Current
#56736 • Original Price: $62
Market Value: $62

10

New

The Egg Nog Pub
North Pole Series™
Issued: 2001 • Current
#56737 • Original Price: $40
Market Value: $40

11

New

LEGO® Building Creation Station
North Pole Series™
Issued: 2001 • Current
#56735 • Original Price: $90
Market Value: $90

12

New

Santa's Sleigh Launch (gift set/5)
North Pole Series™
Issued: 2001
To Be Retired: December 26, 2001
#56734 • Original Price: $75
Market Value: $75

13

New

Bob Cratchit And Tiny Tim
Dickens' Village Series®
Issued: 2001 • Current
#58537 • Original Price: $15
Market Value: $15

14

New

Ghost Of Christmas Present Visits Scrooge
Dickens' Village Series®
Issued: 2001 • Current
#58538 • Original Price: $15
Market Value: $15

15

New

Silver For Sale (set/2)
New England Village®
Series
Issued: 2001 • Current
#56650 • Original Price: $20
Market Value: $20

16

New

Photo Unavailable

Cuckoo Clock Vendor & Cart (set/2)
Alpine Village Series®
Issued: 2001 • Current
#56303 • Original Price: $20
Market Value: $20

17

New

Midtown News Stand (set/2)
Christmas In The City®
Series
Issued: 2001 • Current
#58974 • Original Price: $32.50
Market Value: $32.50

18

New

Planning A Winter Vacation
Christmas In The City®
Series
Issued: 2001 • Current
#58975 • Original Price: $12.50
Market Value: $12.50

Heritage Village Collection® Mid-Year Releases		
	Price Paid	Value
7.		
8.		
9.		
10.		
11.		
12.		
13.		
14.		
15.		
16.		
17.		
18.		
Totals		

19
New

Pretzel Cart
Christmas In The City®
Series
Issued: 2001 • Current
#58973 • Original Price: $22
Market Value: $22

20
New
Artist Rendering,
Not Actual Product

Brick Lift
North Pole Series™
Issued: 2001 • Current
#56809 • Original Price: $17.50
Market Value: $17.50

21
New
Artist Rendering,
Not Actual Product

Just A Cup Of Joe
North Pole Series™
Issued: 2001 • Current
#56811 • Original Price: $22.50
Market Value: $22.50

22
New
Artist Rendering,
Not Actual Product

Little Builders
North Pole Series™
Issued: 2001 • Current
#56810 • Original Price: $16
Market Value: $16

23
New

Crystal Ice King &
Queen (LE-25,000)
Heritage Village Collection®
Issued: 2001
To Be Retired: December 26, 2001
#58976 • Original Price: $20
Market Value: $20

24
New

Gondola (animated)
Heritage Village Collection®
Issued: 2001 • Current
#52511 • Original Price: $85
Market Value: $85

Heritage Village Collection® Mid-Year Releases		
	Price Paid	Value
19.		
20.		
21.		
22.		
23.		
24.		
Totals		

Heritage Village Collection® – Mid-Year Releases

Total Value Of My Collection

Record your collection here by adding the totals from
the bottom of each Value Guide page.

Heritage Village Collection® – Buildings

Page Number	Price Paid	Value	Page Number	Price Paid	Value
Page 31			Page 59		
Page 32			Page 60		
Page 33			Page 61		
Page 34			Page 62		
Page 35			Page 63		
Page 36			Page 64		
Page 37			Page 65		
Page 38			Page 66		
Page 39			Page 67		
Page 40			Page 68		
Page 41			Page 69		
Page 42			Page 70		
Page 43			Page 71		
Page 44			Page 72		
Page 45			Page 73		
Page 46			Page 74		
Page 47			Page 75		
Page 48			Page 76		
Page 49			Page 77		
Page 50			Page 78		
Page 51			Page 79		
Page 52			Page 80		
Page 53			Page 81		
Page 54			Page 82		
Page 55			Page 83		
Page 56			Page 84		
Page 57			Page 85		
Page 58			Page 86		
			Page 87		
Subtotal:			Subtotal:		

	Price Paid	Value
Page Total:		

Total Value Of My Collection

Record your collection here by adding the totals from
the bottom of each Value Guide page.

Heritage Village Collection® – Buildings

Page Number	Price Paid	Value
Page 88		
Page 89		
Page 90		
Page 91		
Page 92		
Page 93		
Subtotal:		

Heritage Village Collection® – Accessories

Page Number	Price Paid	Value
Page 94		
Page 95		
Page 96		
Page 97		
Page 98		
Page 99		
Page 100		
Page 101		
Page 102		
Page 103		
Page 104		
Page 105		
Page 106		
Page 107		
Page 108		
Page 109		
Page 110		
Page 111		
Page 112		
Subtotal:		

Heritage Village Collection® – Accessories

Page Number	Price Paid	Value
Page 113		
Page 114		
Page 115		
Page 116		
Page 117		
Page 118		
Page 119		
Page 120		
Page 121		
Page 122		
Page 123		
Page 124		
Page 125		
Page 126		
Page 127		
Page 128		
Page 129		
Page 130		
Page 131		
Subtotal:		

Heritage Village® – Hinged Boxes and Ornaments

Page Number	Price Paid	Value
Page 132		
Page 133		
Page 134		
Page 135		
Page 136		
Subtotal:		

Page Total:	Price Paid	Value

The Original Snow Village® Collection Overview

Welcome to the snow-covered streets of The Original Snow Village, where neighbors are friendly and families still eat Sunday dinner together. These ceramic, shiny-glazed buildings and accessories give folks a chance to reminisce about the good old days.

Growth Of A Village

It's hard to believe that this collection, inspired by the town of Stillwater, Minnesota, started with only six pieces in 1976. The collection has now grown to feature over 250 buildings, more than 240 accessories and over a dozen ornaments. That is certainly enough to keep collectors on their toes! To celebrate their 25 years of success, Department 56 offered a limited edition piece for each village in 2001. They also offered a special event piece which was only available at Department 56's Silver Anniversary Celebration in St. Paul, Minnesota in the summer of 2001. These pieces, respectively the "Candlerock Lighthouse Restaurant" (LE-30,000) and the "Lowell Inn," join the relatively small ranks of limited edition pieces in Snow Village.

An Eye For Detail

Over the last quarter-century the design of the buildings and accessories in Snow Village has continued to evolve. New technology has resulted in pieces that can be smaller and more detailed at the same time. Just make a quick comparison between the "Village Greenhouse" (1991) and "The Secret Garden Greenhouse" (1998) to see an example. The use of plastic on the newer piece not only looks more like glass, but permits the collector to peek inside. Yet another good example of this is "Uptown Motors Ford®," where viewers can look inside the showroom. Another new trend is larger, elaborate sets with lots of accessories like "Champsfield Stadium" (set/24) and the accessory set "2001 Space Oddity" (set/11). Better make room in your display!

Drive-In Days Are Here Again

Many of the buildings in the Original Snow Village are straight out of the era of bobby socks and poodle skirts – the 1950s! With buildings like "Dinah's Drive-In" and "Rockabilly Records," and classic cars like the "'50s Hot Rod," it's easy to transport yourself

back in time. You can even celebrate the birth of rock and roll with the recently retired "Elvis Presley's Graceland®" set, which came with a classic "1955 Pink Cadillac®" that would have made Elvis proud.

Building It With Style

In 1990, a historic event occurred in Snow Village when two buildings were issued in the new *American Architecture Series*. This was the village's first series, and it celebrates the many distinctive and varied forms of American buildings. So far, 11 buildings have been released, including the stately "Italianate Villa" and the "Carpenter Gothic Bed & Breakfast." One new house was introduced every year (except for in 1993) until 1998, with a new introduction in mid-year 2000.

License To Build

Big names have been moving into town since 1994, when the "Coca-Cola® Brand Bottling Plant" first set up shop. These all-American companies are providing food ("Hershey's™ Chocolate Shop"), travel ("Harley Davidson® Motorcycle Shop") and fun ("Lionel® Electric Train Shop") for all the Snow Village inhabitants, yet never distracting from the collection's downhome charm.

What's New For The Original Snow Village® Collection

This delightful little town gets a bit bigger every year. In December of 2000, 14 new buildings and 31 new accessories turned up in Snow Village, and the town's growth shows no signs of slowing down!

Snow Village Buildings

Abner's Implement Co. (set/2) . . . Whether they need a strong tractor to get all their plowing finished, or replacement parts to keep the furnace going during those cold winter months, villagers can find whatever they need at Abner's.

Buck's County Farmhouse . . . From the warm lights in the windows to the charming rug on the porch rail, everything about this delightful house says, "Come on in and stay awhile."

Buck's County Horse Barn . . . If you're a city slicker who's always wanted to try your hand at riding, this is the place to be! With everything from thoroughbreds to wild mustangs, there's definitely a horse for every rider.

Candlerock Lighthouse Restaurant (LE-30,000) . . . There's no place to relax like Candlerock. The bar here just can't be beat (for ambiance, at least), and the chowder is the best in town!

Creepy Creek Carriage House . . . Does every town have a haunted house? Snow Village certainly does, but don't let the bats in the tower scare you. To complete your collection, this piece is more crucial than creepy.

Crosby House . . . On Christmas Eve, all the town's citizens are invited to celebrate at this stately mansion with music, dinner and dancing. They'll need plenty of room to hold all that revelry!

Frost And Sons 5 & Dime . . . You never know when a shopping spree might strike you! And when it's time to buy a gift – be it Christmas, birthday or just something for that special someone – Frost and Sons has just what you need.

Hauntsburg House . . . We can guess that this place won't have any egg on its windows the morning after Halloween. Those gruesome jack-o'-lanterns in the windows are enough to scare away the most daring would-be hooligan!

The Holiday House . . . This festive family sure went all the way with their Christmas decorations this year. With all those holiday sentiments, Santa sure won't miss this one!

Lowell Inn . . . To celebrate their 25th Anniversary, Department 56 has recreated the charming inn in Stillwater, Minnesota where the inspiration for the Snow Village was born. (Available only at the Department 56 Silver Anniversary Celebration.)

Palm Lounge Supper Club (set/2) . . . The folks in this town are serious about fun, and there's no place to unwind like Palm Lounge. We even heard a rumor that a certain celebrity from Memphis might be stopping by . . .

Timberlake Outfitters . . . Before you head out to the lake for a day of family fun, be sure to stop by "Timberlake Outfitters." With every-thing from canoes to basic outdoor supplies, they're equipped to handle any sporting need.

Totem Town Souvenir Shop . . . When you're looking for kitschy gifts and household stables, Totem Town is the place to be. And be sure to pick up some beef jerky while you're there!

Village Town Hall . . . Running a town this size isn't an easy job. But it's all worth it when you get to light up the town hall for the Christmas season! Everyone wants to be there when the mayor lights up the town tree at the special Yuletide ceremony.

There is never a dull moment in Snow Village. Its inhabitants are always on the go, moving and singing – and even being visited by beings from the stars! Here is a list of the 31 new accessories that have been introduced to the collection to help the villagers along in their busy lives.

The Original Snow Village Collection®
Accessories

'50s Hot Rod (*Classic Cars*™)

1949 Ford Woody Wagon (*Classic Cars*™)

1950 Ford F-1 Pickup (John Deere) (*Classic Cars*™)

1954 Willy's CJ3 Jeep (*Classic Cars*™)

1957 Chevrolet® Bel Air™ (*Classic Cars*™)

1958 Corvette® Roadster (*Classic Cars*™)

1958 John Deere 730 Diesel Tractor (*Classic Cars*™)

1959 Chevrolet® Impala™ Convertible (*Classic Cars*™)

2001 Space Oddity (set/11)

The Abandoned Gas Pump

Buck's County Horse Trailer

Buck's County Stables (set/9)

Buck's County Water Tower

Christmastime Trimming

Elvis Presley's® Autograph (set/3)

Family Canoe Trip (set/3)

Holiday Singers (musical, animated)

Lighting The Jack-O'- Lanterns (set/3)

Mill Falls (animated)

Now Showing – Elvis Presley® Sign

The Old Pickup Truck

On The Beat (set/2)

Pedal Cars For Christmas (set/2)

Perfect Putt (animated)

Roadside Billboards (set/3)

Santa Comes To Town, 2001

Santa's On His Way (musical, animated)

The Tree Lighting Ceremony (set/3)

Windmill By The Chicken Coop

Woodland Carousel (musical, animated)

Yesterday's Tractor

The Original Snow Village Collection® – Mid-Year Releases

Buildings

Christmas Lake Chalet (set/5)

Haunted Barn (set/4)

Stardust Drive-In Theater

Stardust Refreshment Stand (set/7)

Tudor House

Accessories

Crystal Ice King & Queen (LE-25,000)

Fun In The Snow (set/2)

Gondola (animated scene)

Happy New Year (set/4)

Holiday Fun Run

Recent Retirements

Department 56 announced the following Snow Village retirements on November 3, 2000. Each year, the retirements are made public in *USA Today*, as well as on the Department 56 website (*www.department56.com*). Collectors can also pre-register to receive an e-mail listing the retirements directly from the company on the morning of the announcement.

The Original Snow Village®Collection Buildings

- ❏ Center For The Arts (1998)
- ❏ Elvis Presley's Graceland® (2000, set/6)
- ❏ Farm House (1997)
- ❏ The Farmer's Co-op Granary (1998)
- ❏ Gracie's Dry Goods & General Store (1997, set/2)
- ❏ Harley Davidson® Manufacturing (1998, set/3)
- ❏ Haunted Mansion (1998)

The Original Snow Village® Collection Buildings, cont.

- ❏ Hershey's™ Chocolate Shop (1997)
- ❏ Lionel® Electric Train Shop (1998)

- ❏ Lucky Dragon Restaurant (1999)
- ❏ Silver Bells Christmas Shop (2000, set/4)
- ❏ Smokey Mountain Retreat (1996)
- ❏ Starbucks® Coffee (1995)
- ❏ Stick Style House (1998)

The Original Snow Village® Collection Accessories

- ❏ Biplane Up In The Sky (1998)
- ❏ Carnival Tickets & Cotton Candy (1998, set/3)

The Original Snow Village® Collection Ornaments

- ❏ J. Young's Granary (1998)
- ❏ Jingle Belle Houseboat (1999)
- ❏ Lighthouse (1998)
- ❏ Nantucket (1998)

- ❏ Caroling At The Farm (1994)
- ❏ Couldn't Wait Until Christmas (1998)
- ❏ Farmer's Flatbed (1998)
- ❏ Kids Love Hershey's™! (1997, set/2)
- ❏ Let It Snow, Let It Snow (1997)
- ❏ Nativity (1988)
- ❏ Santa Comes To Town, 2000 (LE-2000)
- ❏ Starbucks® Coffee Cart (1995, set/2)
- ❏ Taxi Cab (1987)
- ❏ Uncle Sam's Fireworks Stand (1998, set/2)

- ❏ Pinewood Log Cabin (1998)
- ❏ Queen Anne Victorian (1999)
- ❏ Steepled Church (1998)
- ❏ Street Car (1999)

The Original Snow Village® Collection Top Ten

This list showcases the ten most valuable Snow Village pieces as established by their secondary market value.

Cathedral Church
#5067-4
Issued: 1980 • Retired: 1981
Issue Price: **$36** • Value: **$3,200**

Adobe House
#5066-6
Issued: 1979 • Retired: 1980
Issue Price: **$18** • Value: **$2,700**

Mobile Home
#5063-3
Issued: 1979 • Retired: 1980
Issue Price: **$18** • Value: **$2,100**

Mission Church
#5062-5
Issued: 1979 • Retired: 1980
Issue Price: **$30** • Value: **$1,500**

Skating Rink/Duck Pond Set
#5015-3
Issued: 1978 • Retired: 1979
Issue Price: **$16** • Value: **$1,000**

Stone Church
#5059-1
Issued: 1979 • Retired: 1980
Issue Price: **$32** • Value: **$980**

Stone Church
#5009-6
Issued: 1977 • Retired: 1979
Issue Price: **$35** • Value: **$720**

Diner
#5078-4
Issued: 1986 • Retired: 1987
Issue Price: **$22** • Value: **$695**

Water Tower (John Deere)
#5133-0
Issued: 1988 • Retired: 1991
Issue Price: **$20** • Value: **$680**

General Store (tan)
#5012-0
Issued: 1978 • Retired: 1980
Issue Price: **$25** • Value: **$650**

How To Use Your Collector's Value Guide™

1. Locate your piece in the Snow Village Value Guide. The Original Snow Village® Collection buildings are listed first, followed by Snow Village accessories. Pieces are listed alphabetically within each section. Easy-to-use numerical and alphabetical indexes are located in the back of the book to help you find your pieces (beginning on page 267).

56 Flavors Ice Cream Parlor
Issued: 1990 ¥ Retired: 1992
#51151-9 ¥ Original Price: $42
Market Value: $180

2. Find the market value of your piece. If a variation with secondary market value exists, that value will also be noted (store exclusives are listed in the same manner). If no market value has been established for a piece, it is listed as "N/E" (not established). Pieces currently available at retail stores are listed at their current retail price.

3. Record the price you paid and the secondary market value in the corresponding boxes at the bottom of each page.

Snow Village® Buildings	
Price Paid	Value
1. **$42**	**$180**
2.	
3.	
4.	
5.	
6.	
	$180
Totals	

4. Calculate the value for each page by adding all of the prices in the "price paid" and "value" columns. Be sure to use a pencil so that you can change the totals as your collection grows!

5. Transfer the totals from each page to the "Total Value of My Collection" worksheets for Snow Village, beginning on page 215.

6. Add the totals together to determine the overall value of your collection.

The Original Snow Village® Collection – Buildings

In 1976, Department 56 created a village that has grown from a small town into a sprawling community of over 250 buildings. In 2000, the locals were amazed to see that 13 new edifices sprang up just down the road. It's about time the village had a souvenir shop and a supper club, don't you think?

1

56 Flavors Ice Cream Parlor
Issued: 1990 • Retired: 1992
#5151-9 • Original Price: $42
Market Value: $180

2

2000 Holly Lane (set/11, Event Piece)
Issued: 1999 • Retired: 1999
#54977 • Original Price: $65
Market Value: $100

3

2101 Maple
Issued: 1986 • Retired: 1986
#5043-1 • Original Price: $32
Market Value: $330

4

New

Abner's Implement Co. (set/2)
Issued: 2000 • Current
#55052 • Original Price: $85
Market Value: $85

5

Adobe House
Issued: 1979 • Retired: 1980
#5066-6 • Original Price: $18
Market Value: $2,700

6

Airport
Issued: 1992 • Retired: 1996
#5439-9 • Original Price: $60
Market Value: $88

The Original Snow Village® Collection

	Price Paid	Value
1.		
2.		
3.		
4.		
5.		
6.		
Totals		

7

Al's TV Shop
Issued: 1992 • Retired: 1995
#5423-2 • Original Price: $40
Market Value: $66

8

All Saints Church
Issued: 1986 • Retired: 1997
#5070-9 • Original Price: $38
Market Value: $62

9

. . . *Another Man's Treasure* Garage (set/22)
Issued: 1998 • Current
#54945 • Original Price: $60
Market Value: $60

10

Apothecary
Issued: 1986 • Retired: 1990
#5076-8 • Original Price: $34
Market Value: $102

11

Bakery
Issued: 1981 • Retired: 1983
#5077-6 • Original Price: $30
Market Value: $268

12

Bakery
Issued: 1986 • Retired: 1991
#5077-6 • Original Price: $35
Market Value: $92

The Original Snow Village® Collection		
	Price Paid	Value
7.		
8.		
9.		
10.		
11.		
12.		
13.		
Totals		

13

Bank
Issued: 1982 • Retired: 1983
#5024-5 • Original Price: $32
Market Value: $600

14

Barn
Issued: 1981 • Retired: 1984
#5074-1 • Original Price: $32
Market Value: $440

15

Bayport
Issued: 1984 • Retired: 1986
#5015-6 • Original Price: $30
Market Value: $235

16

Beacon Hill House
Issued: 1986 • Retired: 1988
#5065-2 • Original Price: $31
Market Value: $182

17

Beacon Hill Victorian
Issued: 1995 • Retired: 1998
#54857 • Original Price: $60
Market Value: $83

18

Birch Run Ski Chalet
Issued: 1996 • Retired: 1999
#54882 • Original Price: $60
Market Value: $83

19

Boulder Springs House
Issued: 1996 • Retired: 1997
#54873 • Original Price: $60
Market Value: $78

20

Bowling Alley
Issued: 1995 • Retired: 1998
#54858 • Original Price: $42
Market Value: $62

21

The Brandon Bungalow
Issued: 1997 • Retired: 1999
#54918 • Original Price: $55
Market Value: $65

The Original Snow Village® Collection		
	Price Paid	Value
14.		
15.		
16.		
17.		
18.		
19.		
20.		
21.		
Totals		

The Original Snow Village® Collection – Buildings

The Original Snow Village® Collection – Buildings

22

Brownstone
Issued: 1979 • Retired: 1981
#5056-7 • Original Price: $36
Market Value: $590

23
New

Buck's County Farmhouse
Issued: 2000 • Current
#55051 • Original Price: $75
Market Value: $75

24
New

Buck's County Horse Barn
Issued: 2000 • Current
#55049 • Original Price: $72
Market Value: $72

25
New

Candlerock Lighthouse Restaurant (LE-30,000)
Issued: 2000 • Current
#55045 • Original Price: $110
Market Value: $110

26

Cape Cod
Issued: 1978 • Retired: 1980
#5013-8 • Original Price: $20
Market Value: $400

27

Carmel Cottage
Issued: 1994 • Retired: 1997
#5466-6 • Original Price: $48
Market Value: $63

The Original Snow Village® Collection		
	Price Paid	Value
22.		
23.		
24.		
25.		
26.		
27.		
28.		
Totals		

28

The Carnival Carousel (musical, animated)
Issued: 1998 • Current
#54933 • Original Price: $150
Market Value: $150

29

Carpenter Gothic Bed & Breakfast (set/2)
American Architecture Series
Issued: 2000 • Current
#55043 • Original Price: $75
Market Value: $75

30

Carriage House
Issued: 1982 • Retired: 1984
#5021-0 • Original Price: $28
Market Value: $328

31

Carriage House
Issued: 1986 • Retired: 1988
#5071-7 • Original Price: $29
Market Value: $115

32

Cathedral Church
Issued: 1980 • Retired: 1981
#5067-4 • Original Price: $36
Market Value: $3,200

33

Cathedral Church
Issued: 1987 • Retired: 1990
#5019-9 • Original Price: $50
Market Value: $108

34

Cedar Point Cabin
Issued: 1999 • Current
#55009 • Original Price: $66
Market Value: $66

35

Centennial House
Issued: 1982 • Retired: 1984
#5020-2 • Original Price: $32
Market Value: $330

36

Center For The Arts
Issued: 1998 • Retired: 2000
#54940 • Original Price: $64
Market Value: $68

The Original Snow Village® Collection

	Price Paid	Value
29.		
30.		
31.		
32.		
33.		
34.		
35.		
36.		
Totals		

The Original Snow Village® Collection – Buildings

The Original Snow Village® Collection – Buildings

37

Champsfield Stadium (set/24)
Issued: 1999 • Current
#55001 • Original Price: $195
Market Value: $195

38

Chateau
Issued: 1983 • Retired: 1984
#5084-9 • Original Price: $35
Market Value: $445

39

Christmas Barn Dance
Issued: 1997 • Retired: 1999
#54910 • Original Price: $65
Market Value: $75

40

Christmas Cove Lighthouse
Issued: 1995 • Current
#5483-6 • Original Price: $60
Market Value: $60

The Original Snow Village® Collection		
	Price Paid	Value
37.		
38.		
39.		
40.		
41.		
42.		
Totals		

41

Christmas Lake High School
Issued: 1996 • Retired: 1999
#54881 • Original Price: $52
Market Value: $72

42

The Christmas Shop
Issued: 1991 • Retired: 1996
#5097-0 • Original Price: $37.50
Market Value: $64

43

Church Of The Open Door
Issued: 1985 • Retired: 1988
#5048-2 • Original Price: $34
Market Value: $150

44

Cinema 56
Issued: 1999 • Current
#54978 • Original Price: $85
Market Value: $85

45

Cobblestone Antique Shop
Issued: 1988 • Retired: 1992
#5123-3 • Original Price: $36
Market Value: $83

46

Coca-Cola® Brand Bottling Plant
Issued: 1994 • Retired: 1997
#5469-0 • Original Price: $65
Market Value: $95

47

Coca-Cola® Brand Corner Drugstore
Issued: 1995 • Retired: 1998
#5484-4 • Original Price: $55
Market Value: $88

48

Colonial Church
Issued: 1989 • Retired: 1992
#5119-5 • Original Price: $60
Market Value: $87

49

Colonial Farm House
Issued: 1980 • Retired: 1982
#5070-9 • Original Price: $30
Market Value: $310

50

Congregational Church
Issued: 1984 • Retired: 1985
#5034-2 • Original Price: $28
Market Value: $640

The Original Snow Village® Collection

	Price Paid	Value
43.		
44.		
45.		
46.		
47.		
48.		
49.		
50.		
Totals		

The Original Snow Village® Collection – Buildings

51

Corner Cafe
Issued: 1988 • Retired: 1991
#5124-1 • Original Price: $37
Market Value: $100

52

Corner Store
Issued: 1981 • Retired: 1983
#5076-8 • Original Price: $30
Market Value: $250

53

Country Church
Issued: 1976 • Retired: 1979
#5004-7 • Original Price: $18
Market Value: $385

54

Countryside Church
Issued: 1979 • Retired: 1984
#5058-3 • Original Price: $27.50
Market Value: $270

55

Courthouse
Issued: 1989 • Retired: 1993
#5144-6 • Original Price: $65
Market Value: $200

56

Craftsman Cottage
American Architecture Series
Issued: 1992 • Retired: 1995
#5437-2 • Original Price: $55
Market Value: $80

The Original Snow Village® Collection		
	Price Paid	Value
51.		
52.		
53.		
54.		
55.		
56.		
57.		
58.		
Totals		

57

New

Creepy Creek Carriage House
Issued: 2000 • Current
#55055 • Original Price: $75
Market Value: $75

58

New

Crosby House
Issued: 2000 • Current
#55056 • Original Price: $50
Market Value: $50

59

Cumberland House
Issued: 1987 • Retired: 1995
#5024-5 • Original Price: $42
Market Value: $80

60

Dairy Barn
Issued: 1993 • Retired: 1997
#5446-1 • Original Price: $55
Market Value: $78

61

Delta House
Issued: 1984 • Retired: 1986
#5012-1 • Original Price: $32
Market Value: $300

62

Depot & Train With Two Train Cars (set/2)
Issued: 1985 • Retired: 1988
#5051-2 • Original Price: $65
Market Value: $165

63

Dinah's Drive-In
Issued: 1993 • Retired: 1996
#5447-0 • Original Price: $45
Market Value: $134

64

Diner
Issued: 1986 • Retired: 1987
#5078-4 • Original Price: $22
Market Value: $695

65

Doctor's House
Issued: 1989 • Retired: 1992
#5143-8 • Original Price: $56
Market Value: $115

The Original Snow Village® Collection

	Price Paid	Value
59.		
60.		
61.		
62.		
63.		
64.		
65.		
Totals		

The Original Snow Village® Collection – Buildings

The Original Snow Village® Collection – Buildings

66

Double Bungalow
Issued: 1991 • Retired: 1994
#5407-0 • Original Price: $45
Market Value: $69

67

Duplex
Issued: 1985 • Retired: 1987
#5050-4 • Original Price: $35
Market Value: $155

68

Dutch Colonial
American Architecture Series
Issued: 1995 • Retired: 1996
#54856 • Original Price: $45
Market Value: $70

69

1955 Pink Cadillac®

Elvis Presley's Graceland® (set/6, Event Piece)
Issued: 2000 • Retired: 2000
#55041 • Original Price: $165
Market Value: $170

70

English Church
Issued: 1981 • Retired: 1982
#5078-4 • Original Price: $30
Market Value: $425

71

English Cottage
Issued: 1981 • Retired: 1982
#5073-3 • Original Price: $25
Market Value: $300

72

English Tudor
Issued: 1983 • Retired: 1985
#5033-4 • Original Price: $30
Market Value: $280

The Original Snow Village® Collection

	Price Paid	Value
66.		
67.		
68.		
69.		
70.		
71.		
72.		
Totals		

73

Farm House
Issued: 1987 • Retired: 1992
#5089-0 • Original Price: $40
Market Value: $79

74

Farm House
Issued: 1997 • Retired: 2000
#54912 • Original Price: $50
Market Value: $55

75

The Farmer's Co-op Granary
Issued: 1998 • Retired: 2000
#54946 • Original Price: $64
Market Value: $67

76

Federal House
American Architecture Series
Issued: 1994 • Retired: 1997
#5465-8 • Original Price: $50
Market Value: $74

77

Finklea's Finery: Costume Shop
Issued: 1991 • Retired: 1993
#5405-4 • Original Price: $45
Market Value: $73

78

Fire Station
Issued: 1983 • Retired: 1984
#5032-6 • Original Price: $32
Market Value: $585

79

Fire Station No. 2
Issued: 1987 • Retired: 1989
#5091-1 • Original Price: $40
Market Value: $205

80

Fire Station #3
Issued: 1998 • Current
#54942 • Original Price: $70
Market Value: $70

The Original Snow Village® Collection

	Price Paid	Value
73.		
74.		
75.		
76.		
77.		
78.		
79.		
80.		
Totals		

The Original Snow Village® Collection - Buildings

The Original Snow Village® Collection – Buildings

81

Bass

Trout

Fisherman's Nook Cabins (set/2)
Issued: 1994 • Retired: 1999
#5461-5 • Original Price: $50
Market Value: $70

82

Fisherman's Nook Resort
Issued: 1994 • Retired: 1999
#5460-7 • Original Price: $75
Market Value: $90

83

Flower Shop
Issued: 1982 • Retired: 1983
#5082-2 • Original Price: $25
Market Value: $475

84
New

Frost And Sons 5 & Dime
Issued: 2000 • Current
#55047 • Original Price: $68
Market Value: $68

85

Gabled Cottage
Issued: 1976 • Retired: 1979
#5002-1 • Original Price: $20
Market Value: $385

The Original Snow Village® Collection

	Price Paid	Value
81.		
82.		
83.		
84.		
85.		
86.		
Totals		

86

Gabled House
Issued: 1982 • Retired: 1983
#5081-4 • Original Price: $30
Market Value: $415

87

Galena House
Issued: 1984 • Retired: 1985
#5009-1 • Original Price: $32
Market Value: $385

88

Version 1

Version 2

Version 3

General Store
Issued: 1978 • Retired: 1980
#5012-0 • Original Price: $25
Market Value: **1** – $480 (white) **2** – $650 (tan) **3** – $545 (gold)

89

Giant Trees
Issued: 1979 • Retired: 1982
#5065-8 • Original Price: $20
Market Value: $300

90

Version 1

Version 2

Gingerbread House
Issued: 1983 • Retired: 1984
#5025-3 • Original Price: $24
Market Value: **1** – $400 (coin bank) **2** – $400 (lit house)

91

Glenhaven House
Issued: 1994 • Retired: 1997
#5468-2 • Original Price: $45
Market Value: $68

92

Good Shepherd Chapel & Church School (set/2)
Issued: 1992 • Retired: 1996
#5424-0 • Original Price: $72
Market Value: $90

The Original Snow Village® Collection

	Price Paid	Value
87.		
88.		
89.		
90.		
91.		
92.		
Totals		

The Original Snow Village® Collection – Buildings

93

Gothic Church
Issued: 1983 • Retired: 1986
#5028-8 • Original Price: $36
Market Value: $270

94

Gothic Farmhouse
American Architecture Series
Issued: 1991 • Retired: 1997
#5404-6 • Original Price: $48
Market Value: $68

95

Governor's Mansion
Issued: 1983 • Retired: 1985
#5003-2 • Original Price: $32
Market Value: $325

96

Gracie's Dry Goods & General Store (set/2)
Issued: 1997 • Retired: 2000
#54915 • Original Price: $70
Market Value: $73

97

Grandma's Cottage
Issued: 1992 • Retired: 1996
#5420-8 • Original Price: $42
Market Value: $80

98

Grimsly Manor
Issued: 1999 • Current
#55004 • Original Price: $120
Market Value: $120

The Original Snow Village® Collection		
	Price Paid	Value
93.		
94.		
95.		
96.		
97.		
98.		
99.		
100.		
Totals		

99

Grocery
Issued: 1983 • Retired: 1985
#5001-6 • Original Price: $35
Market Value: $375

100

Harley-Davidson® Manufacturing (set/3)
Issued: 1998 • Retired: 2000
#54948 • Original Price: $80
Market Value: $90

101

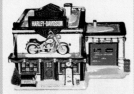

Harley-Davidson® Motorcycle Shop
Issued: 1996 • Current
#54886 • Original Price: $65
Market Value: $65

102

Hartford House
Issued: 1992 • Retired: 1995
#5426-7 • Original Price: $55
Market Value: $85

103

Haunted Mansion (animated)
Issued: 1998 • Retired: 2000
#54935 • Original Price: $110
Market Value: $135

104
New

Hauntsburg House
Issued: 2000 • Current
#55058 • Original Price: $95
Market Value: $95

105

Haversham House
Issued: 1984 • Retired: 1987
#5008-3 • Original Price: $37
Market Value: $285

106

Hershey's™ Chocolate Shop
Issued: 1997 • Retired: 2000
#54913 • Original Price: $55
Market Value: $65

107

Hidden Ponds House
Issued: 1998 • Current
#54944 • Original Price: $50
Market Value: $50

The Original Snow Village® Collection

	Price Paid	Value
101.		
102.		
103.		
104.		
105.		
106.		
107.		
Totals		

The Original Snow Village® Collection – Buildings

108

Highland Park House
Issued: 1986 • Retired: 1988
#5063-6 • Original Price: $35
Market Value: $155

109
New

The Holiday House
Issued: 2000 • Current
#55048 • Original Price: $90
Market Value: $90

110

Holly Brothers Garage
Issued: 1995 • Retired: 1998
#54854 • Original Price: $48
Market Value: $70

111

**Holy Spirit Church
(set/2)**
Issued: 1999 • Current
#55003 • Original Price: $70
Market Value: $70

112

A Home In The Making (set/5)
Issued: 1999 • Current
#54979 • Original Price: $95
Market Value: $95

The Original Snow Village® Collection		
	Price Paid	Value
108.		
109.		
110.		
111.		
112.		
113.		
114.		
Totals		

113

**Home Sweet Home/
House & Windmill
(set/2)**
Issued: 1988 • Retired: 1991
#5126-8 • Original Price: $60
Market Value: $120

114

Homestead
Issued: 1978 • Retired: 1984
#5011-2 • Original Price: $30
Market Value: $260

The Original Snow Village® Collection – Buildings

115

The Honeymooner Motel
Issued: 1991 • Retired: 1993
#5401-1 • Original Price: $42
Market Value: $105

116

Hunting Lodge
Issued: 1993 • Retired: 1996
#5445-3 • Original Price: $50
Market Value: $157

117

The Inn
Issued: 1976 • Retired: 1979
#5003-9 • Original Price: $20
Market Value: $480

118

Italianate Villa
American Architecture Series
Issued: 1997 • Current
#54911 • Original Price: $55
Market Value: $55

119

J. Young's Granary
Issued: 1989 • Retired: 1992
#5149-7 • Original Price: $45
Market Value: $96

120

Jack's Corner Barber Shop
Issued: 1991 • Retired: 1994
#5406-2 • Original Price: $42
Market Value: $85

121

Jefferson School
Issued: 1987 • Retired: 1991
#5082-2 • Original Price: $36
Market Value: $184

122

Jingle Belle Houseboat
Issued: 1989 • Retired: 1991
#5114-4 • Original Price: $42
Market Value: $198

The Original Snow Village® Collection

	Price Paid	Value
115.		
116.		
117.		
118.		
119.		
120.		
121.		
122.		
Totals		

The Original Snow Village® Collection – Buildings

123

Kenwood House
Issued: 1988 • Retired: 1990
#5054-7 • Original Price: $50
Market Value: $145

124

Version 1

Version 2

Knob Hill
Issued: 1979 • Retired: 1981
#5055-9 • Original Price: $30
Market Value: **1** – $360 (gray) **2** – $350 (yellow)

125

Large Single Tree
Issued: 1981 • Retired: 1989
#5080-6 • Original Price: $17
Market Value: $58

126

Last Stop Gas Station (set/2)
Issued: 1999 • Current
#55012 • Original Price: $72
Market Value: $72

127

Lighthouse
Issued: 1987 • Retired: 1988
#5030-0 • Original Price: $36
Market Value: $580

The Original Snow Village® Collection		
	Price Paid	Value
123.		
124.		
125.		
126.		
127.		
128.		
129.		
Totals		

128

Lincoln Park Duplex
Issued: 1986 • Retired: 1988
#5060-1 • Original Price: $33
Market Value: $140

129

Linden Hills Country Club (set/2)
Issued: 1997 • Current
#54917 • Original Price: $60
Market Value: $60

130

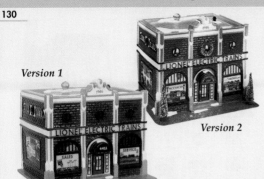

Version 1

Version 2

Lionel® Electric Train Shop
Issued: 1998 • Retired: 2000
#54947 • Original Price: $55
Market Value: **1** – $250 (Allied Model Trains) **2** – $62 (general release)

131

Log Cabin
Issued: 1979 • Retired: 1981
#5057-5 • Original Price: $22
Market Value: $550

132
New

Lowell Inn
(Event Piece)
Issued: 2001 • To Be Retired: 2001
#55059 • Original Price: $85
Market Value: $85

133

Lucky Dragon
Restaurant
Issued: 1999 • Retired: 2000
#55011 • Original Price: $75
Market Value: $80

134

Main Street House
Issued: 1984 • Retired: 1986
#5005-9 • Original Price: $27
Market Value: $245

135

Mainstreet Gift Shop
(GCC Piece)
Issued: 1997 • Retired: 1997
#54887 • Original Price: $50
Market Value: $90

136

Mainstreet Hardware
Store
Issued: 1990 • Retired: 1993
#5153-5 • Original Price: $42
Market Value: $95

The Original Snow Village® Collection

	Price Paid	Value
130.		
131.		
132.		
133.		
134.		
135.		
136.		
Totals		

The Original Snow Village® Collection – Buildings

137

Mansion
Issued: 1977 • Retired: 1979
#5008-8 • Original Price: $30
Market Value: $530

138

Maple Ridge Inn
Issued: 1988 • Retired: 1990
#5121-7 • Original Price: $55
Market Value: $90

139

Marvel's Beauty Salon
Issued: 1994 • Retired: 1997
#5470-4 • Original Price: $37.50
Market Value: $58

140

McDonald's®
Issued: 1997 • Retired: 1999
#54914 • Original Price: $65
Market Value: $75

141

Mission Church
Issued: 1979 • Retired: 1980
#5062-5 • Original Price: $30
Market Value: $1,500

142

Mobile Home
Issued: 1979 • Retired: 1980
#5063-3 • Original Price: $18
Market Value: $2,100

143

Morningside House
Issued: 1990 • Retired: 1992
#5152-7 • Original Price: $45
Market Value: $78

144

Mount Olivet Church
Issued: 1993 • Retired: 1996
#5442-9 • Original Price: $65
Market Value: $88

The Original Snow Village® Collection		
	Price Paid	Value
137.		
138.		
139.		
140.		
141.		
142.		
143.		
144.		
Totals		

145

Mountain Lodge
Issued: 1976 • Retired: 1979
#5001-3 • Original Price: $20
Market Value: $385

146

Nantucket
Issued: 1978 • Retired: 1986
#5014-6 • Original Price: $25
Market Value: $265

147

Nantucket Renovation (LE-1993)
Issued: 1993 • Retired: 1993
#5441-0 • Original Price: $55
Market Value: $90

148

New Hope Church
Issued: 1997 • Retired: 1998
#54904 • Original Price: $60
Market Value: $76

149

New School House
Issued: 1984 • Retired: 1986
#5037-7 • Original Price: $35
Market Value: $260

150

New Stone Church
Issued: 1982 • Retired: 1984
#5083-0 • Original Price: $32
Market Value: $385

151

Nick The Tree Farmer

Nick's Tree Farm

Nick's Tree Farm (set/10)
Issued: 1996 • Retired: 1999
#54871 • Original Price: $40
Market Value: $46

The Original Snow Village® Collection		
	Price Paid	Value
145.		
146.		
147.		
148.		
149.		
150.		
151.		
Totals		

The Original Snow Village® Collection – Buildings

152

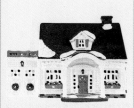

North Creek Cottage
Issued: 1989 • Retired: 1992
#5120-9 • Original Price: $45
Market Value: $75

153

Oak Grove Tudor
Issued: 1991 • Retired: 1994
#5400-3 • Original Price: $42
Market Value: $70

154

**Old Chelsea Mansion
(with book)**
Issued: 1997 • Retired: 1998
#54903 • Original Price: $85
Market Value: $100

155

*Kringle's Toy
Shop*

*Nikki's Cocoa
Shop*

*Saturday Morning
Downtown*

**The Original Snow Village
Start A Tradition Set (set/8)**
Issued: 1997 • Retired: 1998
#54902 • Original Price: $75
Market Value: $98

156

Pacific Heights House
Issued: 1986 • Retired: 1988
#5066-0 • Original Price: $33
Market Value: $110

The Original Snow Village® Collection		
	Price Paid	Value
152.		
153.		
154.		
155.		
156.		
157.		
Totals		

157

New

Palm Lounge Supper Club (set/2)
Issued: 2000 • Current
#55046 • Original Price: $95
Market Value: $95

158

Palos Verdes
Issued: 1988 • Retired: 1990
#5141-1 • Original Price: $37.50
Market Value: $83

159

Paramount Theater
Issued: 1989 • Retired: 1993
#5142-0 • Original Price: $42
Market Value: $190

160

Parish Church
Issued: 1984 • Retired: 1986
#5039-3 • Original Price: $32
Market Value: $335

161

Parsonage
Issued: 1983 • Retired: 1985
#5029-6 • Original Price: $35
Market Value: $365

162

Peppermint Porch Day Care
Issued: 1995 • Retired: 1997
#5485-2 • Original Price: $45
Market Value: $65

163

Pinewood Log Cabin
Issued: 1989 • Retired: 1995
#5150-0 • Original Price: $37.50
Market Value: $70

164

Pioneer Church
Issued: 1982 • Retired: 1984
#5022-9 • Original Price: $30
Market Value: $350

165

Pisa Pizza
Issued: 1995 • Retired: 1998
#54851 • Original Price: $35
Market Value: $52

The Original Snow Village® Collection

	Price Paid	Value
158.		
159.		
160.		
161.		
162.		
163.		
164.		
165.		
Totals		

The Original Snow Village® Collection - Buildings

The Original Snow Village® Collection – Buildings

166

Plantation House
Issued: 1985 • Retired: 1987
#5047-4 • Original Price: $37
Market Value: $110

167

Prairie House
American Architecture Series
Issued: 1990 • Retired: 1993
#5156-0 • Original Price: $42
Market Value: $78

168

Print Shop & Village News
Issued: 1992 • Retired: 1994
#5425-9 • Original Price: $37.50
Market Value: $82

169

Queen Anne Victorian
American Architecture Series
Issued: 1990 • Retired: 1996
#5157-8 • Original Price: $48
Market Value: $80

170

Ramsey Hill House
Issued: 1986 • Retired: 1989
#5067-9 • Original Price: $36
Market Value: $112

171

Red Barn
Issued: 1987 • Retired: 1992
#5081-4 • Original Price: $38
Market Value: $110

172

Redeemer Church
Issued: 1988 • Retired: 1992
#5127-6 • Original Price: $42
Market Value: $76

The Original Snow Village® Collection		
	Price Paid	Value
166.		
167.		
168.		
169.		
170.		
171.		
172.		
Totals		

173

Reindeer Bus Depot
Issued: 1996 • Retired: 1997
#54874 • Original Price: $42
Market Value: $62

174

Ridgewood
Issued: 1985 • Retired: 1987
#5052-0 • Original Price: $35
Market Value: $160

175

River Road House
Issued: 1984 • Retired: 1987
#5010-5 • Original Price: $36
Market Value: $215

176

Rock Creek Mill
Issued: 1998 • Retired: 1998
#54932 • Original Price: $64
Market Value: $112

177

Rockabilly Records
Issued: 1996 • Retired: 1998
#54880 • Original Price: $45
Market Value: $60

178

Rollerama Roller Rink
Issued: 1997 • Retired: 1999
#54916 • Original Price: $56
Market Value: $60

179

Rosita's Cantina
Issued: 1996 • Retired: 1999
#54883 • Original Price: $50
Market Value: $63

180

Ryman Auditorium®
Issued: 1995 • Retired: 1997
#54855 • Original Price: $75
Market Value: $105

The Original Snow Village® Collection		
	Price Paid	Value
173.		
174.		
175.		
176.		
177.		
178.		
179.		
180.		
Totals		

The Original Snow Village® Collection – Buildings

181

St. Anthony Hotel & Post Office
Issued: 1987 • Retired: 1989
#5006-7 • Original Price: $40
Market Value: $112

182

Saint James Church
Issued: 1986 • Retired: 1988
#5068-7 • Original Price: $37
Market Value: $175

183

St. Luke's Church
Issued: 1992 • Retired: 1994
#5421-6 • Original Price: $45
Market Value: $70

184

Santabear Mistletoe Chapel (set/3, Dayton's Piece, LE-2000)
Issued: 2000 • Retired: 2000
#05711 • Original Price: $50
Market Value: N/E

185

School House
Issued: 1979 • Retired: 1982
#5060-9 • Original Price: $30
Market Value: $390

186

The Secret Garden Florist
Issued: 1996 • Current
#54885 • Original Price: $50
Market Value: $50

187

The Secret Garden Greenhouse
Issued: 1998 • Current
#54949 • Original Price: $60
Market Value: $60

The Original Snow Village® Collection		
	Price Paid	Value
181.		
182.		
183.		
184.		
185.		
186.		
187.		
Totals		

188

Service Station
Issued: 1988 • Retired: 1991
#5128-4 • Original Price: $37.50
Market Value: $270

189

Shelly's Diner (set/2)
Issued: 1999 • Current
#55008 • Original Price: $110
Market Value: $110

190

Shingle Victorian
*American Architecture
Series*
Issued: 1996 • Retired: 1999
#54884 • Original Price: $55
Market Value: $63

191

*Oh, Christmas
Tree!*

Silver Bells Christmas Shop (set/4, Event Piece)
Issued: 2000 • Retired: 2000
#55040 • Original Price: $75
Market Value: $85

192

Single Car Garage
Issued: 1988 • Retired: 1990
#5125-0 • Original Price: $22
Market Value: $58

193

Skate & Ski Shop
Issued: 1994 • Retired: 1998
#5467-4 • Original Price: $50
Market Value: $64

The Original Snow Village® Collection		
	Price Paid	Value
188.		
189.		
190.		
191.		
192.		
193.		
Totals		

194

Skating Pond
Issued: 1982 • Retired: 1984
#5017-2 • Original Price: $25
Market Value: $380

195

Skating Rink/Duck Pond Set
Issued: 1978 • Retired: 1979
#5015-3 • Original Price: $16
Market Value: $1,000

196

Small Chalet
Issued: 1976 • Retired: 1979
#5006-2 • Original Price: $15
Market Value: $480

197

Version 1

Version 2

Small Double Trees
Issued: 1978 • Retired: 1989
#5016-1 • Original Price: $13.50
Market Value: **1** – $185 (blue birds) **2** – $58 (red birds)

198

Smokey Mountain Retreat (with magic smoking element)
Issued: 1996 • Retired: 2000
#54872 • Original Price: $65
Market Value: $72

The Original Snow Village® Collection		
	Price Paid	Value
194.		
195.		
196.		
197.		
198.		
199.		
200.		
Totals		

199

Snow Carnival Ice Palace (set/2)
Issued: 1995 • Retired: 1998
#54850 • Original Price: $95
Market Value: $120

200

Snow Village Factory
Issued: 1987 • Retired: 1989
#5013-0 • Original Price: $45
Market Value: $136

201

Snow Village Resort Lodge
Issued: 1987 • Retired: 1989
#5092-0 • Original Price: $55
Market Value: $145

202

Shady Oak Church

Sunday School Serenade

Snow Village Starter Set (set/6)
Issued: 1994 • Retired: 1996
#5462-3 • Original Price: $50
Market Value: $82

203

Snowy Hills Hospital
Issued: 1993 • Retired: 1996
#5448-8 • Original Price: $48
Market Value: $105

204

Snowy Pines Inn

Decorate The Tree

Snowy Pines Inn (set/9, Event Piece)
Issued: 1998 • Retired: 1998
#54934 • Original Price: $65
Market Value: $85

205

Sonoma House
Issued: 1986 • Retired: 1988
#5062-8 • Original Price: $33
Market Value: $155

206

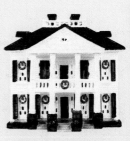

Southern Colonial
American Architecture Series
Issued: 1991 • Retired: 1994
#5403-8 • Original Price: $50
Market Value: $86

207

Spanish Mission Church
Issued: 1990 • Retired: 1992
#5155-1 • Original Price: $42
Market Value: $84

208

Springfield House
Issued: 1987 • Retired: 1990
#5027-0 • Original Price: $40
Market Value: $83

The Original Snow Village® Collection

	Price Paid	Value
201.		
202.		
203.		
204.		
205.		
206.		
207.		
208.		

Totals

The Original Snow Village® Collection - Buildings

The Original Snow Village® Collection – Buildings

209

Spruce Place
Issued: 1985 • Retired: 1987
#5049-0 • Original Price: $33
Market Value: $260

210

Starbucks® Coffee
Issued: 1995 • Retired: 2000
#54859 • Original Price: $48
Market Value: $52

211

Steepled Church
Issued: 1976 • Retired: 1979
#5005-4 • Original Price: $25
Market Value: $600

212

Stick Style House
American Architecture Series
Issued: 1998 • Retired: 2000
#54943 • Original Price: $60
Market Value: $67

213

Stone Church
Issued: 1977 • Retired: 1979
#5009-6 • Original Price: $35
Market Value: $720

214

Stone Church
Issued: 1979 • Retired: 1980
#5059-1 • Original Price: $32
Market Value: $980

215

Stone Mill House
Issued: 1980 • Retired: 1982
#5068-2 • Original Price: $30
Market Value: $530

The Original Snow Village® Collection		
	Price Paid	Value
209.		
210.		
211.		
212.		
213.		
214.		
215.		
Totals		

216

Stonehurst House
Issued: 1988 • Retired: 1994
#5140-3 • Original Price: $37.50
Market Value: $68

217

Stratford House
Issued: 1984 • Retired: 1986
#5007-5 • Original Price: $28
Market Value: $185

218

Street Car
Issued: 1982 • Retired: 1984
#5019-9 • Original Price: $16
Market Value: $370

219

Stucco Bungalow
Issued: 1985 • Retired: 1986
#5045-8 • Original Price: $30
Market Value: $375

220

Summit House
Issued: 1984 • Retired: 1985
#5036-9 • Original Price: $28
Market Value: $370

221

Super Suds Laundromat
Issued: 1999 • Current
#55006 • Original Price: $60
Market Value: $60

222

Swiss Chalet
Issued: 1982 • Retired: 1984
#5023-7 • Original Price: $28
Market Value: $438

223

New

Timberlake Outfitters
Issued: 2000 • Current
#55054 • Original Price: $75
Market Value: $75

The Original Snow Village® Collection		
	Price Paid	Value
216.		
217.		
218.		
219.		
220.		
221.		
222.		
223.		
Totals		

The Original Snow Village® Collection – Buildings

224

New

Totem Town Souvenir Shop
Issued: 2000 • Current
#55053 • Original Price: $68
Market Value: $68

225

Town Church
Issued: 1980 • Retired: 1982
#5071-7 • Original Price: $33
Market Value: $340

226

Town Hall
Issued: 1983 • Retired: 1984
#5000-8 • Original Price: $32
Market Value: $355

227

Toy Shop
Issued: 1986 • Retired: 1990
#5073-3 • Original Price: $36
Market Value: $100

228

Version 2

Version 1

Train Station With 3 Train Cars (set/4)
Issued: 1980 • Retired: 1985
#5085-6 • Original Price: $100
Market Value: **1** – $400 (6 window panes/1 round window in door)
2 – $360 (8 window panes/2 square windows in door)

The Original Snow Village® Collection

	Price Paid	Value
224.		
225.		
226.		
227.		
228.		
229.		
Totals		

229

Trinity Church
Issued: 1984 • Retired: 1986
#5035-0 • Original Price: $32
Market Value: $320

230

Tudor House
Issued: 1979 • Retired: 1981
#5061-7 • Original Price: $25
Market Value: $320

231

Turn Of The Century
Issued: 1983 • Retired: 1986
#5004-0 • Original Price: $36
Market Value: $250

232

Twin Peaks
Issued: 1986 • Retired: 1986
#5042-3 • Original Price: $32
Market Value: $450

233

Uptown Motors Ford®
(set/3)
Issued: 1998 • Current
#54941 • Original Price: $95
Market Value: $95

234

Victorian
Issued: 1979 • Retired: 1982
#5054-2 • Original Price: $30
Market Value: $360

235

Victorian Cottage
Issued: 1983 • Retired: 1984
#5002-4 • Original Price: $35
Market Value: $365

236

Victorian House
Issued: 1977 • Retired: 1979
#5007-0 • Original Price: $30
Market Value: $465

237

Village Bank & Trust
Issued: 1999 • Current
#55002 • Original Price: $75
Market Value: $75

The Original Snow Village® Collection		
	Price Paid	Value
230.		
231.		
232.		
233.		
234.		
235.		
236.		
237.		
Totals		

The Original Snow Village® Collection – Buildings

238

Village Church
Issued: 1983 • Retired: 1984
#5026-1 • Original Price: $30
Market Value: $435

239

Village Greenhouse
Issued: 1991 • Retired: 1995
#5402-0 • Original Price: $35
Market Value: $72

240

Village Market
Issued: 1988 • Retired: 1991
#5044-0 • Original Price: $39
Market Value: $89

241

Village Police Station
Issued: 1995 • Retired: 1998
#54853 • Original Price: $48
Market Value: $70

242

Village Post Office
Issued: 1992 • Retired: 1995
#5422-4 • Original Price: $35
Market Value: $80

243

Village Public Library
Issued: 1993 • Retired: 1997
#5443-7 • Original Price: $55
Market Value: $70

244

Village Realty
Issued: 1990 • Retired: 1993
#5154-3 • Original Price: $42
Market Value: $80

The Original Snow Village® Collection	Price Paid	Value
238.		
239.		
240.		
241.		
242.		
243.		
244.		
Totals		

245

246

247
New

Village Station
Issued: 1992 • Retired: 1997
#5438-0 • Original Price: $65
Market Value: $75

Village Station And Train (set/2)
Issued: 1988 • Retired: 1992
#5122-5 • Original Price: $65
Market Value: $115

Village Town Hall
Issued: 2000 • Current
#55044 • Original Price: $96
Market Value: $96

248

249

250

Village Vet And Pet Shop
Issued: 1992 • Retired: 1995
#5427-5 • Original Price: $32
Market Value: $88

Village Warming House
Issued: 1989 • Retired: 1992
#5145-4 • Original Price: $42
Market Value: $83

Waverly Place
Issued: 1986 • Retired: 1986
#5041-5 • Original Price: $35
Market Value: $305

251

252

Wedding Chapel
Issued: 1994 • Current
#5464-0 • Original Price: $55
Market Value: $55

Williamsburg House
Issued: 1985 • Retired: 1988
#5046-6 • Original Price: $37
Market Value: $147

The Original Snow Village® Collection		
	Price Paid	Value
245.		
246.		
247.		
248.		
249.		
250.		
251.		
252.		
Totals		

The Original Snow Village® Collection - Buildings

253

Woodbury House
Issued: 1993 • Retired: 1996
#5444-5 • Original Price: $45
Market Value: $70

254

Wooden Church
Issued: 1983 • Retired: 1985
#5031-8 • Original Price: $30
Market Value: $350

255

Wooden Clapboard
Issued: 1981 • Retired: 1984
#5072-5 • Original Price: $32
Market Value: $255

256

WSNO Radio
Issued: 1999 • Current
#55010 • Original Price: $75
Market Value: $75

The Original Snow Village® Collection		
	Price Paid	Value
253.		
254.		
255.		
256.		
Totals		

The Original Snow Village® Collection – Accessories

It's easy to make your Snow Village a living, breathing town with the Snow Village accessories available. For 2001, a new Classic Cars™ series was introduced.

1

3 Nuns With Songbooks
Issued: 1987 • Retired: 1988
#5102-0 • Original Price: $6
Market Value: $140

2

New

'50s Hot Rod
Classic Cars™
Issued: 2000 • Current
#55282 • Original Price: $20
Market Value: $20

3

New

1949 Ford Woody Wagon
Classic Cars™
Issued: 2000 • Current
#55288 • Original Price: $20
Market Value: $20

4

New

1950 Ford F-1 Pickup (John Deere)
Classic Cars™
Issued: 2000 • Current
#55285 • Original Price: $20
Market Value: $20

5

New

1954 Willy's CJ3 Jeep
Classic Cars™
Issued: 2000 • Current
#55287 • Original Price: $20
Market Value: $20

6

1955 Ford® Automobiles (6 assorted)
Issued: 1998 • Current
#54950 • Original Price: $10 (each)
Market Value: $10 (each)

7

New

1957 Chevrolet® Bel Air™
Classic Cars™
Issued: 2000 • Current
#55283 • Original Price: $20
Market Value: $20

8

New

1958 Corvette® Roadster
Classic Cars™
Issued: 2000 • Current
#55281 • Original Price: $20
Market Value: $20

The Original Snow Village® Collection

	Price Paid	Value
1.		
2.		
3.		
4.		
5.		
6.		
7.		
8.		
Totals		

9

New

1958 John Deere 730 Diesel Tractor
Classic Cars™
Issued: 2000 • Current
#55284 • Original Price: $20
Market Value: $20

10

New

1959 Chevrolet® Impala™ Convertible
Classic Cars™
Issued: 2000 • Current
#55289 • Original Price: $20
Market Value: $20

11

1964 1/2 Ford® Mustang (3 assorted)
Issued: 1998 • Current
#54951 • Original Price: $10 (each)
Market Value: $10 (each)

12

New

2001 Space Oddity (set/11)
Issued: 2000 • Current
#55118 • Original Price: $125
Market Value: $125

13

New

The Abandoned Gas Pump
Issued: 2000 • Current
#55121 • Original Price: $37.50
Market Value: $37.50

The Original Snow Village® Collection

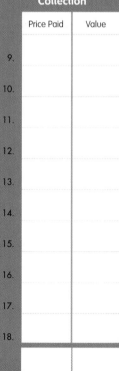

	Price Paid	Value
9.		
10.		
11.		
12.		
13.		
14.		
15.		
16.		
17.		
18.		
Totals		

14

Angels In The Snow (set/2)
Issued: 1999 • Current
#55024 • Original Price: $30
Market Value: $30

15

. . . *Another Man's Treasure* Accessories (set/3)
Issued: 1998 • Current
#54976 • Original Price: $27.50
Market Value: $27.50

16

Apple Girl/Newspaper Boy (set/2)
Issued: 1988 • Retired: 1990
#5129-2 • Original Price: $11
Market Value: $31

17

At The Barn Dance, It's Allemande Left (set/2)
Issued: 1997 • Retired: 1999
#54929 • Original Price: $30
Market Value: $40

18

Version 1   *Version 2*

Auto With Tree
Issued: 1985 • Current
#5055-5 • Original Price: $5
Market Value: **1** – $88 (short/flat) **2** – $6.50 (tall/round)

19

Backwoods Outhouse
Issued: 1999 • Current
#55036 • Original Price: $20
Market Value: $20

20

The Backyard Patio (set/2)
Issued: 1999 • Current
#52836 • Original Price: $40
Market Value: $40

21

Before The Big Game (set/4)
Issued: 1999 • Current
#55019 • Original Price: $37.50
Market Value: $37.50

22

Biplane Up In The Sky (animated)
Issued: 1998 • Retired: 2000
#52731 • Original Price: $50
Market Value: $60

23

Bringing Home The Tree
Issued: 1989 • Retired: 1992
#5169-1 • Original Price: $15
Market Value: $33

24
New

Buck's County Horse Trailer
Issued: 2000 • Current
#55286 • Original Price: $17.50
Market Value: $17.50

25
New

Buck's County Stables (set/9)
Issued: 2000 • Current
#55112 • Original Price: $65
Market Value: $65

26
New

Buck's County Water Tower
Issued: 2000 • Current
#55111 • Original Price: $32.50
Market Value: $32.50

27

Bumper Fun Ride (set/4, animated)
Issued: 2000 • Current
#52500 • Original Price: $98
Market Value: $98

28

Calling All Cars (set/2)
Issued: 1989 • Retired: 1991
#5174-8 • Original Price: $15
Market Value: $72

29

Carnival Tickets & Cotton Candy (set/3)
Issued: 1998 • Retired: 2000
#54938 • Original Price: $30
Market Value: $32

30

Carolers (set/4)
Issued: 1979 • Retired: 1986
#5064-1 • Original Price: $12
Market Value: $122

The Original Snow Village® Collection

	Price Paid	Value
19.		
20.		
21.		
22.		
23.		
24.		
25.		
26.		
27.		
28.		
29.		
30.		
Totals		

The Original Snow Village® Collection – Accessories

The Original Snow Village® Collection – Accessories

31

Caroling At The Farm
Issued: 1994 • Retired: 2000
#5463-1 • Original Price: $35
Market Value: $39

32

Caroling Family (set/3)
Issued: 1987 • Retired: 1990
#5105-5 • Original Price: $20
Market Value: $40

33

**Caroling Through
The Snow**
Issued: 1996 • Retired: 1999
#54896 • Original Price: $15
Market Value: $23

34

The Catch Of The Day
Issued: 1998 • Current
#54956 • Original Price: $30
Market Value: $30

35

Ceramic Car
Issued: 1980 • Retired: 1986
#5069-0 • Original Price: $5
Market Value: $56

36
Ceramic Sleigh
Issued: 1981 • Retired: 1986
#5079-2 • Original Price: $5
Market Value: $64

**The Original Snow Village®
Collection**

	Price Paid	Value
31.		
32.		
33.		
34.		
35.		
36.		
37.		
38.		
39.		
40.		
41.		
42.		
Totals		

37

**Check It Out
Bookmobile (set/3)**
Issued: 1993 • Retired: 1995
#5451-8 • Original Price: $25
Market Value: $40

38
Children In Band
Issued: 1987 • Retired: 1989
#5104-7 • Original Price: $15
Market Value: $35

39

Choir Kids
Issued: 1989 • Retired: 1992
#5147-0 • Original Price: $15
Market Value: $36

40

**Chopping Firewood
(set/2)**
Issued: 1995 • Current
#54863 • Original Price: $16.50
Market Value: $16.50

41

**Christmas At The Farm
(set/2)**
Issued: 1993 • Retired: 1996
#5450-0 • Original Price: $16
Market Value: $28

42

Christmas Cadillac
Issued: 1991 • Retired: 1994
#5413-5 • Original Price: $9
Market Value: $26

43

Christmas Children (set/4)
Issued: 1987 • Retired: 1990
#5107-1 • Original Price: $20
Market Value: $38

44

Christmas Kids (set/5)
Issued: 1997 • Retired: 1999
#54922 • Original Price: $27.50
Market Value: $33

45

Christmas Puppies (set/2)
Issued: 1992 • Retired: 1996
#5432-1 • Original Price: $27.50
Market Value: $40

46

Christmas Trash Cans (set/2)
Issued: 1990 • Retired: 1998
#5209-4 • Original Price: $6.50
Market Value: $18

47

Christmas Visit To The Florist (set/3)
Issued: 1998 • Current
#54957 • Original Price: $30
Market Value: $30

48

New

Christmastime Trimming
Issued: 2000 • Current
#55110 • Original Price: $15
Market Value: $15

49

Classic Cars (set/3)
Issued: 1993 • Retired: 1998
#5457-7 • Original Price: $22.50
Market Value: $32

50

Coca-Cola® Brand Billboard
Issued: 1994 • Retired: 1997
#5481-0 • Original Price: $18
Market Value: $30

51

Coca-Cola® Brand Delivery Men (set/2)
Issued: 1994 • Retired: 1998
#5480-1 • Original Price: $25
Market Value: $35

52

Coca-Cola® Brand Delivery Truck
Issued: 1994 • Retired: 1998
#5479-8 • Original Price: $15
Market Value: $32

53

Cold Weather Sports (set/4)
Issued: 1991 • Retired: 1994
#5410-0 • Original Price: $27.50
Market Value: $50

54

Come Join The Parade
Issued: 1991 • Retired: 1992
#5411-9 • Original Price: $12.50
Market Value: $24

The Original Snow Village® Collection

	Price Paid	Value
43.		
44.		
45.		
46.		
47.		
48.		
49.		
50.		
51.		
52.		
53.		
54.		

Totals

The Original Snow Village® Collection – Accessories

55

Costumes For Sale (set/2)
Issued: 1998 • Current
#54973 • Original Price: $60
Market Value: $60

56

Couldn't Wait Until Christmas
Issued: 1998 • Retired: 2000
#54972 • Original Price: $17
Market Value: $19

57

Country Harvest
Issued: 1991 • Retired: 1993
#5415-1 • Original Price: $13
Market Value: $31

58

Crack The Whip (set/3)
Issued: 1989 • Retired: 1996
#5171-3 • Original Price: $25
Market Value: $34

59

Doghouse/Cat In Garbage Can (set/2)
Issued: 1988 • Retired: 1992
#5131-4 • Original Price: $15
Market Value: $32

60

Down The Chimney He Goes
Issued: 1990 • Retired: 1993
#5158-6 • Original Price: $6.50
Market Value: $24

61

The Dragon Parade
Issued: 1999 • Current
#55032 • Original Price: $35
Market Value: $35

62

Early Morning Delivery (set/3)
Issued: 1992 • Retired: 1995
#5431-3 • Original Price: $27.50
Market Value: $40

63
New

Elvis Presley's® Autograph (set/3)
Issued: 2000 • Current
#55106 • Original Price: $25
Market Value: $25

64

Everybody Goes Skating At Rollerama (set/2)
Issued: 1997 • Retired: 1999
#54928 • Original Price: $25
Market Value: $27

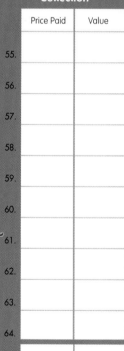

The Original Snow Village® Collection

	Price Paid	Value
55.		
56.		
57.		
58.		
59.		
60.		
61.		
62.		
63.		
64.		
Totals		

65
New

**Family Canoe Trip
(set/3)**
Issued: 2000 • Current
#55116 • Original Price: $48
Market Value: $48

66

Family Mom/Kids, Goose/Girl (set/2)
Issued: 1985 • Retired: 1988
#5057-1 • Original Price: $11
Market Value: **1** – $55 (large) **2** – $47 (small)

67

**Family Winter Outing
(set/3)**
Issued: 1999 • Current
#55033 • Original Price: $10
Market Value: $10

68

Farm Accessory Set (set/35)
Issued: 1997 • Current
#54931 • Original Price: $75
Market Value: $75

69

Farmer's Flatbed
Issued: 1998 • Retired: 2000
#54955 • Original Price: $17.50
Market Value: $20

70

**Feeding The Birds
(set/3)**
Issued: 1994 • Retired: 1997
#5473-9 • Original Price: $25
Market Value: $37

71

**Finding The Bird's
Song (set/2)**
Issued: 1999 • Current
#55020 • Original Price: $25
Market Value: $25

72

**Fire Hydrant And
Mailbox (set/2)**
Issued: 1988 • Retired: 1998
#5132-2 • Original Price: $6
Market Value: $23

73

**Fireman To The Rescue
(set/3)**
Issued: 1998 • Current
#54953 • Original Price: $30
Market Value: $30

The Original Snow Village® Collection

	Price Paid	Value
65.		
66.		
67.		
68.		
69.		
70.		
71.		
72.		
73.		
Totals		

74

Firewood Delivery Truck
Issued: 1995 • Retired: 1999
#54864 • Original Price: $15
Market Value: $20

75

First Deposit
Issued: 1999 • Current
#55023 • Original Price: $14
Market Value: $14

76

First Round Of The Year (set/3, track compatible)
Issued: 1998 • Current
#54936 • Original Price: $30
Market Value: $30

77

Flag Pole
Issued: 1989 • Retired: 1999
#5177-2 • Original Price: $8.50
Market Value: $14

78

Version 1   *Version 2*

For Sale Sign
Issued: 1987 • Retired: 1989
#5108-0 • Original Price: $3.50
Market Value:
1 – $12 (general release) **2** – $20 (blank sign, #581-9)

79

Version 1   *Version 2*

For Sale Sign
Issued: 1989 • Retired: 1998
#5166-7 • Original Price: $4.50
Market Value: **1** – $7 (general release)
2 – $26 (1990 Bachman's Village Gathering Sign)

80

Fresh Frozen Fish (set/2)
Issued: 1990 • Retired: 1993
#5163-2 • Original Price: $20
Market Value: $48

81

Frosty Playtime (set/3)
Issued: 1995 • Retired: 1997
#54860 • Original Price: $30
Market Value: $42

82

Fun At The Firehouse (set/2)
Issued: 1998 • Current
#54954 • Original Price: $27.50
Market Value: $27.50

83

Gifts On The Go (set/2)
Issued: 1999 • Current
#55035 • Original Price: $30
Market Value: $30

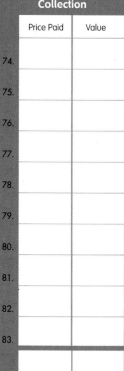

The Original Snow Village® Collection

	Price Paid	Value
74.		
75.		
76.		
77.		
78.		
79.		
80.		
81.		
82.		
83.		
Totals		

The Original Snow Village® Collection – Accessories

84

Girl/Snowman, Boy (set/2)
Issued: 1986 • Retired: 1987
#5095-4 • Original Price: $11
Market Value: $70

85

Going To The Chapel (set/2)
Issued: 1994 • Current
#5476-3 • Original Price: $20
Market Value: $20

86

Grand Ole Opry Carolers
Issued: 1995 • Retired: 1997
#54867 • Original Price: $25
Market Value: $33

87

Harley-Davidson® Fat Boy® & Softail®
Issued: 1996 • Current
#54900 • Original Price: $16.50
Market Value: $17.50

88

A Harley-Davidson® Holiday (set/2)
Issued: 1996 • Retired: 1999
#54898 • Original Price: $22.50
Market Value: $30

89

Harley-Davidson® Sign
Issued: 1996 • Current
#54901 • Original Price: $18
Market Value: $18

90

Harley-Davidson® Water Tower
Issued: 1998 • Current
#54975 • Original Price: $32.50
Market Value: $32.50

91

Hayride
Issued: 1988 • Retired: 1990
#5117-9 • Original Price: $30
Market Value: $66

92

He Led Them Down The Streets Of Town (set/3)
Issued: 1997 • Retired: 1999
#54927 • Original Price: $30
Market Value: $34

93

Heading For The Hills (2 assorted)
Issued: 1996 • Current
#54897 • Original Price: $8.50 (each)
Market Value: $8.50 (each)

94

A Heavy Snowfall (set/2)
Issued: 1992 • Current
#5434-8 • Original Price: $16
Market Value: $16

95

A Herd Of Holiday Heifers (set/3)
Issued: 1993 • Retired: 1997
#5455-0 • Original Price: $18
Market Value: $32

The Original Snow Village® Collection		
	Price Paid	Value
84.		
85.		
86.		
87.		
88.		
89.		
90.		
91.		
92.		
93.		
94.		
95.		
Totals		

The Original Snow Village® Collection – Accessories

96

**Here Comes Santa
(LE-1996)**
Issued: 1996 • Retired: 1996
Various • Original Price: $25
Market Value:
all exclusives – $46
(Fortunoff – $85)

"Here Comes Santa" Versions

Bachman's (#07744), Bronner's (#07745), Broughton (#07748),
Cabbage Rose (#07752), Calabash (#07753), Calico Butterfly (#07751),
Carson Pirie Scott (#07763), Christmas Loft (#07755), Dickens Gift Shop
(#07750), European Imports (#07762), Fibber Magee's (#07747), Fortunoff
(#07741), Gustaf's (#07759), Ingle's Nook (#07754), Limited Edition (#07746),
North Pole City (#07742), Pine Cone (#07740), Royal Dutch (#07760), Russ
Country Gardens (#07756), St. Nick's (#07757), Seventh Avenue (#07758),
Stats (#07749), William Glen (#07743), Young's Ltd. (#07761)

97

**Here We Come A
Caroling (set/3)**
Issued: 1990 • Retired: 1992
#5161-6 • Original Price: $18
Market Value: $32

98

**Hitch Up The
Buckboard
(track compatible)**
Issued: 1997 • Retired: 1999
#54930 • Original Price: $40
Market Value: $46

99

Holiday Hoops (set/3)
Issued: 1996 • Retired: 1999
#54893 • Original Price: $20
Market Value: $25

The Original Snow Village® Collection

	Price Paid	Value
96.		
97.		
98.		
99.		
100.		
101.		
102.		
103.		
104.		
105.		
Totals		

100
New

**Holiday Singers
(musical, animated)**
Issued: 2000 • Current
#52505 • Original Price: $75
Market Value: $75

101

**A Holiday Sleigh
Ride Together
(track compatible)**
Issued: 1997 • Current
#54921 • Original Price: $32.50
Market Value: $32.50

102

**Holy Spirit Baptistery
(music box)**
Issued: 1999 • Current
#55022 • Original Price: $37.50
Market Value: $37.50

103

Home Delivery (set/2)
Issued: 1990 • Retired: 1992
#5162-4 • Original Price: $16
Market Value: $36

104

**A Home For
The Holidays**
Issued: 1990 • Retired: 1996
#5165-9 • Original Price: $6.50
Market Value: $20

105

**How The Grinch Stole
Christmas! – Movie
Premiere**
Issued: 2000 • Current
#55103 • Original Price: $17.50
Market Value: $17.50

The Original Snow Village® Collection – Accessories

106

Is That Frosty?
Issued: 1999 • Current
#55030 • Original Price: $22.50
Market Value: $22.50

107

It's Time For An Icy Treat (set/2)
Issued: 1999 • Current
#55013 • Original Price: $30
Market Value: $30

108

Just Married (set/2)
Issued: 1995 • Current
#54879 • Original Price: $25
Market Value: $25

109

Version 1   Version 2

Kids Around The Tree
Issued: 1986 • Retired: 1990
#5094-6 • Original Price: $15
Market Value: **1** – $65 (large) **2** – $46 (small)

110

Kids, Candy Canes . . . And Ronald McDonald® (set/3)
Issued: 1997 • Retired: 1999
#54926 • Original Price: $30
Market Value: $35

111

Kids Decorating The Village Sign
Issued: 1990 • Retired: 1993
#5134-9 • Original Price: $12.50
Market Value: $34

112

Kids Love Hershey's™! (set/2)
Issued: 1997 • Retired: 2000
#54924 • Original Price: $30
Market Value: $32

113

Kids Tree House
Issued: 1989 • Retired: 1991
#5168-3 • Original Price: $25
Market Value: $59

114

Laundry Day
Issued: 1999 • Current
#55017 • Original Price: $13
Market Value: $13

115

Let It Snow, Let It Snow (track compatible)
Issued: 1997 • Retired: 2000
#54923 • Original Price: $20
Market Value: $25

The Original Snow Village® Collection

	Price Paid	Value
106.		
107.		
108.		
109.		
110.		
111.		
112.		
113.		
114.		
115.		
Totals		

The Original Snow Village® Collection – Accessories

The Original Snow Village® Collection – Accessories

116
New

Lighting The Jack-O'-Lanterns
Issued: 2000 • Current
#55117 • Original Price: $32.50
Market Value: $32.50

117

The Looney Tunes® Animated Film Festival (set/4)
Issued: 1999 • Current
#54983 • Original Price: $40
Market Value: $40

118

Look, It's the Goodyear Blimp (animated)
Issued: 2000 • Current
#55001 • Original Price: $45
Market Value: $45

119

Mailbox
Issued: 1989 • Retired: 1990
#5179-9 • Original Price: $3.50
Market Value: $27

120

Mailbox
Issued: 1990 • Retired: 1998
#5198-5 • Original Price: $3.50
Market Value: $10

121

Man On Ladder Hanging Garland
Issued: 1988 • Retired: 1992
#5116-0 • Original Price: $7.50
Market Value: $22

The Original Snow Village® Collection

	Price Paid	Value
116.		
117.		
118.		
119.		
120.		
121.		
122.		
123.		
124.		
125.		
126.		
127.		
Totals		

122

Marshmallow Roast (set/3)
Issued: 1994 • Current
#5478-0 • Original Price: $32.50
Market Value: $32.50

123

McDonald's® . . . Lights Up The Night
Issued: 1997 • Retired: 1999
#54925 • Original Price: $30
Market Value: $34

124

Men At Work (set/5)
Issued: 1996 • Retired: 1998
#54894 • Original Price: $27.50
Market Value: $36

125
New

Mill Falls (animated)
Issued: 2000 • Current
#52503 • Original Price: $75
Market Value: $75

126

Monks-A-Caroling
Issued: 1983 • Retired: 1984
#6459-9 • Original Price: $6
Market Value: $70

127

Monks-A-Caroling
Issued: 1984 • Retired: 1988
#5040-7 • Original Price: $6
Market Value: $54

128

Moving Day (set/3)
Issued: 1996 • Retired: 1998
#54892 • Original Price: $32.50
Market Value: $44

129

Mush! (set/2)
Issued: 1994 • Retired: 1997
#5474-7 • Original Price: $20
Market Value: $33

130

**Nanny And The
Preschoolers (set/2)**
Issued: 1992 • Retired: 1994
#5430-5 • Original Price: $27.50
Market Value: $43

131

Nativity
Issued: 1988 • Retired: 2000
#5135-7 • Original Price: $7.50
Market Value: $11

132
New

**Now Showing – Elvis
Presley® Sign**
Issued: 2000 • Current
#55105 • Original Price: $30
Market Value: $30

133
New

The Old Pickup Truck
Issued: 2000 • Current
#52868 • Original Price: $30
Market Value: $30

134
New

On The Beat (set/2)
Issued: 2000 • Current
#55119 • Original Price: $35
Market Value: $35

135

**On The Road Again
(set/2)**
Issued: 1996 • Current
#54891 • Original Price: $20
Market Value: $20

136

**On The Way To Ballet
Class (set/3)**
Issued: 1999 • Current
#55031 • Original Price: $27.50
Market Value: $27.50

137

Parking Meter (set/4)
Issued: 1989 • Retired: 1998
#5178-0 • Original Price: $6
Market Value: $13

138

Patrolling The Road
Issued: 1998 • Current
#54971 • Original Price: $20
Market Value: $20

The Original Snow Village® Collection		
	Price Paid	Value
128.		
129.		
130.		
131.		
132.		
133.		
134.		
135.		
136.		
137.		
138.		
Totals		

The Original Snow Village® Collection – Accessories

139
New

Pedal Cars For Christmas (set/2)
Issued: 2000 • Current
#55108 • Original Price: $27.50
Market Value: $27.50

140
New

Perfect Putt (animated)
Issued: 2000 • Current
#52508 • Original Price: $65
Market Value: $65

141

Pets On Parade (set/2)
Issued: 1994 • Retired: 1998
#5472-0 • Original Price: $16.50
Market Value: $25

142

Version 1   Version 2

Pick-Up And Delivery
Issued: 1993 • Current
#5454-2 • Original Price: $10
Market Value:
1 – $10 (general release) **2** – $30 (St. Nick's)

143

Pint-Size Pony Rides (set/3)
Issued: 1993 • Retired: 1996
#5453-4 • Original Price: $37.50
Market Value: $47

The Original Snow Village® Collection

	Price Paid	Value
139.		
140.		
141.		
142.		
143.		
144.		
145.		
146.		
147.		
148.		
149.		
Totals		

144

Pizza Delivery (set/2)
Issued: 1995 • Retired: 1998
#54866 • Original Price: $20
Market Value: $30

145

Poinsettias For Sale (set/3)
Issued: 1995 • Retired: 1998
#54861 • Original Price: $30
Market Value: $41

146

Praying Monks
Issued: 1987 • Retired: 1988
#5103-9 • Original Price: $6
Market Value: $50

147

Preparing For Halloween (set/2)
Issued: 1999 • Current
#54982 • Original Price: $40
Market Value: $40

148

Quality Service At Ford® (set/2)
Issued: 1998 • Current
#54970 • Original Price: $27.50
Market Value: $27.50

149

A Ride On The Reindeer Lines (set/3)
Issued: 1996 • Retired: 1997
#54875 • Original Price: $35
Market Value: $43

150
New

Roadside Billboards (set/3)
Issued: 2000 • Current
#55109 • Original Price: $40
Market Value: $40

151

Rockefeller® Plaza Skating Rink (set/3, musical, animated)
Issued: 2000 • Current
#52504 • Original Price: $125
Market Value: $125

152

Round And Round We Go! (set/2)
Issued: 1992 • Retired: 1995
#5433-0 • Original Price: $18
Market Value: $32

153

Safety Patrol (set/4)
Issued: 1993 • Retired: 1997
#5449-6 • Original Price: $27.50
Market Value: $38

154

Santa Comes To Town, 1995 (LE-1995)
Issued: 1994 • Retired: 1995
#5477-1 • Original Price: $30
Market Value: $48

155

Santa Comes To Town, 1996 (LE-1996)
Issued: 1995 • Retired: 1996
#54862 • Original Price: $32.50
Market Value: $45

156

Santa Comes To Town, 1997 (LE-1997)
Issued: 1996 • Retired: 1997
#54899 • Original Price: $35
Market Value: $42

157

Santa Comes To Town, 1998 (LE-1998)
Issued: 1997 • Retired: 1998
#54920 • Original Price: $30
Market Value: $32

158

Santa Comes To Town, 1999 (LE-1999)
Issued: 1998 • Retired: 1999
#54958 • Original Price: $30
Market Value: $40

159

Santa Comes To Town, 2000 (LE-2000)
Issued: 1999 • Retired: 2000
#55015 • Original Price: $37.50
Market Value: $42

160
New

Santa Comes To Town, 2001 (LE-2001)
Issued: 2000 • Current
#55120 • Original Price: $40
Market Value: $40

161

Santa's Little Helpers
Issued: 1999 • Current
#55025 • Original Price: $27.50
Market Value: $27.50

The Original Snow Village® Collection

	Price Paid	Value
150.		
151.		
152.		
153.		
154.		
155.		
156.		
157.		
158.		
159.		
160.		
161.		
Totals		

The Original Snow Village® Collection – Accessories

203

162

Version 1 *Version 2*

Santa/Mailbox (set/2)
Issued: 1985 • Retired: 1988
#5059-8 • Original Price: $11
Market Value: **1** – $59 (large) **2** – $56 (small)

163

New

Santa's On His Way (musical, animated)
Issued: 2000 • Current
#52502 • Original Price: $65
Market Value: $65

164

School Bus, Snow Plow (set/2)
Issued: 1988 • Retired: 1991
#5137-3 • Original Price: $16
Market Value: $60

165

School Children (set/3)
Issued: 1988 • Retired: 1990
#5118-7 • Original Price: $15
Market Value: $33

166

Scottie With Tree
Issued: 1984 • Retired: 1985
#5038-5 • Original Price: $3
Market Value: $215

167

Send In The Clown!
Issued: 1999 • Current
#55021 • Original Price: $13.50
Market Value: $13.50

168

Service With A Smile (set/2)
Issued: 1995 • Retired: 1998
#54865 • Original Price: $25
Market Value: $32

169

Version 1 *Version 2*

Shopping Girls With Packages (set/2)
Issued: 1986 • Retired: 1988
#5096-2 • Original Price: $11
Market Value: **1** – $55 (large) **2** – $47 (small)

170

Singing Nuns
Issued: 1985 • Retired: 1987
#5053-9 • Original Price: $6
Market Value: $135

171

Sisal Tree Lot
Issued: 1988 • Retired: 1991
#8183-3 • Original Price: $45
Market Value: $95

The Original Snow Village® Collection

	Price Paid	Value
162.		
163.		
164.		
165.		
166.		
167.		
168.		
169.		
170.		
171.		
Totals		

172

Sitting In The Park (set/4)
Issued: 2000 • Current
#55100 • Original Price: $28
Market Value: $28

173

Skate Faster Mom
Issued: 1989 • Retired: 1991
#5170-5 • Original Price: $13
Market Value: $35

174

Skaters & Skiers (set/3)
Issued: 1994 • Current
#5475-5 • Original Price: $27.50
Market Value: $27.50

175

Ski Slope (animated)
Issued: 1998 • Current
#52733 • Original Price: $75
Market Value: $75

176

Sleighride
Issued: 1990 • Retired: 1992
#5160-8 • Original Price: $30
Market Value: $62

177

Sno-Jet Snowmobile
Issued: 1990 • Retired: 1993
#5159-4 • Original Price: $15
Market Value: $35

178

Snow Carnival Ice Sculptures (set/2)
Issued: 1995 • Retired: 1998
#54868 • Original Price: $27.50
Market Value: $38

179

Snow Carnival King & Queen
Issued: 1995 • Retired: 1998
#54869 • Original Price: $35
Market Value: $45

180

Snow Kids (set/4)
Issued: 1987 • Retired: 1990
#5113-6 • Original Price: $20
Market Value: $60

181

Snow Kids Sled, Skis (set/2)
Issued: 1985 • Retired: 1987
#5056-3 • Original Price: $11
Market Value: $50

182

Snow Village Promotional Sign
Issued: 1989 • Retired: 1990
#9948-1 • Original Price: N/A
Market Value: $25

The Original Snow Village® Collection

	Price Paid	Value
172.		
173.		
174.		
175.		
176.		
177.		
178.		
179.		
180.		
181.		
182.		
Totals		

The Original Snow Village® Collection – Accessories

205

The Original Snow Village® Collection – Accessories

183

Snowball Fort (set/3)
Issued: 1991 • Retired: 1993
#5414-3 • Original Price: $27.50
Market Value: $48

184

Snowman With Broom
Issued: 1982 • Retired: 1990
#5018-0 • Original Price: $3
Market Value: $18

185

Special Delivery (set/2)
Issued: 1989 • Retired: 1990
#5148-9 • Original Price: $16
Market Value: $55

186

Special Delivery (set/2)
Issued: 1990 • Retired: 1992
#5197-7 • Original Price: $16
Market Value: $40

187

Spirit Of Snow Village Airplane
Issued: 1992 • Retired: 1996
#5440-2 • Original Price: $32.50
Market Value: $44

188

Spirit Of Snow Village Airplane (2 assorted)
Issued: 1993 • Retired: 1996
#5458-5 • Original Price: $12.50 (each)
Market Value: $42 (each)

189

Starbucks® Coffee Cart (set/2)
Issued: 1995 • Retired: 2000
#54870 • Original Price: $27.50
Market Value: $30

190

Statue Of Mark Twain
Issued: 1989 • Retired: 1991
#5173-0 • Original Price: $15
Market Value: $38

191

Stop Sign (set/2)
Issued: 1989 • Retired: 1998
#5176-4 • Original Price: $5
Market Value: $9

192

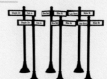

Street Sign (set/6)
Issued: 1989 • Retired: 1992
#5167-5 • Original Price: $7.50
Market Value: $18

193

Stuck In The Snow (set/3)
Issued: 1994 • Retired: 1998
#5471-2 • Original Price: $30
Market Value: $42

194

Taxi Cab
Issued: 1987 • Retired: 2000
#5106-3 • Original Price: $6
Market Value: $12

The Original Snow Village® Collection

	Price Paid	Value
183.		
184.		
185.		
186.		
187.		
188.		
189.		
190.		
191.		
192.		
193.		
194.		
Totals		

195

Terry's Towing (set/2)
Issued: 1996 • Retired: 1999
#54895 • Original Price: $20
Market Value: $26

196

Through The Woods (set/2)
Issued: 1989 • Retired: 1991
#5172-1 • Original Price: $18
Market Value: $33

197

Through The Woods (set/4, animated)
Issued: 1999 • Current
#52791 • Original Price: $75
Market Value: $75

198

Tour The Village
Issued: 1993 • Retired: 1997
#5452-6 • Original Price: $12.50
Market Value: $22

199

Treats For The Kids (set/3)
Issued: 1999 • Current
#55016 • Original Price: $33
Market Value: $33

200

A Tree For Me (set/2)
Issued: 1990 • Retired: 1995
#5164-0 • Original Price: $7.50
Market Value: $18

201
New

The Tree Lighting Ceremony (set/3)
Issued: 2000 • Current
#55104 • Original Price: $65
Market Value: $65

202

Tree Lot
Issued: 1988 • Retired: 1999
#5138-1 • Original Price: $33.50
Market Value: $43

203

Treetop Tree House
Issued: 1996 • Current
#54890 • Original Price: $35
Market Value: $35

204

Trick-Or-Treat Kids (set/3)
Issued: 1998 • Current
#54937 • Original Price: $33
Market Value: $33

205

Two For The Road (track compatible)
Issued: 1998 • Current
#54939 • Original Price: $20
Market Value: $20

206

Uncle Sam's Fireworks Stand (set/2)
Issued: 1998 • Retired: 2000
#54974 • Original Price: $45
Market Value: $48

The Original Snow Village® Collection

	Price Paid	Value
195.		
196.		
197.		
198.		
199.		
200.		
201.		
202.		
203.		
204.		
205.		
206.		
Totals		

207

Up On A Roof Top
Issued: 1988 • Current
#5139-0 • Original Price: $6.50
Market Value: $6.50

208

Up, Up & Away Witch (animated)
Issued: 1998 • Current
#52711 • Original Price: $50
Market Value: $50

209

Uptown Motors Ford® Billboard
Issued: 1998 • Current
#52780 • Original Price: $20
Market Value: $20

210

Village Animated Accessory Track
Issued: 1996 • Retired: 1999
#52642 • Original Price: $65
Market Value: N/E

211

Village Animated All Around The Park (set/18)
Issued: 1994 • Retired: 1996
#5247-7 • Original Price: $95
Market Value: $115

212

Village Animated Skating Pond (set/15)
Issued: 1993 • Current
#5229-9 • Original Price: $60
Market Value: $60

213

Village Animated Ski Mountain
Issued: 1996 • Retired: 1998
#52641 • Original Price: $75
Market Value: $80

214

Village Animated Sledding Hill
Issued: 1997 • Current
#52645 • Original Price: $65
Market Value: $65

215

Village Birds (set/6)
Issued: 1989 • Retired: 1994
#5180-2 • Original Price: $3.50
Market Value: $18

216

Village Express Electric Train Set (set/24)
Issued: 1998 • Current
#52710 • Original Price: $270
Market Value: $270

217

Village Fire Truck
Issued: 1998 • Current
#54952 • Original Price: $22.50
Market Value: $22.50

218

Village Gazebo
Issued: 1989 • Retired: 1995
#5146-2 • Original Price: $27
Market Value: $47

The Original Snow Village® Collection

	Price Paid	Value
207.		
208.		
209.		
210.		
211.		
212.		
213.		
214.		
215.		
216.		
217.		
218.		
Totals		

219

Village Greetings (set/3)
Issued: 1991 • Retired: 1994
#5418-6 • Original Price: $5
Market Value: $11

220

Village Marching Band (set/3)
Issued: 1991 • Retired: 1992
#5412-7 • Original Price: $30
Market Value: $67

221

Village News Delivery (set/2)
Issued: 1993 • Retired: 1996
#5459-3 • Original Price: $15
Market Value: $24

222

Village Phone Booth
Issued: 1992 • Current
#5429-1 • Original Price: $7.50
Market Value: $7.50

223

Village Potted Topiary Pair
Issued: 1989 • Retired: 1994
#5192-6 • Original Price: $5
Market Value: $16

224

Village Service Vehicles (set/3, track compatible)
Issued: 1998 • Current
#54959 • Original Price: $45
Market Value: $45

225

Village Streetcar (set/10)
Issued: 1994 • Retired: 1998
#5240-0 • Original Price: $65
Market Value: $70

226

Village Up, Up & Away, Animated Sleigh
Issued: 1995 • Current
#52593 • Original Price: $40
Market Value: $40

227

Village Used Car Lot (set/5)
Issued: 1992 • Retired: 1997
#5428-3 • Original Price: $45
Market Value: $56

228

Village Waterfall
Issued: 1996 • Retired: 1999
#52644 • Original Price: $65
Market Value: N/E

229

"A Visit With Santa" Versions
Bachman's (#07544) – $56
Fortunoff (#07676) – $56
Lemon Tree (#07684) – $52
Limited Edition (#07641) – $62
Pine Cone (#07730) – $50
Stats (#07650) – $50
William Glen (#07668) – $48
Young's Ltd. (#07692) – $45

A Visit With Santa (LE-1995)
Issued: 1995 • Retired: 1995
Various • Original Price: $25
Market Value: listed above

The Original Snow Village® Collection

	Price Paid	Value
219.		
220.		
221.		
223.		
224.		
225.		
226.		
227.		
228.		
229.		
Totals		

The Original Snow Village® Collection – Accessories

230 Version 1   Version 2

Water Tower
Issued: 1988 • Retired: 1991
#5133-0 • Original Price: $20
Market Value:
1 – $95 (general release)
2 – $680 (John Deere)

231

We're Going To A Christmas Pageant
Issued: 1992 • Retired: 1994
#5435-6 • Original Price: $15
Market Value: $30

232

Welcome To The Congregation
Issued: 1999 • Current
#55014 • Original Price: $15
Market Value: $15

233

The Whole Family Goes Shopping (set/3)
Issued: 1997 • Retired: 1999
#54905 • Original Price: $25
Market Value: $28

234
New

Windmill By The Chicken Coop
Issued: 2000 • Current
#52867 • Original Price: $55
Market Value: $55

235

Winter Fountain
Issued: 1991 • Retired: 1993
#5409-7 • Original Price: $25
Market Value: $63

The Original Snow Village® Collection

	Price Paid	Value
230.		
231.		
232.		
233.		
234.		
235.		
236.		
237.		
238.		
239.		
240.		
241.		
Totals		

236

Winter Playground
Issued: 1992 • Retired: 1995
#5436-4 • Original Price: $20
Market Value: $42

237
New

Woodland Carousel (musical, animated)
Issued: 2000 • Current
#52509 • Original Price: $75
Market Value: $75

238

Woodsman And Boy (set/2)
Issued: 1988 • Retired: 1991
#5130-6 • Original Price: $13
Market Value: $35

239

Woody Station Wagon
Issued: 1988 • Retired: 1990
#5136-5 • Original Price: $6.50
Market Value: $37

240

Wreaths For Sale (set/4)
Issued: 1991 • Retired: 1994
#5408-9 • Original Price: $27.50
Market Value: $52

241
New

Yesterday's Tractor
Issued: 2000 • Current
#52869 • Original Price: $30
Market Value: $30

The Original Snow Village® Collection – Ornaments

Joining the Snow Village ornaments in 2000 were two special edition ornaments which retired the same year. Eight others retired in 2000, and all Snow Village ornaments are now retired.

1

1955 Pink Cadillac® Ornament (Special Edition)
Issued: 2000 • Retired: 2000
#98791 • Original Price: $10
Market Value: $15

2

Elvis Presley's Graceland® Ornament (Special Edition)
Issued: 2000 • Retired: 2000
#98790 • Original Price: $15
Market Value: $20

3

J. Young's Granary
Classic Ornament Series
Issued: 1997 • Retired: 1998
#98632 • Original Price: $15
Market Value: $20

4

J. Young's Granary
Classic Ornament Series
Issued: 1998 • Retired: 2000
#98644 • Original Price: $20
Market Value: $22

5

Jingle Belle Houseboat
Classic Ornament Series
Issued: 1999 • Retired: 2000
#98648 • Original Price: $20
Market Value: $22

6

Lighthouse
Classic Ornament Series
Issued: 1998 • Retired: 2000
#98635 • Original Price: $20
Market Value: $22

7

Nantucket
Classic Ornament Series
Issued: 1997 • Retired: 1998
#98630 • Original Price: $15
Market Value: $21

8

Nantucket
Classic Ornament Series
Issued: 1998 • Retired: 2000
#98642 • Original Price: $20
Market Value: $22

9

Pinewood Log Cabin
Classic Ornament Series
Issued: 1998 • Retired: 2000
#98637 • Original Price: $20
Market Value: $22

10

Queen Anne Victorian
Classic Ornament Series
Issued: 1999 • Retired: 2000
#98646 • Original Price: $20
Market Value: $22

The Original Snow Village® Collection

	Price Paid	Value
1.		
2.		
3.		
4.		
5.		
6.		
7.		
8.		
9.		
10.		
Totals		

11

Steepled Church
Classic Ornament Series
Issued: 1997 • Retired: 1998
#98631 • Original Price: $15
Market Value: $18

12

Steepled Church
Classic Ornament Series
Issued: 1998 • Retired: 2000
#98643 • Original Price: $20
Market Value: $22

13

Street Car
Classic Ornament Series
Issued: 1999 • Retired: 2000
#98645 • Original Price: $20
Market Value: $22

The Original Snow Village® Collection – Mid-Year Releases

On May 11, 2001, Department 56 introduced its mid-year additions to *The Original Snow Village® Collection*. For eager collectors, these buildings and accessories were worth the wait!

1
New

Christmas Lake Chalet (set/5)
Issued: 2001
To Be Retired: December 26, 2001
#55061 • Original Price: $75
Market Value: $75

The Original Snow Village® Collection

	Price Paid	Value
11.		
12.		
13.		
Mid–Year Releases		
1.		
2.		
3.		
4.		
5.		
Totals		

2
New

Haunted Barn (set/4)
Issued: 2001 • To Be Retired: December 26, 2001
#55060 • Original Price: $75
Market Value: $75

3
New

Stardust Drive-In Theater
Issued: 2001 • Current
#55064 • Original Price: $68
Market Value: $68

4
New
Preliminary Design

Stardust Refreshment Stand (set/7)
Issued: 2001 • Current
#55065 • Original Price: $50
Market Value: $50

5
New

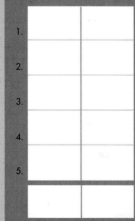

Tudor House
Issued: 2001 • Current
#55062 • Original Price: $60
Market Value: $60

The Original Snow Village® Collection – Ornaments

6
New

Fun In The Snow (set/2)
Issued: 2001 • Current
#55125 • Original Price: $25
Market Value: $25

7
New

Happy New Year (set/4)
Issued: 2001 • Current
#55124 • Original Price: $25
Market Value: $25

8
New

Holiday Fun Run
Issued: 2001 • Current
#55126 • Original Price: $25
Market Value: $25

9
New

Crystal Ice King & Queen (LE-25,000)
Issued: 2001
To Be Retired: December 26, 2001
#58976 • Original Price: $20
Market Value: $20

10
New

Gondola (animated)
Issued: 2001 • Current
#52511 • Original Price: $85
Market Value: $85

Mid-Year Releases

	Price Paid	Value
6.		
7.		
8.		
9.		
10.		
Totals		

Future Releases

Check our website, *CollectorsQuest.com*, for new Snow Village®
releases and record the information here.

The Original Snow Village® Collection	Item #	Status	Price Paid	Value

Page Total:	Price Paid	Value

Total Value Of My Collection

Record your collection here by adding the totals from
the bottom of each Value Guide page.

The Original Snow Village® Collection – Buildings

Page Number	Price Paid	Value
Page 153		
Page 154		
Page 155		
Page 156		
Page 157		
Page 158		
Page 159		
Page 160		
Page 161		
Page 162		
Page 163		
Page 164		
Page 165		
Page 166		
Page 167		
Page 168		
Page 169		
Page 170		
Page 171		
Page 172		
Page 173		
Page 174		
Page 175		
Page 176		
Page 177		
Page 178		
Page 179		
Page 180		
Page 181		
Page 182		
Page 183		
Page 184		
Page 185		
Subtotal:		

The Original Snow Village® Collection – Buildings

Page Number	Price Paid	Value
Page 186		
Page 187		
Page 188		
Subtotal:		

The Original Snow Village® Collection – Accessories

Page Number	Price Paid	Value
Page 189		
Page 190		
Page 191		
Page 192		
Page 193		
Page 194		
Page 195		
Page 196		
Page 197		
Page 198		
Page 199		
Page 200		
Page 201		
Page 202		
Page 203		
Page 204		
Page 205		
Page 206		
Page 207		
Page 208		
Page 209		
Page 210		
Subtotal:		

The Original Snow Village® Collection – Ornaments

Page Number	Price Paid	Value
Page 211		
Page 212		
Subtotal:		

	Price Paid	Value
Page Total:		

Other Department 56® Collectibles Overview

Throughout the years, Department 56 has introduced many other buildings and accessories in addition to the Heritage Village and Snow Village lines. Alone or inside the traditional D56 community, these additional pieces add a bit of flavor to any collection.

Literary Classics®

This series was launched in 1998 and brings great works of literature to life. Favorites like *Little Women*, Tom Sawyer and the legendary Sherlock Holmes have all been represented.

Seasons Bay™

Seasons Bay is the perfect Victorian seaside resort and, best of all, this village is year-round. Complementing the buildings are painted pewter accessories depicting activities from all four seasons. The collection was first released in 1988 with six buildings which were available in "first edition" versions.

Storybook Village®

This village breathes life into favorite children's nursery rhymes, fairy tales and books. From the "Mother Goose Book Cellar" to "Cinderella's Dress Shop" (set/2), each piece is accompanied by whimsical accessories to make you feel that fairytales can come true.

Other Collectibles

In 2000 and 2001, Department 56 created more magic with lighted pieces based on the favorites *How The Grinch Stole Christmas!* and Harry Potter™, including several *Harry Potter™ Secret Boxes*.

To honor Bachman's, Department 56 has made exclusive pieces available only at that store's Village Gathering events. Department 56 also issued a three building collection called *Bachman's Hometown Series* in 1987 and 1988.

Another small collection, *Meadowland*, was introduced in 1979. It consisted of two buildings and two accessories, which were then retired only a year after their release. And in 1996, Department 56 produced pieces for H.J. Heinz Co. and State Farms Insurance to market through their *Profile Series®*.

Several event pieces have also been issued to benefit the Ronald McDonald House®, while other pieces have been available only in Canada and for members of various village collector's clubs.

What's New For Other Department 56® Collectibles

Here are the new 2001 releases for some of Department 56's other villages and collections. There are plenty of new buildings and accessories to add to collectors' booming villages!

Other Department 56® Buildings

Historical Landmark™ Series

St. Paul Cathedral . . . If you're lucky enough to be attending the Department 56 Silver Anniversary Celebration, you can pick up the "St. Paul Cathedral." This replica of a real cathedral in St. Paul, Minnesota, features a special copper dome. Part of the proceeds from this piece will help fund a dome restoration project on the real building. *(As of this printing, the color and design of this piece had not yet been finalized.)*

Hot Properties!

Town Hall (set/3) . . . The citizens of Whoville congregate and sing their songs at the "Town Hall." This whimsical building is the perfect place to erect the town tree and foil the Grinch's plans to ruin Christmas.

Literary Classics®

Sherlock Holmes – 221B Baker Street (set/3, with book) . . . "The game is afoot" with the great consulting detective's famous London residence. Figurines of Sherlock Holmes and his ever-faithful friend, Dr. Watson, come with the set, along with a copy of Sir Arthur Conan Doyle's *A Study in Scarlet & The Sign of Four.*

Seasons Bay®

Breezy Hill Stables . . . All the horses at Breezy Hill are set for a day of riding. Whether you're an experienced rider or a blushing novice, the equestrian trainers will show you how to sit in that saddle like a pro.

East Cape Cottages (set/2) . . . There's no place like the seashore for a relaxing vacation, especially when you've got a boat of your own to explore the waters. This set includes a traditional two-story cottage, and a smaller home, each with its own attached boat!

Garden Valley Vineyards . . . The wine that flows from this stately mansion just can't be beat. Every night, the owners hold a tasting contest to name the season's best! But it's only available in a limited edition of 5,600 pieces, so if you have a taste for it, you'd better grab it while you still can!

Storybook Village®

Cinderella's Dress Shop (set/2) . . . Now everyone can be the belle of the ball when they stop by "Cinderella's Dress Shop." Whether you're trying to snare a prince or just want to look your best, this fashionable shop will have the perfect creation.

The Emerald City (set/2) . . . Dorothy™, Toto™, The Tin Man™, The Cowardly Lion™ and The Scarecrow™ are following The Yellow Brick Road™ all the way to "The Emerald City." This imposing fortress is sure to make you feel like you're right there with them!

Frosty Frolic Castle (set/2, musical) . . . This chilly castle is just chock full of wintertime fun. Join the Snowbabies™ in their rowboat – they left just enough room for you – as they make their first appearance in Storybook Village®.

Rapunzel's Hair Salon . . . Finally, Rapunzel is sharing her amazing hair secrets with the rest of the world! And even if your hair isn't long enough to make a ladder, you're still sure to get the perfect new 'do at this chic and new salon.

Rudolph's Red-Nosed Lighthouse (set/4) . . . Now Rudolph® can guide all kinds of travelers with his vividly painted, red-beaconed lighthouse. Ships at sea will find wintry travel much easier (and even festive) with Rudolph® to light their way!

Other Department 56® Accessories

Hot Properties!

Harry's Inheritance (Hinged Secret Box)

Golden Snitch™ In Flight (Hinged Secret Box)

Hermione Granger™ (Hinged Secret Box)

Hogwarts™ School Of Witchcraft And Wizardry (Lighted Scene)

Journey To Hogwarts™ (Lighted Scene)

The Mirror Of ERISED™ (Hinged Secret Box)

Musical Sleigh (musical, U.S. only)

Professor Of Potions (Hinged Secret Box)

Under The Invisibility Cloak (Hinged Secret Box)

Miscellaneous*

56 Ball Ornament

56 Bell Ornament

Footbridge

One Village Place Ornament

*(Pieces available only at Department 56 Silver Anniversary Celebration.)

Seasons Bay® Series

Summer – Evening Of Horseback Riding (set/2)

Fresh Seafood By The Shore

Patriotic Decorations (set/7)

Pull Together

Fall – Gathering Grapes (set/2)

Winter – A Sleigh Ride With Santa (set/2)

Other Department 56® Mid-Year Releases

Seasons Bay® Series

Seaside Inn

Storybook Village® Collection

Hansel And Gretel's Sweets Shop (set/4)

Rudolph's Bunk House (set/2)

Wizard Of Oz Tea Set (set/5)

Hot Properties!
Lord Of The Rings –

Arwen™, The Elven Princess (Resin Ornament; Secret Box)

Bag End (gift set/2)

Frodo™ And Bilbo™ (Resin Ornament; Secret Box)

Galadriel™ The Elven Queen (Waterglobe)

Gandolf™ The Gray (Resin Ornament; Secret Box)

Gimli™ (Resin Ornament)

Gimli™ And Legolas™ (Secret Box)

Hobbits In Hiding (Waterglobe)

Legolas (Ornament)

The Lord Of The Rings (Ornament Hanger)

Moria Mines Entrance (Picture Frame)

The One Ring (Picture Frame; Resin Ornament)

Orthanc (Blown Glass Ornament)

Prancing Pony (Blown Glass Ornament)

Ring Of Power (Ornament Stand)

The Ringbearer (Waterglobe)

Ringwraiths, Servants of Sauron™ (Waterglobe)

Rivendell (Blown Glass Ornament)

Saruman™ (Resin Ornament; Secret Box)

Saruman's™ Chamber (Waterglobe)

The Shire (Blown Glass Ornament)

Strider™ (Resin Ornament; Secret Box)

How The Grinch Stole Christmas –

Countdown To Christmas (Advent Tree, set/25)

How To Use Your Collector's Value Guide™

1. *Locate* your piece in the Value Guide. In "Other Department 56® Collectibles," the buildings are listed first, followed by accessories. Both sections are broken down alphabetically by series or collection and then by piece name. The *Hot Properties!* line is

located in its entirety at the end of the value guide section. If you have difficulty finding your piece, refer to the numerical and alphabetical indexes in the back of the book, beginning on page 267.

Hometown Boarding House
Issued: 1987 ▼ Retired: 1988
#670-0 ▼ Original Price: $34
Market Value: $275

2. *Find* the market value of your piece. If no market value has been established, it is listed as "N/E" (not established). If a piece is still current and available at stores, the market value reflects the retail value.

Bachman's Hometown Series Buildings	Price Paid	Value
1.	$34	$275
2.		
3.		
Meadowland Buildings		
4.		
5.		
Miscellaneous Buildings		
6.		
7.		
Totals		$275

3. *Record* the price you paid for the piece and its secondary market value in the corresponding boxes at the bottom of the page.

4. *Calculate* the value for the page by adding all the boxes in each column. Be sure to use a pencil so you can change the totals as your collection grows.

5. *Transfer* the totals from each page to the "Total Value of My Collection" worksheet for Other Department 56 Collectibles on page 241.

6. *Add* all of the secondary market value totals together to determine the overall value of your collection.

Other Department 56® Collectibles – Buildings

1

Hometown Boarding House
Issued: 1987 • Retired: 1988
#670-0 • Original Price: $34
Market Value: $275

2

Hometown Church
Issued: 1987 • Retired: 1988
#671-8 • Original Price: $40
Market Value: $370

3

Hometown Drugstore
Issued: 1988 • Retired: 1989
#672-6 • Original Price: $40
Market Value: $625

4

Countryside Church
Issued: 1979 • Retired: 1980
#5051-8 • Original Price: $25
Market Value: $625

5

Thatched Cottage
Issued: 1979 • Retired: 1980
#5050-0 • Original Price: $30
Market Value: $680

6

Painting The White Picket Fence

The Adventures Of Tom Sawyer – Aunt Polly's House (set/5, w/book)
Literary Classics®
Issued: 2000 • Current
#58600 • Original Price: $90
Market Value: $90

7

Bachman Greenhouse (Bachman's Piece)
Issued: 1998 • Retired: 1998
#2203 • Original Price: $60
Market Value: $88

Bachman's Hometown Series Buildings		
	Price Paid	Value
1.		
2.		
3.		
Meadowland Buildings		
4.		
5.		
Miscellaneous Buildings		
6.		
7.		
Totals		

223

Miscellaneous – Buildings

8

Bachman's Flower Shop (Bachman's Piece)
Issued: 1997 • Retired: 1997
#8802 • Original Price: $50
Market Value: $115

9

Canadian Trading Co. (Canadian Piece For Dickens' Village®)
Issued: 1997 • Retired: 1998
#58306 • Original Price: $65 (U.S.)
Market Value: $138 (U.S.)

10

Collectors' Club House (set/2)
Issued: 1998 • Retired: 1998
#54800 • Original Price: $56
Market Value: $125

11

Photo Unavailable

Fire Station No. 1 (State Farm Piece)
The Profile Series®
Issued: 2000 • Current
#05709 • Original Price: N/A
Market Value: N/E

12

The Great Gatsby West Egg Mansion (set/4, with book)
Literary Classics®
Issued: 1999 • Current
#58939 • Original Price: $135
Market Value: $135

13

Photo Unavailable

Heinz Evaporated Horseradish Factory (H.J. Heinz Co. Piece)
The Profile Series®
Issued: 2000 • Current
#05710 • Original Price: $32
Market Value: $32

Miscellaneous Buildings

	Price Paid	Value
8.		
9.		
10.		
11.		
12.		
13.		
14.		
15.		
Totals		

14

Heinz Grocery Store (H.J. Heinz Co. Piece)
The Profile Series®
Issued: 1998 • Retired: 1999
#05600 • Original Price: $34
Market Value: N/E

15

Heinz House (H.J. Heinz Co. Piece)
The Profile Series®
Issued: 1996 • Retired: 1997
#7826 • Original Price: $27
Market Value: $95

16

The House That
❤ Built™ 1998
(Event Piece)
Issued: 1998 • Retired: 1998
#2210 • Original Price: N/A
Market Value: $300

17

Independence Hall
(set/2)
Historical Landmark Series™
Issued: 1998 • Retired: 2000
#55500 • Original Price: $110
Market Value: $120

18

Little Women **The**
March Residence
(set/4, w/book)
Literary Classics®
Issued: 1999 • Retired: 2000
#56606 • Original Price: $90
Market Value: $100

19

Main Street Memories
(State Farm Piece)
The Profile Series®
Issued: 1997 • Retired: 1997
#56000 • Original Price: $35.50
Market Value: $125

20

The Original Bachman
Homestead (LE-7,500)
Issued: 1999 • Retired: 1999
#02255 • Original Price: $75
Market Value: $125

21

Ronald McDonald
House® "The House
That ❤ Built"
(Event Piece)
Issued: 1997 • Retired: 1997
#8960 • Original Price: N/A
Market Value: $370

22
New

Sherlock Holmes –
221B Baker Street
(set/3, w/book)
Literary Classics®
Issued: 2000 • Current
#58601 • Original Price: $90
Market Value: $90

23
New

Preliminary
Design

St. Paul Cathedral
(Event Piece)
Historical Landmark Series™
Issued: 2001 • To Be Retired: 2001
#58919 • Original Price: $150
Market Value: $150

Miscellaneous Buildings

	Price Paid	Value
16.		
17.		
18.		
19.		
20.		
21.		
22.		
23.		
Totals		

Miscellaneous – Buildings

24

The Times Tower (set/3)
Issued: 1999 • Retired: 1999
#55510 • Original Price: $185
Market Value: $330

25

City Lights (set/12)
Issued: 1999 • Retired: 1999
#13612 • Original Price: $335
Market Value: N/E

26

Law Office, Inc.
Issued: 1999 • Retired: 1999
#13606 • Original Price: $50
Market Value: N/E

27

Mediterranean Mortgage Co.
Issued: 1999 • Retired: 1999
#13600 • Original Price: $30
Market Value: N/E

28

Monopoly® Bank & Trust
Issued: 1999 • Retired: 1999
N/A • Original Price: N/A
Market Value: N/E

Miscellaneous Buildings		
	Price Paid	Value
24.		
Monopoly® Brand Citylights™ Buildings		
25.		
26.		
27.		
28.		
29.		
30.		
Totals		

29

Newsstand Daily
Issued: 1999 • Retired: 1999
#13602 • Original Price: $37.50
Market Value: N/E

30

Old St. James Hospital
Issued: 1999 • Retired: 1999
#13603 • Original Price: $37.50
Market Value: N/E

31

Opera Du Jardin
Issued: 1999 • Retired: 1999
#13605 • Original Price: $45
Market Value: N/E

32

Oriental Express
Issued: 1999 • Retired: 1999
#13601 • Original Price: $37.50
Market Value: N/E

33

Police Department
Issued: 1999 • Retired: 1999
#13604 • Original Price: $37.50
Market Value: N/E

34

Yorkshire Grand Hotel
Issued: 1999 • Retired: 1999
#13607 • Original Price: $60
Market Value: $60

35

Bay Street Shops (set/2, First Edition)
Issued: 1998 • Retired: 1999
#53301 • Original Price: $135
Market Value: $138

36

Bay Street Shops (set/2)
Issued: 1998 • Current
#53401 • Original Price: $135
Market Value: $135

37

New

Breezy Hill Stables
Issued: 2000 • Current
#53447 • Original Price: $68
Market Value: $68

38

Chapel On The Hill (First Edition)
Issued: 1998 • Retired: 1999
#53302 • Original Price: $72
Market Value: $75

Monopoly® Brand Citylights™ Buildings

	Price Paid	Value
31.		
32.		
33.		
34.		

Seasons Bay® Buildings

35.		
36.		
37.		
38.		

Totals

Seasons Bay® – Buildings

39

Chapel On The Hill
Issued: 1998 • Current
#53402 • Original Price: $72
Market Value: $72

40
New

East Cape Cottages (set/2)
Issued: 2000 • Current
#53448 • Original Price: $95
Market Value: $95

41
New

Garden Valley Vineyards (LE-5,600)
Issued: 2000 • Current
#53446 • Original Price: $125
Market Value: $125

42

The Grand Creamery (First Edition)
Issued: 1998 • Retired: 1999
#53305 • Original Price: $60
Market Value: $65

43

The Grand Creamery
Issued: 1998 • Current
#53405 • Original Price: $60
Market Value: $60

Seasons Bay® Buildings

	Price Paid	Value
39.		
40.		
41.		
42.		
43.		
44.		
Totals		

44

Grandview Shores Hotel (First Edition)
Issued: 1998 • Retired: 1999
#53300 • Original Price: $150
Market Value: $157

45

Grandview Shores Hotel
Issued: 1998 • Retired: 2000
#53400 • Original Price: $150
Market Value: $153

46

**Inglenook Cottage #5
(First Edition)**
Issued: 1998 • Retired: 1999
#53304 • Original Price: $60
Market Value: $65

47

Inglenook Cottage #5
Issued: 1998 • Retired: 2000
#53404 • Original Price: $60
Market Value: $63

48

**Mystic Ledge
Lighthouse (LE-5,600)**
Issued: 2000 • Retired: 2000
#53445 • Original Price: $96
Market Value: $400

49

**Parkside Pavilion
(set/2)**
Issued: 1999 • Current
#53411 • Original Price: $65
Market Value: $65

50

**Parkside Pavilion
(set/9, Event Piece)**
Issued: 1999 • Retired: 2000
#53412 • Original Price: $75
Market Value: $85

**Side Porch Café
(First Edition)**
Issued: 1998 • Retired: 1999
#53303 • Original Price: $50
Market Value: $53

Seasons Bay® – Buildings

Seasons Bay® Buildings		
	Price Paid	Value
45.		
46.		
47.		
48.		
49.		
50.		
51.		
Totals		

229

Seasons Bay® – Buildings

52

Side Porch Café
Issued: 1998 • Current
#53403 • Original Price: $50
Market Value: $50

53

Springlake Station
Issued: 1999 • Current
#53413 • Original Price: $90
Market Value: $90

54

Stillwaters Boathouse
Issued: 1999 • Current
#53414 • Original Price: $70
Market Value: $70

55

The Butcher, Baker And Candlestick Maker (set/2)
Issued: 1999 • Retired: 2000
#13186 • Original Price: $75
Market Value: $130

56

New

Cinderella's Dress Shop (set/2)
Issued: 2000 • Current
#13203 • Original Price: $50
Market Value: $50

57

New

The Emerald City (set/2)
Issued: 2000 • Current
#13201 • Original Price: $95
Market Value: $95

58

New

Frosty Frolic Castle (set/2, musical)
Issued: 2000 • Current
#13205 • Original Price: $95
Market Value: $95

Seasons Bay® Buildings

	Price Paid	Value
52.		
53.		
54.		
55.		

Storybook Village® Buildings

56.		
57.		
58.		
Totals		

59

Goldilocks Bed And Breakfast (set/4)
Issued: 1996 • Retired: 1999
#13193 • Original Price: $95
Market Value: $145

60

H.D. Diddle Fiddles (set/4)
Issued: 1998 • Current
#13183 • Original Price: $75
Market Value: $75

61

Hickory Dickory Dock (set/3)
Issued: 1996 • Retired: 1998
#13195 • Original Price: $95
Market Value: $195

62

Humpty Dumpty Café (set/4)
Issued: 1997 • Current
#13181 • Original Price: $95
Market Value: $95

63

Lambsville School (set/5)
Issued: 1996 • Retired: 1999
#13194 • Original Price: $95
Market Value: $160

64

Lil' Boy Blue Petting Farm (set/3)
Issued: 1999 • Current
#13172 • Original Price: $75
Market Value: $75

65

Mary Quite Contrary Flower Shop (set/5)
Issued: 1997 • Retired: 2000
#13180 • Original Price: $95
Market Value: $130

66

An Old House In Paris That Was Covered With Vines (set/9)
Issued: 1998 • Current
#13185 • Original Price: $75
Market Value: $75

Storybook Village® Buildings		
	Price Paid	Value
59.		
60.		
61.		
62.		
63.		
64.		
65.		
66.		
Totals		

Storybook Village® – Buildings

67

Old Woman Cobbler (set/5)
Issued: 1996 • Retired: 1999
#13191 • Original Price: $95
Market Value: $145

68

P. Peter's (set/3)
Issued: 1998 • Current
#13184 • Original Price: $75
Market Value: $75

69

Peter Piper Pickle And Peppers (set/4)
Issued: 1996 • Retired: 1998
#13192 • Original Price: $95
Market Value: $130

70

Queen's House Of Cards (set/8)
Issued: 1999 • Current
#13173 • Original Price: $85
Market Value: $85

71

New

Rapunzel's Hair Salon
Issued: 2000 • Current
#13204 • Original Price: $50
Market Value: $50

72

New

Rudolph's Red-Nosed Lighthouse (set/4)
Issued: 2000 • Current
#13202 • Original Price: $95
Market Value: $95

Storybook Village® Buildings		
	Price Paid	Value
67.		
68.		
69.		
70.		
71.		
72.		
73.		
74.		
Totals		

73

T.L. Pigs Brick Factory (set/6)
Issued: 1998 • Retired: 2000
#13182 • Original Price: $95
Market Value: $145

74

'Twas The Night Before Christmas (set/6, Parkwest/NALED Piece)
Issued: 2000 • Current
#13175 • Original Price: $75
Market Value: $75

Value Guide — Department 56® Villages

Other Department 56® Collectibles – Accessories

1

Aspen Trees
Issued: 1979 • Retired: 1980
#5052-6 • Original Price: $16
Market Value: $375

2

Sheep (set/12)
Issued: 1979 • Retired: 1980
#5053-4 • Original Price: $12
Market Value: $300

3 New

56 Ball Ornament (Event Piece)
Issued: 2001 • To Be Retired: 2001
#97702 • Original Price: $15
Market Value: $15

4 New

Photo Unavailable
56 Bell Ornament (Event Piece)
Issued: 2001 • To Be Retired: 2001
#97703 • Original Price: $15
Market Value: $15

5

Bachman's Wilcox Truck (Bachman's Piece)
Issued: 1997 • Retired: 1997
#8803 • Original Price: $29.95
Market Value: $53

6

The First House That ❤ Built (Event Piece)
Classic Ornament Series
Issued: 1999 • Retired: 1999
#98774 • Original Price: $16.50
Market Value: N/E

7 New

Footbridge (Event Piece)
Issued: 2001 • To Be Retired: 2001
#52910 • Original Price: $15
Market Value: $15

8

Photo Unavailable
Heinz Hitch (H.J. Heinz Co. Piece)
The Profile Series®
Issued: 1999 • Current
N/A • Original Price: $39
Market Value: $39

9

Horse Drawn Squash Cart (Bachman's Piece)
Issued: 1995 • Retired: 1995
#0753-6 • Original Price: $50
Market Value: $97

10

Lighted Sign
Monopoly® Brand Citylights™
Issued: 1999 • Retired: 1999
#13610 • Original Price: $17.50
Market Value: N/E

11

New Year's Millennium Waterglobe
Issued: 1999 • Retired: 2001
#20008 • Original Price: $32.50
Market Value: N/E

Meadowland Accessories

	Price Paid	Value
1.		
2.		

Miscellaneous Accessories

3.		
4.		
5.		
6.		
7.		
8.		
9.		
10.		
11.		
Totals		

233

Miscellaneous – Accessories

12

New

**One Village Place
Ornament (Event Piece)**
Issued: 2001 • To Be Retired: 2001
#97700 • Original Price: $15
Market Value: $15

13

**Ronald McDonald
House® Ornament
(Event Piece)**
Issued: 1997 • Retired: 1997
#8961 • Original Price: $7.50
Market Value: N/E

14

**Say It With Flowers
(Bachman's Piece)**
Issued: 1998 • Retired: 1998
#2204 • Original Price: $30
Market Value: N/E

15

**Tending The
Cold Frame
(Bachman's Piece)**
Issued: 1998 • Retired: 1998
#2208 • Original Price: $35
Market Value: $60

16

Times Tower
Classic Ornament Series
Issued: 1999 • Retired: 1999
#98775 • Original Price: $25
Market Value: $28

17

**Village Express Van
(Canadian Piece For
Heritage Village)**
Issued: 1992 • Retired: 1996
#5865-3 • Original Price: $25 *(U.S.)*
Market Value: $90 *(U.S.)*

Miscellaneous Accessories

	Price Paid	Value
12.		
13.		
14.		
15.		
16.		
17.		

Seasons Bay® Spring Accessories

	Price Paid	Value
18.		
19.		
20.		
21.		
22.		
23.		

Totals

18

**Arriving At The
Station (set/5)**
Issued: 1999 • Current
#53416 • Original Price: $32.50
Market Value: $32.50

19

The Garden Cart
Issued: 1998 • Current
#53327 • Original Price: $27.50
Market Value: $27.50

20

The Garden Swing
Issued: 1999 • Current
#53415 • Original Price: $13
Market Value: $13

21

I'm Wishing
Issued: 1998 • Current
#53309 • Original Price: $13
Market Value: $13

22

**Relaxing In A Garden
(set/3)**
Issued: 1998 • Current
#53307 • Original Price: $25
Market Value: $25

23

**A Stroll In The Park
(set/5)**
Issued: 1998 • Current
#53308 • Original Price: $25
Market Value: $25

24

Sunday Morning At The Chapel (set/2)
Issued: 1998 • Current
#53311 • Original Price: $17
Market Value: $17

25

4th Of July Parade (set/5)
Issued: 1998 • Current
#53317 • Original Price: $32.50
Market Value: $32.50

26

A Day At The Waterfront (set/2)
Issued: 1998 • Current
#53326 • Original Price: $20
Market Value: $20

27
New

Evening Of Horseback Riding (set/2)
Issued: 2000 • Current
#53601 • Original Price: $30
Market Value: $30

28

Fishing In The Bay
Issued: 1998 • Current
#53313 • Original Price: $13
Market Value: $13

29
New

Fresh Seafood By The Shore
Issued: 2000 • Current
#53604 • Original Price: $27.50
Market Value: $27.50

30

Gently Down The Stream
Issued: 1999 • Current
#53418 • Original Price: $25
Market Value: $25

31

A Grand Day Of Fishing
Issued: 1998 • Current
#53419 • Original Price: $25
Market Value: $25

32

Here Comes The Ice Cream Man (set/4)
Issued: 1998 • Current
#53314 • Original Price: $35
Market Value: $35

33

Lifeguard On Duty
Issued: 1999 • Current
#53423 • Original Price: $20
Market Value: $20

34
New

Patriotic Decorations (set/7)
Issued: 2000 • Current
#53605 • Original Price: $12
Market Value: $12

35

The Perfect Wedding (set/7, with book)
Issued: 1999 • Current
#53417 • Original Price: $25
Market Value: $25

Seasons Bay® Spring Accessories

	Price Paid	Value
24.		

Seasons Bay® Summer Accessories

	Price Paid	Value
25.		
26.		
27.		
28.		
29.		
30.		
31.		
32.		
33.		
34.		
35.		
Totals		

Seasons Bay® – Accessories

36
New

Pull Together
Issued: 2000 • Current
#53600 • Original Price: $35
Market Value: $35

37

An Afternoon Picnic (set/3)
Issued: 1999 • Current
#53420 • Original Price: $18
Market Value: $18

38

Back From The Orchard
Issued: 1998 • Current
#53320 • Original Price: $27.50
Market Value: $27.50

39

A Bicycle Built For Two
Issued: 1999 • Current
#53421 • Original Price: $17.50
Market Value: $17.50

40
New

Gathering Grapes (set/2)
Issued: 2000 • Current
#53602 • Original Price: $25
Market Value: $25

41

Rocking Chair Readers (set/2)
Issued: 1999 • Current
#53422 • Original Price: $15
Market Value: $15

42

Trick Or Treat (set/4)
Issued: 1998 • Current
#53319 • Original Price: $25
Market Value: $25

43

Afternoon Sleigh Ride
Issued: 1998 • Current
#53322 • Original Price: $27.50
Market Value: $27.50

44

A Day Of Holiday Shopping (set/3)
Issued: 1999 • Current
#53425 • Original Price: $25
Market Value: $25

45

The First Snow
Issued: 1999 • Current
#53426 • Original Price: $15
Market Value: $15

46

Fun In The Snow (set/2)
Issued: 1998 • Current
#53323 • Original Price: $15
Market Value: $15

47

Singing Carols In Town
Issued: 1999 • Current
#53427 • Original Price: $22.50
Market Value: $22.50

Seasons Bay® Summer Accessories		
	Price Paid	Value
36.		
Seasons Bay® Fall Accessories		
37.		
38.		
39.		
40.		
41.		
42.		
Seasons Bay® Winter Accessories		
43.		
44.		
45.		
46.		
47.		
Totals		

48

Skating On The Pond (set/2)
Issued: 1998 • Current
#53324 • Original Price: $20
Market Value: $20

49

New

A Sleigh Ride With Santa (set/3)
Issued: 2000 • Current
#53603 • Original Price: $35
Market Value: $35

50

Storybook Village Collection Sign
Issued: 1999 • Current
#13169 • Original Price: $10
Market Value: $10

51

3 Men In A Tub Stackable Teapot And Cup (set/3)
Issued: 1997 • Retired: 1999
#13329 • Original Price: $15
Market Value: N/E

52

Cinderella (set/5)
Issued: 1997 • Current
#13326 • Original Price: $32.50
Market Value: $32.50

53

Cinderella Stackable Teapot And Cup (set/3)
Issued: 1997 • Retired: 1999
#13327 • Original Price: $15
Market Value: N/E

54

Hey Diddle Diddle (set/5)
Issued: 1996 • Current
#13303 • Original Price: $32.50
Market Value: $32.50

55

Hickory Dickory Dock (set/5)
Issued: 1996 • Current
#13302 • Original Price: $32.50
Market Value: $32.50

56

Humpty Dumpty (set/5)
Issued: 1997 • Current
#13324 • Original Price: $32.50
Market Value: $32.50

57

Humpty Dumpty Stackable Teapot And Cup (set/3)
Issued: 1997 • Current
#13328 • Original Price: $15
Market Value: $15

58

Little Boy Blue (set/5)
Issued: 1996 • Current
#13316 • Original Price: $32.50
Market Value: $32.50

59

Little Miss Muffet (set/5)
Issued: 1996 • Current
#13318 • Original Price: $32.50
Market Value: $32.50

Seasons Bay® Winter Accessories		
	Price Paid	Value
48.		
49.		
Storybook Village® Accessories		
50.		
Storybook® Teapots		
51.		
52.		
53.		
54.		
55.		
56.		
57.		
58.		
59.		
Totals		

Seasons Bay® – Accessories

Storybook® Teapots

60
Little Red Riding Hood (set/5)
Issued: 1996 • Current
#13317 • Original Price: $32.50
Market Value: $32.50

61
Mother Goose (set/5)
Issued: 1996 • Current
#13300 • Original Price: $32.50
Market Value: $32.50

62
Mother Goose Stackable Teapot And Cup (set/3)
Issued: 1997 • Retired: 1999
#13330 • Original Price: $15
Market Value: N/E

63
Peter Pumpkin (set/5)
Issued: 1996 • Retired: 1999
#13314 • Original Price: $32.50
Market Value: N/E

64
Tea And Coffee (set/5)
Issued: 1997 • Current
#13325 • Original Price: $32.50
Market Value: $32.50

65
Three Bears (set/5)
Issued: 1996 • Current
#13301 • Original Price: $32.50
Market Value: $32.50

Storybook® Teapots

	Price Paid	Value
60.		
61.		
62.		
63.		
64.		
65.		

Hot Properties!

66.		
67.		
68.		
69.		
70.		
71.		

Totals

66
A Gift For Cindy Lou Who

Cindy Lou Who's House
How The Grinch Stole Christmas!
Issued: 2000 • Current
#59004 • Original Price: $75
Market Value: $75

67
New

Town Hall
How The Grinch Stole Christmas!
Issued: 2000 • Current
#59034 • Original Price: $75
Market Value: $75

68

Harry And Hagrid At Gringotts™ (secret box, LE-2000)
Issued: 2000 • Retired: 2000
#59012 • Original Price: $27.50
Market Value: $32

69

Harry And The Sorting Hat (secret box, LE-2000)
Issued: 2000 • Retired: 2000
#59010 • Original Price: $19.50
Market Value: $30

70

Harry Potter™ (secret box, LE-2000)
Issued: 2000 • Retired: 2000
#59008 • Original Price: $19.50
Market Value: $30

71

Harry Potter™ Animated Scene
Issued: 2000 • Current
#59006 • Original Price: $125
Market Value: $125

72

New

Photo Unavailable

**Harry's Inheritance
(hinged secret box)**
Issued: 2000 • Current
#59019 • Original Price: $24
Market Value: $24

73

**The Golden Snitch™
(secret box, LE-2000)**
Issued: 2000 • Retired: 2000
#59007 • Original Price: $12.50
Market Value: $30

74

New

Photo Unavailable

**Golden Snitch™ In Flight
(hinged secret box)**
Issued: 2000 • Current
#59020 • Original Price: $13.50
Market Value: $13.50

75

**Hedwig™ The Owl
(secret box, LE-2000)**
Issued: 2000 • Retired: 2000
#59009 • Original Price: $19.50
Market Value: $30

76

New

**Hermione Granger™
(hinged secret box)**
Issued: 2000 • Current
#59017 • Original Price: $24
Market Value: $24

77

New

**Hermione™ The
Bookworm
(secret box, LE-2000)**
Issued: 2000 • Retired: 2000
#59011 • Original Price: $19.50
Market Value: $35

78

New

Photo Unavailable

**Hogwarts™ School
Of Witchcraft And
WIzardry**
Issued: 2000 • Current
#59036 • Original Price: $75
Market Value: $75

79

New

Photo Unavailable

Journey To Hogwarts™
Issued: 2000 • Current
#59027 • Original Price: $75
Market Value: $75

80

New

Photo Unavailable

**The Mirror Of ERISED™
(hinged secret box)**
Issued: 2000 • Current
#59018 • Original Price: $24
Market Value: $24

81

New

Musical Sleigh
*How The Grinch Stole
Christmas!*
#59035 • Original Price: N/A
Market Value: N/E

82

New

**Professor Of Potions
(hinged secret box)**
Issued: 2000 • Current
#59016 • Original Price: $27.50
Market Value: $27.50

83

New

**Under The
Invisibility Cloak
(hinged secret box)**
Issued: 2000 • Current
#59015 • Original Price: $24
Market Value: $24

Hot Properties!

	Price Paid	Value
72.		
73.		
74.		
75.		
76.		
77.		
78.		
79.		
80.		
81.		
82.		
83.		
Totals		

Other Department 56® Collectibles – Mid-Year Releases

The following are the mid-year releases for the *Seasons Bay® Series, Storybook Village® Collection* and *Hot Properties!* line, introduced on May 11, 2001.

1
New

Seaside Inn
Seasons Bay® Series
Issued: 2001 • Current
#53449 • Original Price: $68
Market Value: $68

2
New

Hansel And Gretel's Sweets Shop (set/4)
Storybook Village® Collection
Issued: 2001 • Current
#13210 • Original Price: $50
Market Value: $50

3
New

Rudolph's Bunk House (set/2)
Storybook Village® Collection
Issued: 2001 • Current
#13206 • Original Price: $75
Market Value: $75

4
New

Artist Rendering, Not Actual Product

Wizard Of Oz Tea Set (set/5)
Storybook Village® Collection
Issued: 2001 • Current
#13211 • Original Price: $40
Market Value: $40

Mid-Year Releases

	Price Paid	Value
1.		
2.		
3.		
4.		
Totals		

4

Other Mid-Year Releases
Hot Properties!

Advent Tree
❏ Countdown To Christmas (*How The Grinch Stole Christmas*, set/25, #59037, $50)

Frames
❏ Moria Mines Entrance (*Lord of the Rings*, #59081, $18.50)
❏ The One Ring (*Lord of the Rings*, #59079, $10)

Gift Sets
❏ Bag End (*Lord of the Rings*, set/2, #59038, $50)

Ornaments
❏ Arwen™, The Elven Princess (*Lord of the Rings*, resin, #59061, $12.50)
❏ Frodo™ And Bilbo™ (*Lord of the Rings*, resin, #59062, $10)
❏ Gandolf™ The Gray (*Lord of the Rings*, resin, #59065, $10)
❏ Gimli™ (*Lord of the Rings*, resin, #59067, $10)
❏ Legolas (*Lord of the Rings*, #59083, $10)
❏ The Lord Of The Rings (*Lord of the Rings*, ornament hanger, #59078, $2.50)
❏ The One Ring (*Lord of the Rings*, resin, #59076, $7.50)
❏ Orthanc (*Lord of the Rings*, blown glass, #59060, $17.50)
❏ Prancing Pony (*Lord of the Rings*, blown glass, #59068, $17.50)
❏ Ring Of Power (*Lord of the Rings*, ornament stand, #59077, $12.00)
❏ Rivendell (*Lord of the Rings*, blown glass, #59059, $17.50)
❏ Saruman™ (*Lord of the Rings*, resin, #59063, $10)
❏ The Shire (*Lord of the Rings*, blown glass, #59058, $17.50)
❏ Strider™ (*Lord of the Rings*, resin, #59066, $10)

Secret Boxes
❏ Arwen™, The Elven Princess (*Lord of the Rings*, #59049, $20)
❏ Frodo™ And Bilbo™ (*Lord of the Rings*, #59044, $20)
❏ Gandalf™ The Gray (*Lord of the Rings*, #59050, $20)
❏ Gimli™ And Legolas™ (*Lord of the Rings*, #59045, $20)
❏ Saruman™ (*Lord of the Rings*, #59047, $20)
❏ Strider™ (*Lord of the Rings*, #59046, $20)

Waterglobes
❏ Galadriel™, The Elven Queen (*Lord of the Rings*, #59043, $25)
❏ Hobbits In Hiding (*Lord of the Rings*, #59042, $40)
❏ The Ringbearer (*Lord of the Rings*, #59039, $30)
❏ Ringwraiths, Servants of Sauran™ (*Lord of the Rings*, #59041, $35)
❏ Saruman's™ Chamber (*Lord of the Rings*, #59040, $30)

Miscellaneous
❏ Grimsly Manor (waterglobe, #52932, $50)

Total Value Of My Collection

Record your collection here by adding the totals from
the bottom of each Value Guide page.

Buildings

Page Number	Price Paid	Value
Page 224		
Page 225		
Page 226		
Page 227		
Page 228		
Page 229		
Page 230		
Page 231		
Page 232		
Page 233		

Accessories

Page 234		
Page 235		
Page 236		
Subtotal:		

Accessories, cont.

Page Number	Price Paid	Value
Page 237		
Page 238		

Storybook Tea Pots

Page 239		
Page 240		
Subtotal:		

	Price Paid	Value
Page Total:		

Secondary Market Overview

When Department 56 makes its annual retirement announcement, collectors scramble to buy up the pieces. So where do you turn when the retailers finally run out of stock? Look to the secondary market! It's not actually a physical place, but a complex web of buyers and sellers who use several methods to find each other.

Leave No Stone Unturned

The best place to start your hunt is at your local retailer. Retailers are a great source of information. They may be able to introduce you to other collectors in the area and give you information about collector shows and events. These shows attract dealers from all over the country and are a great opportunity to find that elusive piece. Another option is an exchange (see our list on page 244). An exchange usually provides a mailing where collectors list the pieces they are selling with prices. There is usually a subscription fee for the list and the exchange may charge a percentage of the purchase price for coordinating the sale. And don't overlook classified ads in your local newspaper. Someone in your area might have just what you're looking for.

One of the fastest-growing secondary market venues is the Internet. You can find websites for secondary market dealers and individual collectors with pieces for sale. You can also find sellers through bulletin boards, chat rooms and mailing lists. Other popular places to buy and sell are Internet auction sites. Remember, many of these same sources are useful when selling a piece, too.

The Secondary Market Trampoline

Like the stock market, prices on the secondary market tend to fluctuate and often these changes are unpredictable. Supply and demand is one of the major factors affecting market price. If there are too many pieces available, the price will fall. If there are too few, the price may skyrocket. This is why many limited edition, exclusive pieces and variations become so valuable on the secondary market.

Prices for individual pieces are largely affected by the condition of the piece and its packaging. Do your best to avoid chips and breakage – that means letting your kids play "Godzilla versus Snow Village®" is *not* a good idea! The original packaging is also important. If it is damaged or missing, the price can drop dramatically. Pieces which fetch the highest value are those that are MIB (mint in box) and have only been removed from their boxes to be inspected. Whenever you purchase a piece, you should always inspect it and make sure you got what you paid for.

However, don't forget that the most important rules of collecting are to have fun and buy pieces that you like! Remember that the market is fickle. If you collect purely for investment and prices drop, you will be sorely disappointed. So, enjoy hunting down and capturing those hard to find pieces and watching your village grow one house (or more!) at a time.

EXCHANGES, DEALERS & NEWSLETTERS

Fifty-Six™ (formerly the Quarterly)
(general information – *a must!*)
Department 56, Inc.
P.O. Box 44056
One Village Place
Eden Prairie, MN 55344-1056
(800) 548-8696
www.department56.com

56 Directions
Jeff & Susan McDermott
364 Spring Street Ext.
Glastonbury, CT 06033
(860) 633-8192
www.56directions.com

Collectible Exchange, Inc.
6621 Columbiana Road
New Middletown, OH 44442
(800) 752-3208
www.colexch.com

The Cottage Locator
Frank & Florence Wilson
211 No. Bridebrook Rd.
East Lyme, CT 06333
(860) 739-0705

Donna's Collectible Exchange
703 Endeavor Drive South
Winter Springs, FL 32708
(800) 480-5105
www.donnascollexch.com

New England Collectibles Exchange
Bob Dorman
201 Pine Avenue
Clarksburg, MA 01247-4640
(413) 663-3643
www.collectiblesbroker.com

The Village Chronicle
Peter & Jeanne George
757 Park Ave.
Cranston, RI 02910
(401) 467-9343

Villages Classified
Paul & Mirta Burns
P.O. Box 34166
Granada Hills, CA 91394-9166

Protecting Your Investment

It's taken time, effort and money to build up your collection – now it's time to make sure that you are covered in the event of unforeseen circumstances. Insuring your collection is a wise move, and one that doesn't have to be costly or difficult. The process can be broken down into three simple steps, which are outlined below.

1. *Assess* the current value of your Department 56 collection. If it is quite large, you may want to have it professionally appraised. Otherwise, you can do it yourself by consulting a reputable price guide such as the Collector's Value Guide™.

2. *Determine* the amount of coverage you need. Collectibles are often covered under a basic homeowner's or renter's policy, but ask your agent if your policy covers fire, theft, flood, hurricanes, earthquakes and damage or breakage from routine handling. Additionally, determine whether your policy covers claims at "current replacement value" – the amount it would cost to replace items at their current value if they were lost, damaged or stolen. If the amount of insurance does not cover your collection, you may want to add a Personal Articles Floater or a Fine Arts Floater ("rider") to your policy. There are a number of insurance companies which specialize in collectibles insurance and can work with you to make sure your collection is adequately covered.

3. *Keep* up-to-date documentation of your collectible pieces and their values. Save your receipts and consider photographing each item, making sure to show variations, artist signatures and other special features in the photograph. Keep this documentation in a safe places, such as a safe deposit box, or make two copies and give one to a friend or relative.

Variations

Like any collectible made by artists, no two pieces with the same name are exactly alike. But sometimes a significant difference appears, like a color or design change. Some of the changes are the result of human error, but sometimes Department 56 decides to change the look of the piece. The version of the piece that differs from the standard is considered to be a variation. Not all variations will affect the value of the piece, but some will see a high value on the secondary market.

A Chameleon Act

One of the most obvious variations is a color change. Sometimes it is the color of the entire piece or it might just be a detail or trim that changes color.

"Peggotty's Seaside Cottage," the charming upside-down boat home from David Copperfield, first appeared in 1989 with a gray porcelain hull. It was later released in its intended dark green color.

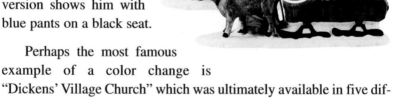

The *Dickens' Village* "Ox Sled" first featured a driver with tan pants on a green seat. Another version shows him with blue pants on a black seat.

Perhaps the most famous example of a color change is "Dickens' Village Church" which was ultimately available in five different colors. The white version became the most valuable.

"Under The NCC Umbrella," released in 2000 and 2001, is an example of purposeful color variations. This special event piece is being offered to club members in five different colors and is itself a repaint of "Under The Bumbershoot."

Back To The Drawing Board

Many pieces also undergo design changes either to correct an error or just to make the piece look better.

When the *New England Village* "Amish Family" (set/3) was first introduced, it featured a man with a mustache. It wasn't until after the accessory was released that Department 56 found out that the Amish prohibit wearing mustaches. So in the new version, the man sports only a beard.

"Ada's Bed And Boarding House" featured not only a color change but also a variation in the piece's design. Two versions have the rear steps as part of the mold, while the third version's steps have been attached separately.

In the *Disney Parks Village* piece, "Mickey's Christmas Carol," one version's dormer windows sport spires, while the other version's have no spires.

Another accessory with a design change is the *New England Village* piece "Sleighride" (also known as "Dickens' Sleighride"). One version shows the driver with a thin scarf, while the other has a thick scarf.

Use That Spellcheck!

Another common variation is a misspelling, which usually occurs on the bottomstamp.

"Blythe Pond Mill House" in *Dickens' Village* lost an "l" on some pieces and became "By The Pond" on the bottomstamp.

The "Nicholas Nickleby Cottage" also featured a misspelled bottomstamp, "Nickolas Nickelby," using a "k" instead of an "h" in the first name.

The "Crooked Fence Cottage" and "J. Lytes Coal Merchant" both had versions which featured mistakes on their bottomstamps, not in their names, but in the descriptions. "Crooked Fence Cottage" said "Seires" instead of "Series" and "J. Lytes Coal Merchant" said "Vallage" instead of "Village."

"Kensington Palace" (set/23) differed from the norm and had a mistake on its box. The first version was marked "Princess of Whales" and was later corrected to say "Princess of Wales."

The Best Things Come In Small Packages

As technology improves, Department 56 can make its pieces both smaller and more detailed. Some accessories showed this change in the middle of their production run. Both "Kids Around The Tree" and "Family Mom/Kids, Goose Girl" (set/2) have a smaller version featuring more detail.

Just For You!

Although not really variations, Department 56 often releases exclusives based on existing pieces. They are usually available through a specific retailer or group and are often highly coveted by collectors because of their limited availability and uniqueness.

To see all of the variations with value, check out the Value Guide section of this book!

SO WHAT'S AN ARTIST PROOF?

Before a piece is released to the public, artists in the Department 56 studio usually produce a test piece called an Artist Proof. They use this prototype to test things such as color scheme and firing results. There are only a few of these proofs made and even fewer leave the studio and find their way into collectors' hands. Therefore, proofs can fetch a high price on the secondary market for collectors lucky enough to find them.

History 101 – The Stories Behind The Buildings

Ever wondered what some of your favorite Department 56 buildings would look like if they were life-sized? Well, many of them have been inspired by actual buildings, and the stories behind those real-life historic structures are just as fascinating as their miniature counterparts.

Big Ben

Most people seem to think that this memorable name applies to the huge clock tower outside Parliament in London. But in fact, the name Big Ben doesn't refer to the tower at all, but to the giant bell inside. The gigantic thirteen-ton bell was cast and rang for the first time in 1859. Unfortunately, it cracked after a mere two months! But it is still in use today, and that crack gives Big Ben its distinctive off-tune sound which is used to literally "ring in" the New Year for expectant crowds in London every year.

Gad's Hill Place

As a youngster, Charles Dickens would often pass by the formidable Gad's Hill Place in the village of Higham in Rochester, Kent. Noticing his son's interest in the 18th Century home, Dickens' father once remarked to him that, if he "were to be very persevering and work very hard, [he] might someday come to live in it." Then at the height of his literary success in 1856, Dickens did indeed buy the house,

taking up residence there four years later. It was at Gad's Hill that Dickens lived out his remaining years, while working on his unfinished opus, *The Mystery of Edwin Drood.* Built by James Stevens in 1780, the home has since become a private school. But fans of Charles Dickens still flock there.

Independence Hall

When the city of Philadelphia finished building the Pennsylvania State House in 1753 (after 21 years of construction), no one could have known the part it was to play in the history of an entire nation.

It was the building where, during the Revolutionary War, the Declaration of Independence would be signed by the Continental Congress. Later the Constitution would be drafted here. And it was where Benjamin Franklin was even rumored to playfully trip other delegates from his seat! That's a very impressive run of history for a building that originally contained the city dog pound, isn't it?

The Old Globe Theater

In 1599, an English theater company (which included the writer, and occasional actor, William Shakespeare) called the Lord Chamberlain's Men worked together to build a theater in London. In the end, they crafted the Globe Theater, easily the most famous amphitheater in Great Britain, even if it no longer stands today.

It was the place where lords and ladies in box seats shared space with the lowliest peasant to view all the greatest plays of the time, including Shakespeare's own work. The spectators got an especially realistic view of the action in 1613,

when a cannon fired during a production of *Henry VIII* set fire to the Globe's thatched roof, and burned the theater to the ground. Hastily rebuilt a year later, the second Globe Theater would enjoy success until the Puritans closed it down in 1642 and their leader, Oliver Cromwell had it torn down two years later. It would be over two hundred years before anyone was able to rebuild such a majestic place.

St.-Martin-In-The-Fields Church

When the first recorded church went up at this London site in 1222, it was surrounded by fields where the monks from Westminster Abbey grazed their animals and grew vegetables.

It wasn't until 1726 when this design of Scottish-born architect James Gibbs finally came to life. But many traditionalists were unhappy with its unconventional design. It's a good thing few people listened to them, because St.-Martin-in-the-Fields is regarded as one of London's prime tourist attractions. It not only remains a fully functioning and popular church, but its architecture has influenced many churches across the pond in New England.

St. Nikolaus Kirche

It was just a parish church in Oberndorf, Austria, and the original building isn't even there any more. But, on Christmas Eve 1818, that one tiny church would change the way the world celebrated Christmas.

Due to a broken organ at the church, Father Joseph Mohr was looking for a way to still have music at his Christmas Eve service. After Mohr had a poem he had written set to music by his friend Franz Gruber, the two men serenaded the congregation with the song "Stille Nacht." But we all know the song they invented as "Silent Night," heard for the very first time at St. Nikolaus Kirche and now sung all over the world at Christmastime.

Sir John Falstaff Inn

After Charles Dickens miraculously survived a traumatic train wreck in 1865, it was to a Kent public house called the Falstaff Inn that he went to fortify his spirits, telling the innkeeper, "I never thought I should be here again." But the house's history goes back even further than that.

Named for Sir John Falstaff, a devious character in William Shakespeare's *Henry IV*, the inn was conveniently located across the street from Gad's Hill. And in 1676, the inn got some notoriety when legendary English highwayman Swift Nick (a.k.a. John Nevison) robbed a man nearby, and rode his horse all the way from Kent to York to establish his alibi. Later, local folklore would attribute the ride to Dick Turpin instead – another criminal who was executed in York.

Tower Of London

For over nine centuries now, this stone fortress has guarded the banks of London's Thames River. But it didn't spring up overnight.

After conquering England for himself in 1066, William the Conqueror set about constructing forts and castles of his own all over the island, and chose the city of London as the location for the grandest of them all. Originally, it was just a small fortification, but over time, English monarchs built it up into a combination castle and prison. It became notorious for its political prisoners and executions.

Today, it houses the British Crown Jewels and the Royal Ravens. Legend has it that if the ravens ever leave the tower, the whole Commonwealth of England will fall. No one is too worried, though, since their wings are clipped!

Department 56® Product Spotlight

Department 56® isn't just villages! For many years, this company has been producing several other lines of collectibles and giftware. If you're looking to start a new collection or just want something to spruce up your home, there's a Department 56 product for you.

Candle Crown™ Collection

First released in 2000, this line of porcelain candle extinguishers continues to grow in number. Three numbered, limited edition sets were made available in bone china with 23-karat gold accents, and these same pieces were also available as porcelain open editions. Since then, many new open edition pieces have been released including collections like *African Safari Animals*, *A Christmas Carol* and a *Seasonal Collection*. Also, two porcelain limited edition pieces, "Father Time – 2000" (LE-2000) and "Lady Liberty" (LE-5,600) have been released.

Silhouette Treasures® Collection

These elegant porcelain figurines have been a collector favorite since 1987. The collection began with a Victorian lamplighter and three carolers, known collectively as *Lamplighter*. Soon more figures were added and the collection was renamed *Winter Silhouette*™. The line gradually expanded to include items such as ornaments, musicals and even lighted scenes. Now called the *Silhouette Treasures® Collection*, there are 74 pieces, including 17 new releases this year.

Snowbabies™ Figurines

These delightful, wintertime children have been warming hearts since 1986. Artist Kristi Jensen Pierro created these cherubic children in their nubby, glittery snowsuits in a collection that now numbers over 200 pieces. The line includes figurines, ornaments, hinged boxes, pewter miniatures, tree toppers and more.

In 1998, licensed properties came to *Frosty Frolic Land*™ with *The Guest Collection*™. These pieces featured popular characters from properties like *"Looney Tunes"* and *The Wizard of Oz*. This year Rudolph® makes his appearance. Then in 2000, the first pieces in *Snowbabies Starlight Games*™ *Collection* were introduced, depicting the Snowbabies competing in athletic events.

This year the *Snowbabies Babies On The Farm* have made their first appearance in the collection, with their bright red suit jackets and farm animal friends.

Once the flowers come up, it's time to take out the *Snowbunnies*®, the springtime cousins of the *Snowbabies*™ *Collection*. These bunny-suited toddlers are perfect for Easter because many feature pastel accents. Collectors can also eagerly look forward to annual bisque Easter animals.

Tabletop And Giftware

Since its earliest days, Department 56 has offered a diverse line of home decor products as well. From the kitchen to the bathroom and everywhere in between, these pieces will brighten up any space. One of the newest collections is the *Fresco*™ tabletop line. Inspired by the bold colors of impressionist paintings, these pieces are hand painted in Italy in bright blue and yellow. If you still want more Department 56 in your life, be sure to check out their giftware items like the *Just Ducky*™ collection and *Under The Mistletoe*.

Collectors' Display Ideas

In this section, three collectors have shared both their displays and some great tips for our readers. Hopefully this information will give you some new ideas for your next display to get those creative juices flowing!

Don't Waste That Space!

An empty dresser top presents the perfect opportunity
to show off many of your pieces.

Matt Lake of West Virginia has been collecting and displaying his villages since 1994. He even maintains a web site (*www.iolinc.net/mlake/dept56.htm*) devoted to his collection. So where does he display his vast and varied villages? Anywhere he can find room! Don't be limited by your card tables – any flat and stable surface can be the foundation for your village. So, let your imagination take over and look for unconventional places to showcase your houses. Don't skip rooms like the bathroom and kitchen or places like stairways. Matt displays his *Little Town of Bethlehem* collection under his Christmas tree and even uses a window cornice to display some of his additional *Christmas in the City* pieces.

The "Village Animated Skating Pond" makes a great centerpiece
for this display with buildings naturally curved around it.

Taking On A Giant

Pete Sloan of Georgia was first bitten by the village bug in 1988 when he received his first piece for Christmas. His display grew so large in fact, that he eventually filled the display window at a store he managed in Florida. One year his helpers, his wife Pam and his mother Mary, even threatened not to pitch in if his village got any larger! Although his collection consists mainly of Snow Village

This multi-tiered Snow Village display has a very realistic look. Pete made the mountains in his display using simple craft materials.

pieces, Pete is not afraid to mix and match pieces from other villages and even other companies (gasp!) if they will enhance the display. However, if you do this, make sure to select items with the right scale and if they're not shiny, try spraying them with a clear gloss spray.

If you want to tackle a large display, Pete has several recommendations. Throughout the year he keeps a journal where he can jot down ideas for his coming display. Planning different areas is important, real towns always have sections (e.g., residential, business and ski areas) and it is easiest to work on one section at a time. While setting up, Pete recommends a base of 2" styrofoam. Also, don't face all your houses in the same direction. Create several levels and use

lots of trees and other accessories. Don't be afraid to use multiples of an accessory or figure – placing them apart from each other and turning them in different directions gives the illusion of different pieces. Check out *www.petes-display.com* for more great ideas!

To give them a more natural look, Pete modified his "Village Animated Ski Mountain" and "Village Animated Sledding Hill." He removed as much of the bases as he could and then sank them into the styrofoam.

Spring Is In The Air

Marilu LeBel of Virginia has been collecting and displaying her *Dickens' Village* and *Disney Parks Village* pieces since 1996. Her inspiration for this spring display came about quite by accident. While packing up her winter display, she couldn't find the boxes for

her "Chelsea Market Flower Monger & Cart" (set/2) or the Lord & Taylor version. So there the pieces sat on her coffee table. But when she went to her local craft store for another project, she spotted a flower-cart shaped plant stand. Eureka! She now had the perfect way to display her boxless flower

ᵍThis colorful springtime display proves that your villages can be displayed year round. In addition to her flower sellers, Marilu also added her blue "Under The NCC Umbrella"

sellers. Marilu says that this display wasn't too hard and that beginners shouldn't shy away. Here's how she did it:

Step 1. Fill the cart level to the top with floral foam.

Step 2. Cut scrapbooking paper (or other sturdy, thick paper) to fit around the inside of the cart and slip it in between the foam and the sides of the cart. This will help hide the foam.

Step 3. Measure and cut green felt to fit on top of the foam.

Step 4. Measure and cut wire ribbon and run it through the top of the cart.

Step 5. Add your pieces and decorate as desired. Marilu used miniature baskets filled with flowers cut from taper candle rings. You can use floral foam in the baskets or hot glue to hold your flowers in place. Have a look around your craft store for other flowers and flower-making materials.

To see more of Marilu's photos visit: *http://albums.photo-point.com/j/AlbumIndex?u=840698&a=12420642&f=0*

Display Success With "Dr. S"

Display guru, "Dr. S" is back again, ready to help both beginners and advanced "displayers" enhance their growing villages. This time, he's here with easy-to-follow instructions for building country roads and loading docks to add that special touch to your scene.

The Quick Country Road

You will need:

- Foam core board
- Plaster or Sculptamold
- Paint mixing sticks cut to various lengths
- Small trees and bushes
- Brown paint
- HO model railroad ballast or clean sand

Step One: Look at your city or town, planning the direction for your country expansion. On your base material – plywood homasote or similar material – sketch your new country road, beginning at the end of the paved surface you may have done earlier. This is not the road to ruin, but only to the less settled countryside . . . it does not need potholes.

Step Two: Overlay your sketch with a layer of foam core board or homasote – you can purchase thin homasote from a hobby supply store or craft store. Do not use cardboard since you will be using water based paint – water and paper are not friendly to each other. When you are comfortable with the design, move on to step three. Remember, cars need space to drive past each other. We subscribe to the theory that you do not want to create accident sites.

Step Three: Using pieces of those always useful paint mixing sticks, coat your road surface with a thin coat of plaster or Sculptamold. The plaster will provide a prototypical uneven surface. The Sculptamold (again, at hobby or craft stores) will give you a much more uneven surface, typical of a road less traveled. You decide where this path will take you! Plaster sets quickly, but Sculptamold sets slowly, making it a great material for people who cannot decide what they want . . .

Remember that roads have edges, so don't forget to taper the edges into the surrounding grass, weeds or bushes. The area surrounding the road can be covered in the same material applied thinly, but painted in greens, browns and golds.

Step Four: Paint the road surface with whatever shades of brown paint you like. If this is a beach road, use light tan. If you are in the forest, use dark brown. If you are in an industrial area, mix shades of gray and brown. You get the idea? Most importantly, take some photos of your favorites roads, and have them near you when you do this. Paint is cheap. Even if it takes three or four coats to get the color you want, keep trying. This is also a peaceful, cheap alternative to therapy – you can lose yourself in the fantasy world at virtually no cost!

When you are happy with the color, sprinkle the sand onto the road surface so that it is completely covered. Model railroad ballast is cheap and sand from the sides of the road is even cheaper (for New

Englanders, spring brings lots and lots of sand from the sides of the road as the snow melts) – you are the king, and you get to decide what is right for your kingdom. This is a bit like being Darth Vader of the mini-world . . .

Step Five: The base is in place, the rest is art. Remember those photos of roads you have liked? Remember photos from travel magazines? Make your world match. You may purchase trees from model and hobby shops, adding them to meet your plan. Even tree stumps are available. Clumps of grass can be made from brushes, and bare trees from sticks. The key is that you need to make this look like it makes you happy!

The Quick Loading Dock

The backs of your businesses may face an alley, a road or a parking lot. So, they need an outside storage platform to accept deliveries. If the ground slopes away from the building, the loading dock becomes essential to business.

This quick loading dock fills the bill nicely. The dimensions are suitable for Department 56-scale buildings. You can build it in any size or shape you need – remember, you are the ruler of the Empire.

You will need:

- Lengths of wood 1/8" (or larger) square
- Wooden coffee stirrers
- Wood stain or art markers
- Water-soluble white glue or carpenters' glue

Step One: Develop your plan. It is easier to start with a low loading dock for your first adventure, and work up from there – just like adding a deck on your house. Look at your buildings and decide where you might want an addition. Cut cardboard in the approximate size and shape of your loading dock and trim it to fit.

Step Two: Paint or stain all the wood in the color you like. You may also build it and paint later, but if you are using stain, the glue will not absorb it, leaving little white spots – not a good thing.

Step Three: Place the outline of the shape onto a piece of waxed paper – the paper will prevent you from gluing your loading dock to the kitchen table.

Trace the outline onto the paper. Now place the 1/8" (or larger) square wood in a frame arrangement, approximately one inch apart as viewed in the photo.

To avoid moving everything when you touch one piece, use a SMALL dot of glue to glue the framework to the underlying waxed paper. This will separate easily later.

Lay the coffee stirrers (or "stripwood" purchased at a local hobby store) at right angles to the framework. Don't be fussy – this is a loading dock, not coffee table. Real loading docks have holes and rough lumber. Go for it!

Step Four: Let everything dry for 24 hours or you will make a mess of your work. It is tempting to try to see how it looks next to the building, but don't!

Step Five: Remove the floor assembly from the waxed paper. If it does not pull off, use a small hobby knife to cut away the excess. This is like vacuuming – no one will see what's underneath, so relax, don't worry. Cut the leg support to length and glue to the underside of the loading dock floor.

Place it where you want it. If you like it, go make another one! There is no end to this project, because every commercial and industrial building could use one. You can even build them for friends!

Current Display Pieces

Giving your village display that perfect "touch" can be accomplished by adding display accessories. Department 56 provides a wide variety from which to choose. In the following list, items that are designed for a specific village or series – Heritage Village, Snow Village, *Seasons Bay*, *Dickens' Village* or *North Pole Woods* – are labeled (HV), (SV), (SB), (DV) or (NPW). New pieces for 2001 are marked with an asterisk (*).

Fences

- ❏ Birch Fence (set/4) (NPW) . 52878*
- ❏ Candy Cane Fence 52664
- ❏ Corral Fence. 52746
- ❏ Holly Split Rail Fence (set/4). 52722
- ❏ Holly Split Rail Fence
  With Seated Children 52723
- ❏ Snow Fence, White (SV) . . 52657
- ❏ Victorian Wrought Iron
  Fence Extension (HV). 52531
- ❏ Victorian Wrought Iron
  Fence With Gate
  (set/5) (HV) 52523
- ❏ Village Halloween
  Fence (set/2). 52702

Snow

- ❏ Clear Ice. 52729
- ❏ Glistening Snow. 53362
- ❏ Pine Scented Fresh
  Fallen Snow 52848
- ❏ Real Plastic Snow. 49981
- ❏ Village Blanket Of New
  Fallen Snow 49956
- ❏ Village Crushed Ice 52908*
- ❏ Village First Frost
  Snow Crystals 52906*
- ❏ Village Fresh Fallen Snow . 49979
- ❏ Village Ice Crystal
  Blanket Of Snow 52841

Trees

- ❏ Autumn Trees (set/4) 53383
- ❏ Craggy Oak Tree 52748
- ❏ Decorated Sisal Trees
  (set/2, asst.) 52714

Trees, Cont.

- ❏ Flowering Potted Trees
  (2 asst.) 53332
- ❏ Green Glitter Sisal Trees
  (set/2). 52902*
- ❏ Holly Hedges (set/4). 52900*
- ❏ Holly Topiaries (set/4) 52899*
- ❏ Holly Tree & Bush (set/2) . 52901*
- ❏ Icy Tree, Lg. 52891*
- ❏ Icy Trees, Med. (set/2) 52890*
- ❏ Icy Trees, Sm. (set/3) 52889*
- ❏ Metal Bare Branch Trees
  (set/6). 52931*
- ❏ Mini Sisal Evergreens. 52763
- ❏ Natural Evergreens (set/8) . 52885*
- ❏ Natural Evergreens (set/16) . 52886*
- ❏ Planter Box Topiaries 53334
- ❏ Potted Topiaries 53370
- ❏ Spring/Summer
  Trees (set/4) 53382
- ❏ Storybook Village Collection
  Landscape Set (set/6) 13179
- ❏ Summer Pine Trees With
  Pine Cones (set/3) 52771
- ❏ Tinsel Trims (set/8) 52713
- ❏ Village Autumn
  Maple/Birch Tree (set/4). . . 52655
- ❏ Village Bare Branch
  Trees (set/6) 52623
- ❏ Village Birch Cluster 52631
- ❏ Village Fiber Optic
  Trees (set/2) 52888*
- ❏ Village Flexible Sisal
  Hedge, Sm. (set/3) 52596
- ❏ Village Flexible Sisal
  Hedge, Lg. (set/3). 52662
- ❏ Village Flocked Pine
  Trees (set/2) 56715

Trees, cont.

- ❏ Village Frosted
  Shrubbery (set/24) 52843
- ❏ Village Frosted Spruce
  (set/2) 52637
- ❏ Village Frosted
  Topiaries (set/16) 52842
- ❏ Village Frosty Light
  Trees (set/2) 52844
- ❏ Village Halloween
  Spooky Tree 52770
- ❏ Village Hybrid Landscape
  (set/22) 52600
- ❏ Village Icicle Trees (set/3) . 56722
- ❏ Village Jack Pines (set/3) . . 52622
- ❏ Village Landscape (set/14) . 52590
- ❏ Village Landscape
  Starter Set (set/6) 52898*
- ❏ Village Palm Trees (set/2). . 52820
- ❏ Village Peppermint
  Trees (set/3) 56721
- ❏ Village Pequot Pine, X-Lg.. 52819
- ❏ Village Pequot Pines (set/3) . 52818
- ❏ Village Porcelain Pine
  Trees (set/4) 59001
- ❏ Village Snowy Evergreen
  Trees, Lg. (set/5) 52614
- ❏ Village Snowy Evergreen
  Trees, Med. (set/6) 52613
- ❏ Village Snowy Scotch
  Pines (set/3) 52615
- ❏ Village Twinkling Lit
  Shrubs, Green (set/4) 52824
- ❏ Village Twinkling Lit
  Shrubs, White (set/4) 56724
- ❏ Village Twinkling Lit
  Town Tree 52837
- ❏ Village Twinkling Lit
  Trees, Green (set/3) 52823
- ❏ Village Twinkling Lit
  Trees, White (set/3) 56723
- ❏ Village Twinkling Tip Tree. . 52781
- ❏ Village Winter Birch (set/6). 52636
- ❏ Village Winter Green
  Spruce (set/3) 52892*
- ❏ Village Wintergreen
  Pines (set/3) 52660
- ❏ Village Wintergreen
  Pines (set/2) 52661
- ❏ Winter Pine Trees With
  Pine Cones (set/3) 52772
- ❏ Winter Trees (set/4) 53384

Miscellaneous Accent Pieces

- ❏ Adirondack Chairs
  (set/4) (SB) 53436
- ❏ Balsam Fir Incense
  (pack/15) 52881*
- ❏ Beach Front (set/3) 53355
- ❏ Beach Front
  Extensions (set/4) 53374
- ❏ Bears In The Birch 52743
- ❏ Birch Bridge (NPW) 52876*
- ❏ Birch Gazebo (NPW) 52877*
- ❏ Birds Out Back (set/2) 52866*
- ❏ Buffalo On The Prairie 52865*
- ❏ Candy Cane Bench 52669
- ❏ The Dockhouse (set/2) 52863*
- ❏ Fabric Cobblestone Road . . 52884*
- ❏ Festive Front Yard 52506*
- ❏ Fieldstone Entry Gate 52718
- ❏ Fieldstone Stairway 52826
- ❏ Fieldstone Wall (set/6) 52717
- ❏ Fieldstone Wall
  With Apple Tree 52768
- ❏ Flowering Vines (set/2). . . . 53344
- ❏ Frosty Light Sprays (set/2) . 52682
- ❏ Garden Fountain (set/9) . . . 53330
- ❏ Garden Gazebo 53338
- ❏ Garden Park Bench. 53333
- ❏ Geranium Window Box . . . 53345
- ❏ Good Fishing 56643*
- ❏ Grassy Ground Cover
  (3.5-oz. bag) 53347
- ❏ Green 52739
- ❏ Haunted Front Yard 52924*
- ❏ Harvest Decorating (set/12) . 53431
- ❏ Ivy Vines (set/4) 53377
- ❏ Lattice Obelisk (set/2) 53376
- ❏ Majestic Woodland
  Birds (set/2) 52814
- ❏ Mountain Lion's Den 52864*
- ❏ Nativity Sand 41430
- ❏ Peppermint Road,
  Curved Section 52667
- ❏ Peppermint Road,
  Straight Section 52666
- ❏ Personalize Your Village
  Accessories (set/5) 52811
- ❏ Pinecone Path, Straight and
  Curved (set/6, NPW) 52874*
- ❏ Potted Flowers (12 Asst.) . . 53331
- ❏ Putting Green 52740

Miscellaneous Accent Pieces, cont.

- Revolving Display Stand . . 52640
- Road Construction Signs (set/2, SV) 52680
- Sandy Beach (SB) 53433
- Seasons Bay Christmas Garlands & Wreaths (set/14, SB) 53429
- Seasons Bay Park (set/8, SB) 53428
- Seasons Bay Sign (SB). . . . 53343
- Slate Stone Path, Straight . . 52719
- Slate Stone Path, Curved . . 52767
- Stone Footpath Sections (set/6). 53375
- Stone Stairway 52725
- Stone Wall With Sisal Hedge 52724
- Swinging Under The Old Oak Tree. 52769
- Tacky Wax 52175
- Telephone Poles (set/6) (SV). 52656
- Thoroughbreds (set/5). 52747
- Trout Stream, The. 52834
- Two Lane Paved Road (SV). 52668
- Village Autumn Moss (4 asst.). 52802
- Village Brick Road (set/2) . 52108
- Village Brick Town Square. 52601
- Village Camden Park Cobblestone Road (set/2) . . 52691
- Village Cats & Dogs(set/6). 52828
- Village "Christmas Eave" Trim. 55115
- Village Cobblestone Road (set/2) 59846
- Village Cobblestone Town Square 52602
- Village Country Road Lampposts (set/4). 52663
- Village Craggy Cliff Platform 52794
- Village Craggy Cliff Extensions 52795
- Village FALLen Leaves (3-oz. bag) 52610
- Village Ground Cover (2 asst.) 52840
- Village Halloween Scene . . 52933*
- Village Halloween Set (set/22). 52704

Miscellaneous Accent Pieces, cont.

- Village Holiday Cobblestone Road 56447
- Village Ice Crystal Gate & Walls (set/14). 56716
- Village Ice Crystal Walls (set/6). 56717
- Village Junkyard. 52861*
- Village Log Pile 52665
- Village Lookout Tower. . . . 52829
- Village Mill Creek Campsite 52894*
- Village Mill Creek, Curved Section. 52634
- Village Mill Creek Pond. . . 52651
- Village Mill Creek, Straight Section 52633
- Village Mill Creek Wooden Bridge 52653
- Village Mountain (set/14). . 52280
- Village Mountain Backdrop (set/2). 52574
- Village Mountain Stream . . 52909*
- Village Park Bench. 52851
- Village Pink Flamingos (set/4) 52595
- Village Real Gravel (3 Asst.) 52839
- Village Red Wrought Iron Park Bench 56445
- Village Sign And Bench . . . 52882*
- Village Smokehouse 52880*
- Village Spring/Summer Moss (4 Asst.) 52803
- Village Stone Curved Wall/Bench (set/4) 52650
- Village Stone Footbridge . . 52646
- Village Stone Holly Corner Posts And Archway (set/3). . . 52648
- Village Stone Trestle Bridge. 52647
- Village Stone Wall 52629
- Village Tall Stone Walls (set/4). 52825
- Village Wooden Canoes (set/3). 52830
- Village Wooden Rowboats (set/3). 52797
- Village Wrought Iron Park Bench. 52302
- Wolves In The Woods. 52765
- Wooden Pier (set/2) 52766

Miscellaneous Accent Pieces, cont.

Lighted Accent Pieces

Lighted Accent Pieces, cont.

Village Brite Lites

Glossary

accessory — a piece designed to enhance village buildings, typically non-lit miniature figurines.

animated — a piece capable of movement.

bottomstamp — also called an "understamp," an identifying mark on the underside of a collectible. Department 56 buildings have a bottomstamp which includes the village name, the title of the piece, the copyright date and the company logo.

event piece — a piece specially made for sale only at Department 56 promotional events.

exchange — a secondary market service, listing pieces that collectors wish to buy or sell.

exclusive — a piece made especially for, and only available through, a specific store, exposition or buying group.

first edition — a piece with limited production. In *Seasons Bay*®, there were first edition pieces with special decals, as well as different colors and attachments than the open edition piece.

issue date — for Department 56, the year of production is considered the year of "issue," although the piece may not become available to collectors until the following year.

issue price — the retail price of an item when it is first introduced.

mint-in-box — a piece that comes in its original box and is in "good as new" condition. This usually adds to the item's value.

open edition — a piece with no predetermined limitation on time or size of production run.

release date — the year a piece becomes available to collectors. For most pieces, the release date is the year following the issue date.

series — a grouping within a collection that is based on a certain theme, such as the *American Architecture Series*.

track compatible — pieces that can stand alone, but are made to go with animated tracks.

Numerical Index

Numerical Index

Alphabetical Index

– Key –

All village pieces are listed below in alphabetical order. The first number refers to the piece's location within the Value Guide section and the second to the box in which it is pictured. Items that are not pictured are listed as "NP."

Alphabetical Index

	Pg.	Pic.
	Pg.	**Pic.**

Alphabetical Index

Alphabetical Index

Acknowledgements

CheckerBee Publishing would like to thank Matt Lake, Jeff & Susan McDermott, Mr. Sierakowski, Frank & Florence Wilson and all the Department 56 retailers and collectors who contributed their valuable time to assist us with this book.